20.00

920.02
BAC

Bach, Jonathan
Above the Clouds

0-688-11760-0

DATE DUE		
JUN 3 '93		
JUN 1 '93		
JUL 10 '93		
MAR 9 '94		
MAY 24 '95		
JUN 14 '95		
APR 19 '96		
OCT 06 1998		
OCT 12 1998		
OCT 31 1998		
DEC 22 2000		
JUL 16 2003		

Above the Clouds

A REUNION OF FATHER AND SON

Jonathan Bach

WILLIAM MORROW AND COMPANY, INC.

NEW YORK

It is the policy of William Morrow and Company, Inc., and its imprints and affiliates, recognizing the importance of preserving what has been written, to print the books we publish on acid-free paper, and we exert our best efforts to that end.

Library of Congress Cataloging-in-Publication Data
Bach, Jonathan.
    Above the clouds / by Jonathan Bach.
      p. cm.
    ISBN 0-688-11760-0
    1. Bach, Richard—Biography—Family. 2. Authors, American—20th
century—Biography.   3. Fathers and sons—United States—Biography.
4. Bach, Jonathan—Family.   I. Title.
PS3552.A255Z57 1993
387.7'092—dc20
    [B]   92-26185
                                                            CIP

Printed in the United States of America

3 4 5 6 7 8 9 10

BOOK DESIGN BY MICHAEL MENDELSOHN

Above
the Clouds

PROLOGUE

All I wanted was sun.

When I heard the weather report, I knew nature was going to challenge my right to a suntan. But there I was anyway, lying on a towel at Greenlake Park north of Seattle, reading through an early untitled version of what is now this book.

True to the mid-May forecast, the sun was obscured by clouds. One minute it would light up the page so brightly I'd have to put on my sunglasses to read, the next minute I could barely make out the letters as clouds slowly passed. Round about page 107, the light-then-dark and the heat-then-chill on my back was driving me crazy.

I turned over and sighed. "Hey. Sun. Make up your mind."

The sun listened and it was bright. But clouds lined up to the west, waiting to hide it, and I felt bad for blaming the sun. It was just doing its job.

Clouds were the culprits.

It doesn't take long in life to discover we can't control the weather, and we accept that. We try to accept other Unchangeables and, in trying, most of us realize our insignificance. We try to make the cutest girl in the class love us, but she has eyes on the handsome jerk in the back row. We try to get our boyfriend to be more romantic, but we can't get him away from the TV.

So what if, in the midst of our disappointment, the Unchangeable becomes the Changeable?

And what if we discovered that it wasn't coincidence that we got what we wished for, but that *we* made it happen? And what if we learned that we could do it again, then routinely?

This book is my answer.

This book is about what happened after my father, author Richard

Bach, left my family when I was two years old. This is what I did about the Unchangeable clouds that masked my sun for the next twenty years. This is what I did after I decided not to be a slave to heat-then-chill and bright-then-dark, a slave to thinking of him and feeling abandoned, then going for long periods of contentment and vowing never to think of him again, only to find that he would always creep back into my thoughts.

This is what I did to feel good about being Richard Bach's son.

That was all I'd wanted.

Jonathan Bach

CHAPTER ONE

In 1970, Daddy walked out the screen door of our house and drove away. Three years later, I started to learn why.

August 1973

Something bad had happened.

Mom looked very serious as she gathered my two brothers, three sisters, and me into the living room of our Michigan home. Her expression was the same as when I put up a fuss about going to bed.

After Mom sat on the couch and we all sat down on the floor, she spoke.

"Daddy won't be called 'Daddy' anymore," she said. "His Daddy-part died."

There didn't seem to be any reaction from us. Kris, my oldest sister at fifteen years old, looked at the carpet while Bethany, three and a half, leaned against her. Beside them was eleven-year-old Rob, who looked just as serious as Mom. Nine-year-old Erica looked pensive, and Jim, seven, looked like he normally did when he assembled puzzles.

I sat there, borrowing everybody's expressions because I didn't know what to think of what Mom had said. I was only five.

So I leaned against Kris and imagined that Daddy, a very tall, thin, mustached man, was now in a wheelchair. In my mind he had stitches across his stomach where they'd removed the dead part because of some kind of accident.

"But he's still the captain of the family," Mom said. "So he will be called Captain from now on."

11

I updated my five-second-old image. Daddy wore a black captain's cap like the one I had seen in my picture books.

That's pretty good for him to be a captain even though he is sick, I thought.

After Mom's talk, which only lasted another minute, I went to the book and brought it to Kris and Beth.

"That man is a captain," I said to Beth, pointing to a picture of a smiling man standing on a ship.

"That's right," Kris said cheerily.

"But he's not sick. He feels good. See? He's smiling."

She nodded.

For some reason, her eyes were wet.

Chapter Two

For the next seven years, as my family moved from Michigan to Massachusetts to Vermont, I rarely thought of the man named Captain. I never saw him, never spoke to him, but occasionally Kris or Rob would mention something about the funny things he used to say. I didn't understand, but I told myself I wasn't old enough.

I never knew why we had to move so much, but I never asked. Mom said we were moving and that was all I needed to know. It was Law.

Law was also when Mom said that dinnertime, bedtime, go-to-your-room-time was now, not later. Law was anything Kris or Rob or Erica or Jim said. Law was anything the kindergarten, first-grade, second-grade, or third-grade teacher said.

But for my friends, the only Law that seemed to matter to them, the Law that reigned most supreme, was Father Law.

At my friends' houses after school, fathers were the guys who fixed things, built things, painted things. They were the Masters of the Home and they were the strongest people on the planet. They were brave, capable, bulletproof. And when they drove in the driveway at 5:15 in the afternoon, they were people to be feared. They made me nervous with their power.

Fathers were the guys who came to Open House at elementary school with every mom except mine. They were the guys who got clay ashtrays my classmates made for Father's Day. They were baseball coaches and scout leaders. They were the names on the second signature line on the bottom of the parental consent forms we had to return to our teachers the next day.

These men were called "dads" by my best friends Duane and Bobby and Brad and Shawn. Dads built tree houses and minibikes, wrestled with my friends in front of the TV, shot B-B-gun targets with them in the backyard.

My friends would help their dads tap maple trees for syrup, they'd hold the flashlight while their dads worked under the truck, or help them pump out the water that leaked into the basement.

Dads allowed my friends to ride snowmobiles without supervision in the fields behind their houses, allowed them to bring their military medals to school, to use their fishing lures as long as they put them back in the tackle box when they were done.

But dads were redundant.

Why does somebody need a dad when a mom can take care of everything? I thought as I walked home from my fourth-grade buddy's house. He couldn't go bike-riding because his dad wanted him to finish painting the small shed in his backyard.

My other buddies—all of their moms were home when they came home, had their lunches packed for school in the morning, and were always in the kitchen doing something. I never saw any moms try to fix the water heater, change the oil in the car, or change the bulb in the outside floodlight.

Once I saw Shawn's mom drive a tractor, but that's the closest any mom came to being as versatile as mine. And out of all the moms *and* dads I'd seen, not one of them could do what my mom did best.

Mom flew airplanes.

That was the greatest thing about her. She worked at little airports, one in each state we'd lived. Not major international airports, but little ones with one runway surrounded by acres of flat grassy field and enough space to tie down thirty or forty planes.

That's where I spent most of my time, watching planes come and go while Mom worked in the hangar, helping other guys put cloth fabric and extremely potent turpentine-smelling stuff called butyrate dope on antique airplane frames. She only had to tell me once that the fumes were really bad and to back way away. I'd see her with the white mask that only covered her face and worry what might happen if she forgot to wear it.

So it is 1977, and Sugarbush airport in Warren, Vermont, is the latest airport Mom worked. School had adjourned for the summer, so

Sugarbush became the center of the family activity.

While Kris, nineteen, was in Colorado for the summer working as a camp counselor, fifteen-year-old Rob was on vacation from the same private Michigan high school Kris had been attending. He spent a lot of time at the airport learning to fly, and he paid for his lessons by working at the airport's little restaurant.

Thirteen-year-old Erica was learning to fly, too, but she was learning in engineless planes called gliders. When she wasn't flying, she paid for her lessons by "running the line"—helping the airport staff attach motor-driven planes to gliders with a hundred-and-fifty-foot rope and push them into position for takeoff.

Eleven-year-old Jim rarely came to the airport. He stayed home alone, reading, watching TV. He'd show up once in a while, when there was an airshow or an airport picnic, but he didn't like being near airplanes when he couldn't fly them. He hated not being old enough to learn to fly.

Beth was eight and she stayed close to the terminal as she watched the planes come and go. She'd practice gymnastics in the grass, and every now and then help wash and wax planes, especially the spots underneath the fuselage; other than me, she was the only other person who could slither underneath.

As Mom sold airplane rides behind the glass flight counter which displayed maps, rulers, and a few Sugarbush airport T-shirts for sale, I swatted flies in the office, pumped gas when the pilots would let me, and ran back and forth from the taxiway to the airport restaurant, bringing towpilots and airport workers cold drinks and sandwiches.

I watched Erica's and Rob's takeoffs and landings and eavesdropped when flight instructors taught preflight—what parts of the airplane to check before getting in. I was proud to see my brother and sister learn to fly like all the older pilots who came in the office and asked me why I wasn't flying too. I was ashamed to admit I preferred life on the ground. I never told them I got sick most of the time. I didn't need to remind myself of my handicap—that flying was only fun when there wasn't enough wind to bend a blade of grass.

But, still, I loved airplanes.

On the ground, I was an airplane expert. I could identify any plane that landed, I knew who owned what airplane, and I knew airport talk like "base leg," "final approach," and "run-up." Mom taught me what the letters stood for on the sides of all planes and she even taught me how to talk to an airplane on the radio if she stepped out of the office.

On most of the summer weekends, there were gatherings at nearby airports called airshows and fly-ins which attracted lots of people who came to see planes: planes with one wing on top, planes with one wing on the bottom, planes with wings on the top and the bottom, planes with one engine, two engines, three engines, planes with a little wheel at the tail, planes with a nosegear, planes that did neat tricks in the air, planes called "antiques" that just sat on the ground to be seen and not touched.

After all the planes did their tricks in the air, Mom would start selling rides to the spectators in her starburst red-white-and-blue Tiger Moth biplane. After every landing she made, I'd take the bottle of Fantastic and a clean rag from the plane's baggage compartment and wipe the bugs off the propeller and the oil that had leaked and wind-streaked from under the engine to the tailwheel. And every so often I'd spray the hand-painted red "Bette Bach" on the side of the cockpit panel, whether it needed it or not.

When the oil and bugs were wiped away, I'd make sure nobody smoked around the airplane, put a hand through the delicate fabric that covered it, or wandered past the yellow rope that separated the crowd from the airplanes. I'd make sure the Tiger Moth's six-foot prop didn't have anybody near it when Mom yelled "Clear," started the engine, and began flying rides. I'd make sure the passengers stepped only on the black, rough part of the wing near the fuselage as they got into the front cockpit.

"The seat belt's kinda tricky," I'd yell over the choking antique engine, strapping in passengers who had just paid ten dollars for as many minutes in the air. Oily exhaust and strong propwash would blast us while Mom sat in the pilot's seat checking instruments.

I'd step off the wing when the passenger was ready, then I'd give Mom a thumbs-up, feeling just as important as real-life Air Force ground crew I had seen at bigger airshows. The next second after my signal, violent propwash from increased throttle would pin the collar on my white flight suit against my neck, blowing grass and dirt into my eyes. The people who waited in line would always turn away, holding their hats and their purses as they tried to shield their eyes from flying earth. As much as my eyes would squint and water, I never turned my back on the colorful biplane until it shrank to a pepper speck in the ocean sky.

Mom seemed to be the only woman pilot alive. Except for Mom's best friend, June, every pilot who walked through the airport office door was male.

Any one of them could be my father and I wouldn't recognize him.

CHAPTER THREE

My experiences at the airport were so much fun that I felt compelled to make something more out of them.

So I started writing.

One of my first stories at age nine was titled *Flight 703*. In two pencil-scratched pages, it told about a former airline captain who, when flying as a passenger one day, decided to get up from his seat and help the pilot with a particularly difficult flight.

. . . "I think you should fly above the clouds until the rain stops," Mr. Belgrim said to the pilot and co-pilot.

"You think we should, Joe?" said the pilot.

"Why not?" said the co-pilot.

Suddenly, the plane jerked upward above the puffy clouds.

They landed safely at Daytona Beach airport and this time, everybody got out. The plane didn't make anymore flights that day. Everybody either stayed at campsites or hotels.

The next day the sky was as blue as blue can be. Flight 703 was off the ground at 8:30 A.M. This time it was headed for New York City.

From then on the plane was careful.

Mom liked the story. And the second after her "This is very good, Jonny," I wanted to be a writer when I grew up.

CHAPTER FOUR

Words, sentences, paragraphs, story ideas came to me, sometimes faster than I could write them. I felt like a grown-up reporter, taking notes from a fast-talking politician inside my head.

I showed Mom my collections of sentences when she wasn't busy cooking dinner or running errands. I waited until she had a quiet moment, usually just before she went to bed.

"This is great stuff for a nine-year-old, Jonny," she said one night in the dim light of her bedroom lamp. "You've definitely got your father's genes for writing."

I thought of the word *father* and all my friends' dads as I dangled my pajama-ed feet over the side of her king-size bed.

But my father's jeans? I suspected she wasn't referring to denim.

"Jeans?" I asked.

"Genes. G-E-N-E-S. It means you've got an inherited talent. It means you've got it in you to be a writer," she said, her eyes warm and hopeful.

"Genes," I said, hoping to work that new word into my next story. "So where did I get them?"

"See those books over there?"

She pointed to a bookshelf in the darkest corner of the room.

"Can you turn on the light?" I said, pointing to the nightstand lamp on the other side of the bed. I wanted her to dissolve whatever demons lived over in that gloomy corner.

She did.

I got up and walked over to books.

"That section there, to your left, is all your father's stuff."

I turned my head sideways to read the vertical book titles on that special shelf.

Stranger to the Ground
Biplane
Nothing by Chance
A Gift of Wings
Illusions
Jonathan Livingston Seagull

"Hey, this one on the end has my name on it!"

"That's where you got your name," she said proudly.

I had to look inside.

"Can I see it?"

"Sure, but don't take all night there. I'm getting a little tired."

"Okay, okay," I said, taking the book quickly from the shelf.

The cover was deep navy blue with a ghost-white, hazy-traced seagull image. *Jonathan Livingston Seagull* was in yellow letters, *by Richard Bach* in white.

I opened to the first page and looked for each time my name was mentioned. Some of the pages had nothing but pictures of seagulls.

"Remember Captain Mac?" Mom asked me from her bed.

"No," I said. But his name sounded familiar.

"He was your father's flying buddy a long time ago. He's mentioned in *Nothing by Chance*," Mom said to me from her bed. "Your middle name comes from him, Stuart MacPherson."

I looked up at the orange book with the words *Nothing by Chance*.

"Does he spell Stuart the same way as me?"

"Mm hmm."

I kept *Seagull* open as I took the book off the shelf.

On the cover was a picture of a biplane which flew silhouetted against a beautiful setting orange sun.

The plane looked like it might be a Parks 2A. I'd seen one at an antique fly-in a few months before.

Underneath the silhouetted biplane, that Richard Bach name demanded my attention again; on this cover, it was printed in bold, black letters.

I was no longer interested in guys named Stuart, silhouetted biplanes, or pictures of seagulls. I tried hard to remember something about Captain.

"How come he never visits?" I asked.

Mom cleared her throat.

"Because he doesn't want to be a daddy."

"Oh yeah," I said, remembering the bad accident and the wheelchair.

CHAPTER FIVE

In a wistful voice, Mom continued talking about Dick Bach. She told me he used to be a great father, that they had shared thirteen wonderful years of marriage until he decided to escape from it.

She told me they had met during high school and he had been an Air Force pilot and a free-lance writer.

She told me that finding a decent husband and marrying was what everybody did in those days, but things happened between Dick Bach and her that were magical. They practiced Christian Science, she said, a belief that there are spiritual causes for ordinary events. She told me a lot of unusual things happened with her and Dick—cuts that healed instantly, premonitions, astounding coincidences, telepathy between them.

She told me I had been born with spinal meningitis, that I wasn't expected to live, and if by some miracle I stayed alive, that at the very least I would be deaf and in a wheelchair.

Wow . . . I thought. *I almost died . . .*

She held my hand for a few seconds while she spoke.

"You showed them all, Jonny. When you just kept feeling better and better, I knew you were a miracle baby."

I asked if *Jonathan Livingston Seagull* had been written about me.

"No," she said. "*Jonathan* was an idea that came to him when he was walking on a beach," she said as I held the book in my hands. "He heard a voice telling him to write it and that's exactly what he did. But you *are* named after it, yes."

"So the book came first?" I asked.

"Oh, yes, but it wasn't always a book. When you were born it was just a short story. The first part of the story was written in '58 and it sat in the bottom file cabinet for ten years until he dusted it off and finished it just when you were born. That's why we named you Jonathan."

When she said that, I felt special and powerful, like it was my birthday and I got to choose what I wanted for dinner and dessert.

"There were lots of times we'd be struggling for money and a check would come just in time to buy food. But even though it didn't happen all the time, we never gave up hope. There was no doubt in my mind that Dick was going to be a famous author. That was our dream—him writing, me editing his stuff. In the meantime, I took care of you guys and let him have his privacy to work. That's just the way it had to be."

She told me he had taught her to fly in the early years of their marriage. He had given the Tiger Moth to her after the divorce and when *Jonathan Livingston Seagull* was a new success.

Mom got out of her bed, joined me in the corner, and started sorting through a pile of envelopes. Inside one of them was a copy of *Time* magazine, dated November 13, 1972.

I sat with her on the edge of the bed as she showed me the magazine. My father was on the cover, looking just like I remembered him—strong cheekbones, a thin, long face, a high forehead, and a mustache.

"This is a story about him. Of course, I only got a paragraph," she said, turning to where the article started. There were a few other pictures of him: one flying a biplane, one of him smiling slightly.

"This is you and Beth," she said, pointing to the small boy and girl who were being held in Mom's arms as she stood surrounded by four other children.

"What did they say about us?" I asked. "Can I read this?"

"Sure," she said, getting back into bed. "But you won't find anything in there about Pauline. She was Dick's friend who believed in his writing, especially *Jonathan Livingston Seagull*. They wrote to each other a lot and then finally she asked him to come to New York because she needed him and . . ." She sighed. "He went."

Mom paused for a few seconds. Something about her voice told me I should stop asking questions.

But she continued.

"After he came back, he started to change. He didn't like me asking questions about her and he got real defensive. On top of that, he decided he wasn't a good father to you kids. Eventually he just left."

I looked at the floor. This was very adult stuff I knew I wasn't old enough to understand.

"It wasn't long before he had millions of dollars. I didn't ask for any of it, and he didn't send any more than child support."

I asked her if he'd ever written about the family.

"No," she said, helplessly. "As much as I wish he would recognize you children, he just doesn't. He never has and I doubt he ever will."

Mom told me other bits of trivia—that he didn't believe in birthdays or Christmas or any holidays, so he didn't send cards. She told me he didn't believe in marriage and he'd vowed never to get married again. She told me he lived in Florida now and owned lots of planes.

I didn't care that he had left. I couldn't miss what I'd never had.

Richard Bach was my father and I felt neither pain nor happiness. It was just a fact.

CHAPTER SIX

At the airport one day a few weeks after I sat in Mom's room learning about my father, I buckled another passenger into the Tiger's front cockpit as Mom sat in the cockpit behind. A few minutes later, I watched it climb the sky for what seemed to be the millionth time in my life. That's when the million-and-first potential passenger spoke to me as she waited for Mom to return.

It was right after an airshow, and though most of the spectators had gone, the yellow rope that had separated them from the taxiway and the other airplanes was still up.

"That's quite a biplane," the woman said as I looked away from the sky.

"Sure is," I said, folding my collar down again. The woman looked younger than Mom. She was taller too.

"Built in 1944 and solid as a rock," I said proudly.

"Really? 1944 . . ."

"Yep. The de Havilland Tiger Moth 82A was used as a trainer in the British air force," I said, telling her what Mom had taught me months ago.

"You really know your business, don't you?" the woman said as I approached the yellow rope.

"Yep," I said, stopping at the rope and staying on the important side of it. "Only because that's my mom's plane."

"Oh, really?" the woman said with raised eyebrows.

I pulled slightly at my name tag, making sure the sun didn't keep her from seeing the words on it.

" 'Jonathan Bach—Ground Crew,' " she said, reading the tag. She paused, tilted her head and asked, "This is just a wild guess, but have you ever heard of a book called *Jonathan Livingston Seagull?*"

I smiled with pride.

"My father wrote it," I said confidently.

I looked down at the grass, not knowing what else to say. The smile stayed, but I didn't feel I deserved the pleasure of being Richard Bach's son because I didn't know much about him.

"Well, I'll be darned!" she said. "Imagine that!"

I scanned my memory for what little I did know.

"Mom says he gave her the biplane," I said, smoothing the grass with my foot. "And he used to write articles for *Flying* magazine." I tried to remember something else. "But I can't say much else because I haven't seen him and because my mom isn't married to him anymore and he's somewhere in Florida."

The woman seemed to understand.

"Oh, that's too bad."

I looked at the grass.

"Well," she said, "she must be quite a special mother."

"The best," I said, looking up from the grass and into the woman's thin face and blue eyes.

I told her that Mom belonged to this special group called the Ninety-Nines, a group of women pilots from all over the country. The group was named to commemorate the first ninety-nine women pilots who answered Amelia Earhart's request for a meeting of women pilots sometime long ago.

"Or something like that," I said. "You'll have to ask my mom about it. I don't remember all the things she told me."

We talked about the rarity of women pilots and the beauty of antique planes and the thrills of airshows. Then the bald wheels of Mom's biplane touched the long carpet of grass parallel to the asphalt runway.

I anticipated her next question because so many people had asked it.

"Landing on the grass makes it easier on the tires," I said.

The woman nodded and stepped many steps ahead of me to get a better look at the biplane.

I looked at the grass.

Richard Bach was my father and it was more than just a fact. There was a specialness to it, like being on the other side of the yellow rope.

My thoughts dissolved in the crescendo of the approaching Tiger's sputtering engine. I had a job to do.

Mom quickly turned the airplane back toward the runway and kept the propeller spinning, pushing soft wind-exhaust into my face as I helped the previous passenger out of the front cockpit.

The man shouted thanks to Mom and gave me a ten-dollar bill for the ride and two extra dollar bills. I saluted him after he saluted me. He told me thanks and walked away. He smoothed his windblown hair, wiped his watery eyes, and yelled "Woooo!" to a crowd of cheering friends on the other side of the yellow rope.

I strapped the new lady passenger in and again watched Mom and her biplane fly away.

In the background buzzes of arriving and departing airplanes, the thought of my father returned. To me, that woman passenger wasn't just the last ride of the day. Her observation of my name was proof, confirmation, of my uniqueness. A stranger had recognized my name, guessed correctly who my father was without me saying anything.

It hit me that I was not Kristel or Rob or Erica or Jim or Bethany. I was the one named after a book just as real as every textbook I'd ever read at school.

I was Jonathan.

I felt immediately older, more mature. I felt I should live up to the honor. But I made a vow to be careful never to be arrogant about it around anybody, especially my brothers and sisters. They probably felt bad not being named Jonathan.

After the biplane touched again on the dark emerald grass and taxied over to my services as ground crew, after I helped the lady out, after I took her ten-dollar bill and received her thanks and "Nice talking with you, Jonathan," I looked at Mom.

Her face was a shade of sunburn, decorated with a smudge of oil. The dingy cream-colored fur collar of her leather flight jacket was a darker cream from another day's worth of oil exhaust. Her goggles, now on her forehead, had left a light red goggle outline around her eyes.

There was no one else to fly, so I suspected she couldn't wait to shut the plane off and get some coffee as she usually did.

The engine's idle didn't fade.

"That's all of them!" I yelled to her as I approached the cockpit.

She shook her head, smiled, and pointed to the empty front cockpit. It must be calm up there.

I trusted my mom, but I looked at the windsock near the runway, just to make sure her definition of calm agreed with mine. The windsock was limp.

I nodded and smiled back.

Three minutes later, the big painted-white 22 at the end of the runway rolled backward as the deafening full-throttle engine powered us aloft. As the rest of the runway shrank below, wind whistled in the wires that bridged the top wing and the bottom wing.

Even though I'd made many flights in the Tiger, each time was like the first. Being part of the sky never gets boring.

Faint oil-exhaust perfume blew past me, mixed with the smell of my leather helmet, and my chest was sore from excitement.

We were level with a sun that was becoming as orange as the cover of *Nothing by Chance*. It cast its fire on the few puffs of clouds that lingered over the horizon.

I leaned out of the cockpit and felt the push of eighty miles an hour against my face. The air was chilly, but I rolled my sleeves up anyway and unfastened my belt to see more of the quilt of Vermont farmland below. The weathered barns, rusty silos, the specks of cows, every white church steeple, every green mountain: all of it was mine. No one else was in the sky to claim it.

Aside from birthdays and Christmases, this was nine-year-old heaven—a thousand feet above the world on a calm day with Mom: the rare woman pilot Bette Bach.

I saw her in the rearview mirror over the front cockpit. The goggles covered most of her face.

I scooched up higher in my seat so she could see me better. As soon as she caught my stare, I gave her a thumbs-up. She smiled at me, not an ounce of disapproval that I was out of my seatbelt.

It didn't matter that Mom had told me about Richard. She was all the parents I wanted.

CHAPTER SEVEN

It was a year later, another summer, and I was again at the airport. But I was not Mom's ground crew. She didn't seem to fly rides anymore. She spent more and more time in the airport office as I worked the line near the runway with my sister Erica, helping the airport staff coordinate takeoffs and landings for sailplane rides.

I crouched at the tail of an L-19 towplane, working quickly to get the eyelet on the end of a rope to fit into a latchlike device just above the plane's little tailwheel.

The towplane's engine occasionally missed a cylinder spark, spinning the propeller erratically, but it managed to push gentle wind back to me. Though the plane sounded ready for the scrap pile, I knew it was about to spit forth incredible power.

If I didn't get the rope latched soon, the pilot of the plane and the other pilot sitting in the unattached motorless glider a hundred and fifty feet behind me would not be pleased.

It's this stupid plane's fault, I thought, trying not to wince at the pain I was causing myself as I pressed hard against the latch.

The L-19 wasn't an ordinary plane, it was a relic: a prehistoric single-engine, high-wing powerhouse used in the military. The plane looked as if it had flown through a lot of missions. There were dents all over the thing, and a few small bulletlike holes that defied repair. There was no paint on the dull-silver plane, except for a faded registration number and a few places of chipped color. Those colored specks were near the biggest dents—remnants, I presumed, from collisions with other planes that *did* have paint.

Jon Fineman was the perfect pilot for that airplane. The airport staff called him Big Jon to avoid confusion with me, and he was taller than

29

the three other male towpilots, standing over six feet tall, weighing about two hundred thirty pounds.

He dressed in frayed, oil-stained, short-sleeved button shirts that looked as if they had been the substitute for gas caps in antique airplanes. With those gas-cap shirts he always wore cut-off jeans, a bandanna headband, and old sneakers.

I thought Mom was joking when she said he was an engineering manager at IBM during the week. There was a chance it could be true, because he only flew on weekends, but I just couldn't picture him in a suit and tie. When I saw him come to the airport one Friday afternoon in a dress shirt and pants, I believed her.

"Big Jon!" I shouted to him from beside the rudder. "I can't get the latch to go!"

He looked at me through black horn-rimmed glasses, his headband doing little to dam the sweat and keep it out of his eyes. It must have been ninety degrees on that day. Even with the shuddering, choking plane's door open, he swam in twenty additional cockpit degrees as he tried to hear what I was saying.

"Wiggle the lever arm a little! Right as you're pressing down!"

I went back to the latch, hoping it would work for me this time.

It did.

I gave him a thumbs-up. He returned the gesture with a smile.

I ran back to the glider, hooked it up to the L-19, took my place at the end of the glider's left wing and held it off the ground. Without my help, the glider's wing would drag along the ground on takeoff like the downed end of a seesaw.

I faced forward to the L-19, raised my left arm, and made a talking motion with my left hand. Big Jon eased the towplane forward easily until the slack in the rope was gone.

I held up my vertical open palm toward him when the glider jolted slightly, then gave him another thumbs-up. I gave the same to the pilot of the pristine, brilliant-white, high-performance sailplane at the end of my right arm. The woman pilot nodded to me and pressed first on the left rudder pedal, then the right, and then again more quickly, making the rudder wave back and forth.

That was the signal to Big Jon. All systems go.

Jon wagged the towplane's rudder and pushed its throttle all the way forward, unleashing a roar like a squadron of World War II bombers. The roar bounced off the mountains surrounding Sugarbush Valley and came back to me as I ran, holding the wing of the accelerating glider until it got too fast for me. By then, enough air was rushing past the wing so it could support itself in flight.

A hundred feet later, I slowed from a run to a jog to a walk and watched the tandem planes lift into the cloudless July bluescape.

From just outside the airport's little office, Mom watched them go too. She shaded her eyes as they flew into the sun.

She liked Big Jon. She seemed to watch every takeoff he made, and he quickly became more than just another towpilot to her. She even invited him over for dinner a few times.

He told us he'd been in Vietnam, told us stories about how he'd been a Navy gunner, manning a .50-caliber machine gun on a destroyer. He'd also been a paratrooper, and he told us how the wind had caught his parachute once when he landed and dragged him miles over rocks and downed trees and even a barbed-wire fence. He had the scars to prove it.

He seemed to be a living war-movie character—he was always strong, confident, heroic, capable, and an all-around buddy to everyone. He was a folksy, no-nonsense fellow, born in California, raised in Vermont. At the end of every day, he'd be attached to a glass of Jack Daniel's and water—a concoction he referred to as a "Miller Time."

By the third time he came to dinner, we knew something was up.

He started calling me Ace, which I liked much better than Little Jon, and true to the war-movie image, he seemed like a decent guy. Erica, Jim, and Beth seemed to like him too. He took us out for ice cream and for rides in his Volkswagen convertible.

The rest of the family speculated that it might lead somewhere if things kept going the way they were.

I didn't know what to think. I hoped that their relationship wouldn't develop into anything. Nothing about the Bach family needed changing.

Chapter Eight

It was late afternoon after dinner, three weeks and six dinners since Big Jon had become more than "just a towpilot" to Mom. Erica, Jim, and Beth had been excused from the table, but I hadn't finished eating my Brussels sprouts. Mom said I had to, but I wanted to go outside and play with Jim and Beth. I whined and complained about having to stay at the table, hoping Mom would give in as she sometimes did.

Mom held her ground.

I knew Jim and Beth were building these great dams down at the stream, having all kinds of fun with fast-moving water, so I decided to forget the sprouts. Mom would get over it. I'd eat them next time. I'd gotten away with it before. Besides, she was more tolerant these days.

I got up, walked across the living room and started up the stairs to my bedroom to get my boots.

Big Jon was still at the table, across from where I'd been. Mom was just coming back to sit down after clearing some dishes.

I made it to the first stair.

"What did your mother tell you about vegetables?" Big Jon said to me loudly.

I took the second step, stopped to hear what he had to say.

"I know, but I'll eat them when I come back."

Mom spoke to me as I reached the third step.

"Jonny, no. Vegetables now. Then you can go. Don't make it tough for me," Mom said, sitting down.

My vegetables were really cold, definitely inedible.

"Oh, Mom. You can't really expect . . ."

Big Jon got up from the table and approached me.

I froze, wondered what he was doing.

He snatched my right hand off the stair railing, grabbed my right

32

wrist, and held it firmly. He looked at me as if he were forging steel.

"You do what your mother tells you," he said. "Otherwise, you can eat nothing from now on. Understand?"

I pulled away, tense with chills of fear. An iron ball lodged in my throat, slowing my breath. I'd never felt threatened before, not even in the few fights I'd had with Jim. I never felt more scared.

"O . . . okay . . . yes . . ." I said, looking to Mom for help.

She looked at Jon, didn't say anything to him.

"Just go up to your room for a while," she said to me.

Big Jon let go and I ran up the eleven steep steps, trying not to collapse into tears on the way.

There was no door to my room, and I was scared he would follow me up and hit me. I got into bed and under the covers, and let myself heave and cry for the next half hour.

Mom didn't say anything to him or come up and make me feel better. I didn't want to believe that my mom, that fearless, capable superparent, could be scared. I couldn't imagine her like those other moms who let their husbands make all the decisions. Would she now say things like, "If it's okay with Big Jon, it's okay with me"?

I prayed intensely that she would not marry this guy, this virtual stranger.

Ever.

CHAPTER NINE

In September of that same year, Mom married Big Jon.

As I'd feared, he brought strict rules to the family. They seeped into the crevices where my brothers, sisters, and I used to play. The cleanliness of our rooms was monitored more closely. So too our attention to chores and our negative attitudes about the work. Scrubbing the counter, taking out the trash, feeding the cats, chores that still brought my brothers and sisters a weekly allowance, were now leisure work compared to the cords and cords of wood we had to cut, split, carry, and stack.

Leaving a cupboard door open the third time after being told to close it resulted in a one-dollar fine. Leaving the gas cap off the gas can a certain number of times resulted in another financial penalty.

Laziness was a luxury.

Big Jon's maxim was, "You support the family, the family will support you." What he really meant was, "Pull your weight or don't live under my roof." Even though he had moved into our house, nobody debated whether it was his roof or ours. We did as we were told.

But even though I never got used to the new structure, I considered it to be a worthwhile trade for Mom's new happiness. I assumed Erica, Jim, and Beth felt the same.

His effect on Mom was obvious to me. She didn't seem to sigh as much during the arguments between me and Beth; she didn't seem as tired or sad. She had energy, smiled a lot more, slept a lot less.

A year after they married, we moved to another little Vermont town called Alburg, this one in the northwest corner of the state. We were told that was the most suitable place to build an airstrip for the Tiger, Big Jon's Cessna 170, and his other plane, an antique Bowers Flybaby.

By 1980, Kris had been on her own for a few years, away at an Iowa university. Rob was old enough to be on his own too. He stayed in the town we moved from, working in a deli to support himself. That left Erica, Jim, Beth, and me to share the work in this new house.

There were cows and pigs to feed, which wasn't all that bad a chore until the animals disappeared one day while we were at school and came back a few weeks later from a place I'd never heard of: a slaughterhouse. The cows and pigs we had fed so religiously were now little deli-wrapped green packages in the large freezer out in the shed. It was disturbing. We had fed those animals, those living, breathing creatures, that were now frozen green bricks. I was glad I hadn't named them. But as long as I didn't think about where it came from, the meat tasted better than any we bought at the store.

We all helped to build a two-car garage, which we called "the annex." It had a two-bedroom apartment over it so we wouldn't have to keep sharing bedrooms. We built a barn, a tractor shed, a seventeen-hundred-foot runway in the back acreage, and a two-plane hangar.

None of us was used to a farm atmosphere, not even Astra, the Shetland sheepdog we'd had for five years. It was as if the farm knew Astra could have no place there. The place seemed too rugged for her, as it did for the rest of us. Just when we were starting to adapt, Astra was struck and killed by the school bus.

No one was more affected by Astra's death than my brother Jim. He had called her "my dog," and none of us argued with that. He played with her more than anyone else, so I figured he had a right to consider her his dog.

Jim and Big Jon buried her in the runway we were clearing in back of the house. None of the rest of us could bear to watch.

But while the rest of us went to school the next day after Astra was killed, Jim stayed home. He didn't say much, stayed in his room, was last to the dinner table that day and for a long time after.

A few days after Astra was killed, Big Jon brought home a golden retriever named Conner. In the first ten minutes, Big Jon had him trained not to go beyond the kitchen linoleum and into the carpeted dining room. His strong voice and a stronger stare were the only training methods he used. Conner learned the rules as fast as we, probably because he was just as intimidated. Maybe he, like us, thought Jon wasn't joking when he talked about using a two-by-four to help the training process.

Out of all the aspects of life with this new stepfather, Erica, Jim, Beth, and I dreaded no chore more than getting the wood cut and split before the winter. That, like a lot of other things, was a new activity for us. In the days before Mom got married, we got our wood from a truck that came loaded with the stuff already cut and split. All we had to do was stack it. Now our alarm clocks had to be set to ring at 6:00 A.M. on Saturdays to trek out to the back acreage and cut it ourselves.

"Happy dreams," I said to Erica one night before a Saturday morning. "Hope you don't have nightmares about tomorrow."

"*Wood*mares is more like it!" Erica said.

I agreed.

On wood days Big Jon was a drill sergeant. Erica, Jim, Beth, me, even Mom, none of us was the military type, but we were all enlisted, like it or not.

There was no way I could think of him as head of the family. That sacred position was held by the man whose name was on those books on Mom's shelf.

Why couldn't Captain have stayed? What was so bad about us?

CHAPTER TEN

Erica reached over and turned the alarm off.

Reveille.

I squinted at the daylight through the translucent curtains. There wasn't much sun out there.

I fought for another minute of sleep, thinking how painful the cold autumn day would be.

"Get up, Jonny," Erica said, sleepily. "We gotta do wood."

Aren't there laws restricting work for twelve-year-olds? I thought.

Big Jon opened the door to our room.

"Hey, Jonny, up. Let's go. And for you both: I just saw Beth and Jim's room upstairs and I was appalled at it."

I gulped, sat up in bed immediately. Erica had only managed to open the sweater drawer of her dresser before he came in, and she sorted through it much more slowly now, as if sifting through earthquake wreckage.

"I'll tell you guys the same thing I told them. Keep it clean or you'll be sleeping in the barn. I mean it," he said, punctuating every other word with a finger point and a frown.

He was deadly serious.

"I mean, the cows are neater than you guys."

He wasn't trying to make a joke.

I gulped again, didn't dare look at Erica or Big Jon.

"Look at me," he said.

I strained to look at him.

"You got it?"

"Yeah, I got it," I said with a quiet, shaky voice. Erica said the same with her back to him. She was looking at the floor.

"Okay. Ten minutes. Oh, and make sure the little Homelite saw gets sharpened this morning," he said to me, frowning.

I nodded.

He left the door open and walked upstairs.

I took a deep, nervous breath and started to get dressed. Erica pulled two more drawers open and sorted more quickly what to wear.

"I don't think this room is too bad," she said, looking at a few clothes on the floor.

It was good to hear her talk.

"Neither do I," I said. "I'd rather sleep with the cows than be in this house," I said softly, laughing a little.

She chuckled too, and the heavy air in the room dissolved.

Ten minutes later, after a quick, fend-for-yourself breakfast, Erica, Jim, Beth, and I assembled in the kitchen, putting on our boots and coats. None of us said anything. Jim looked tired and mad, Beth looked confused, Erica looked the most ready to work, but seemed just as reluctant to face the day.

Mom put on her boots with the rest of us.

I was the first out the door and headed to the little shed where the chain saws were kept. It was my job to make sure they were sharpened, oiled, and ready. The two chain saws were always there.

But not today. One was missing.

"What the . . . where's the little Homelite?" I asked myself, searching the shed for it.

I looked in the garage, in the other shed where the tractor was kept, in the shed where general everything stuff was kept, and in the back of the truck. It was nowhere.

Big Jon probably knew where it was.

I shuddered at the thought of asking him anything, but I had to find it and sharpen it or I'd be punished.

I was about to go into the house to ask him when I saw him coming out. Erica followed a few feet behind him, Beth after her. Jim lagged behind.

"Got the saw ready to go?" Big Jon said to me forcefully.

"Not yet. I can't find it."

"Weren't you supposed to sharpen it?"

Big Jon continued to walk, his heavy, slow steps crunching gravel.

He stopped just in front of me. Erica, Beth, and Jim passed him, heading for the truck nearby.

"Yeah, I know. I was about to, but . . . "

"When did I tell you to sharpen it?"

I felt chills, swallowed.

"This morning."

"No," he said firmly. "When did I tell you to sharpen it?"

I looked at the gravel and remembered.

"A few days ago, I think."

"You mean three days ago," he said calmly.

"Yeah," I said.

"What?"

"Three days ago," I said louder.

Chills, an iron ball in my throat, my heart beating faster.

"Yep," he said. "Oh, it's okay, just bring the ax with you when you come out to the field."

The ball swelled in my throat. I never used an ax on the days we cut wood. I hadn't known we owned an ax.

"The ax?" I said, clearing my throat. "If I could find the Homelite, I'd sharpen it."

"The Homelite's up at Marken's," he said. "I brought it up there yesterday."

Yesterday.

I fought tears, ashamed of my bad memory.

"When's it gonna be . . . "

"Won't be ready until Monday," Big Jon said, glaring at me. "So bring the ax when you come out. Got it?"

I felt water in my eyes.

"Yes." I sniffed quickly.

His eyes stayed sharp on me for a second, then he walked indifferently to the driver's side of the truck.

I gasped for a breath, turned, and went into the shed. It was nice to be out of his sight, but I hoped my brother and sisters could see me. I saw Mom pass by the shed, about to get into the truck. I didn't want to create a big scene by telling her how I felt. She'd probably just tell me, as she had before, that Jon's way of teaching responsibility was just something we had to get used to, as much as *she* didn't like it sometimes.

I lifted the rusty ax from its place in the wall and let the tears come, falling hard on the shed's oily wooden floor.

Days when I flew with Mom in the heavenly freedom of a clear Vermont summer seemed like someone else's memories.

CHAPTER ELEVEN

A few yards away from the tree I was cutting, the sputtering hydraulic log splitter was hard at work. Erica loaded short logs on the flat steel platform, Mom operated the hydraulic cylinder that pushed the logs against a stationary steel blade, Jim took the wood as it split and threw it onto the truck, and Beth brought freshly cut logs over to a pile near Erica.

We'd been working an hour before Big Jon came over to me where I was slowly chipping away at a stingy piece of elm.

"I don't expect you to go the whole day cutting with the ax," he said. "But I *do* want you to learn about responsibility."

I nodded, looked at the forest floor, wiped my sweaty brow with my soiled-gloved hand.

"The Homelite's in the car," he said.

I shook my head in disgust. No tears this time, just frustration and anger.

In the car? It's been in the damn car all this time?

I walked the half mile back to the garage, calling him a son of a bitch at every other step.

There are fathers and there are dads. Big Jon was neither to me.

A dad would never do this to me, I thought. *A dad is not a guy to be feared.*

We ended at two that afternoon—seven straight hours of cutting, carrying, splitting, loading, unloading, stacking.

Beth walked down the driveway to check the mail, Erica followed her, and I went in the house with Jim. He went back up to his room to sleep and I searched the kitchen cupboards for food while Mom took off her boots.

Big Jon got in the truck to go into town.

As the tailgate of the pickup truck turned out of the driveway, I sat down on my bed in the next room, soaking up a bit of freedom as I held a day-old doughnut from the kitchen cupboard.

It was one of those rare times I could be lazy.

I didn't know why, but I felt like writing for the first time in months. It was a feeling I hadn't had since Mom married Jon. Fears of him changing my life against my will had squelched my creativity. To write under the shadow of this man now living in the house was scary. I was afraid he would make me do something more productive, something more consistent with "supporting the family."

I suspected that Mom would surely come to my rescue, threaten to divorce him if he ever prevented me from expressing whatever natural talent I had. It'd be like bumping into the class bully after school: since you're outside school grounds, for him to hit you violates serious civil rights guaranteed under the Constitution.

Writing could become my new refuge, a safety zone from the bully and the adult world where kids had to do as they were told.

But I thought about that day when Big Jon grabbed my wrist, and my faith that Mom could protect me dwindled to nothing.

I suspected that Captain could protect me if he knew me better. I reminded myself I didn't know that much about *him,* and for the first time, not knowing much made me feel incomplete, like handing in a book report to a teacher after I'd lazily skimmed the chapters.

Kris and Rob knew him well because they had been my age when he left, but they didn't say much about him. Erica and Jim had flown out to Los Angeles to see him earlier that year and they came back with lots of good things to tell: he had a big house and a pool and showed them around the city, took them shopping, made pan-bread, asked a lot of questions, talked about all kinds of things like what Erica and Jim wanted to do when they got older.

They also said Captain had a new wife, that her name was Leslie Parrish, and she was really, really nice.

I didn't care how nice she was. He had married her instead of remarrying Mom. Hadn't Mom said he vowed never to marry again?

I realized it must have been *us kids* he left. Words hit me from long ago confirming that: his daddy-part died.

But Erica and Jim said they had such a great time . . .

Richard had bought Jim one of those expensive electronic kits with the panel and the wires and other assorted gizmos. Jim thought Captain was a great guy.

I didn't know what to think. I figured they liked him so much because they were older and could understand him better. But if they had fun, maybe Beth and I could too. I knew Kris and Rob had already spent time with him, and I learned Beth and I were the next to go.

I tried to put my confusion aside.

Married. Mom had married, so maybe that wasn't so bad. For a second I wondered why they couldn't have just married each other again. But I didn't allow myself to think that way. Trying to postulate about impossibilities would only have led to more confusion.

In my room, Dick Bach's old Smith-Corona typewriter rested on the desk next to the window by Erica's bed.

Erica came in the room as I put the paper in the carriage. I thought she was going to say something about my being on her side of the room again, and I was prepared to argue again that there was no room on my side to type. She didn't say anything, but I waited until she left to start writing.

I took a breath and thought.

After what had happened with Big Jon that morning, Richard had a better chance of being my "dad" than Big Jon. The vague, misty image of him didn't seem so cloudy anymore.

I didn't know what to say to my father. I just knew I wanted to say something.

I thought of the few stories I had just written for my sixth-grade English composition class, read them over, screened them to make sure they were as entertaining as I wanted them to be. There was one I had written about the hassles of mowing a small graveyard and another about playing video games.

I put a fresh piece of paper in the typewriter and started a letter.

September 2, 1980
Dear Captain,

I wanted to write you and say that I am writing a few stories. Your books are on the shelf with the other flying ones, but I haven't read them yet. I want to be a writer too someday.

Mom said it's in the genes, but I still need some practice. Maybe I'll be good enough to write a whole book someday. For now, there's work around the house and sometimes I don't feel like writing.

Someday all the wood will be split already and I can have time to do more writing! I wish! Still, I still manage to get some writing done so it isn't too bad.

The stories I sent will give you a good idea of the things I'm doing and my writing style. Feel free to comment on them as much as you want. Like I said, I still need to make a few more drafts before they are as good as they can be, but they're not bad the way they are now.

Hope you are fine and that all is well.

Hope you can write me a letter soon!

Love,
JONATHAN

I scrolled the letter out of the typewriter and read it twice more. A few minutes later, I asked Mom for Richard's address.

She gave it to me without asking why I wanted it, but I suspected she wanted to know.

"I'm sending him some of my stories. Is that okay?"

She cleared her throat.

"Sure. I think he'd love to see what you've written."

I hoped I wasn't making her feel bad, but there was no way to know for sure. She seemed genuinely supportive. So, with a murky conscience, I put the letter in the mailbox. I felt daring and adventurous, a bit more free from Big Jon's authority.

Back in the house, I let my weight press into the couch and stared at the bookshelf against the wall. There was that sacred section of Bach books in every house we'd ever had, now in the den of this house.

The cover of *Nothing by Chance* radiated like an orange beacon. Mom said it was about flying, not as philosophical as *Jonathan Livingston Seagull*. I decided I wasn't old enough to get into weird stuff and reading about flying would be better.

I went to the shelf, took the book out. The cover was as mystical as when I had first seen it.

I opened to the first chapter, wondering why it had never occurred to me to read it until then.

Chapter one.

The river was wine beneath our wings—dark royal June Wisconsin wine. It poured deep purple from one side of the valley to the other, and back again. The highway leaped across it once, twice, twice more, a daring shuttlecock weaving a thread of hard concrete.

I stopped reading.

Big Jon was home, the pickup's tires grinding gravel as he turned back up the driveway. I felt that iron ball again, this time in my stomach.

What's he doing back so fast?

I closed the book, wedging my finger between pages zero and one. I got to my room as fast as I could. I hadn't cleaned an inch of it since he woke me up that morning.

I harvested clothes off the floor like a frantic berrypicker, scared that Big Jon would come in.

But my fear wasn't as strong as it usually was. There was a part of me, a new part, that didn't seem to care if he saw the room messy, no matter what his threat was that morning.

That opening paragraph was the reason.

With his words, my father put me back in the front seat of the Tiger Moth, flying with Mom over the Sugarbush Valley.

Chapter Twelve

A week later, it came.

"You got a letter from Richard," Erica said to me as she came into our room. She threw it to me while Beth leafed through the new L. L. Bean catalog on Erica's bed.

The letter drifted ungracefully down to me on my bed, landing on my open motorcycle magazine.

"Cool! He answered my letter!"

"You wrote him? What'd you say?" Erica asked.

"I just told him I was writing stuff. Y'know, that little arcade story I showed you and you said it was pretty good?"

"Yeah . . . "

"Well, I figured since you and Jim went out to see him, I'd send him a letter to tell him about me before it was my turn to go."

"And mine too," Beth said.

"Yeah, yeah, and yours."

I opened the letter, feeling a flutter of excitement in my stomach.

I made sure Big Jon was out of sight, returned to my bed, and started to read Richard's typewritten words.

September 11, 1980
Dear Jonathan,

What a strange letter you write! Happy and sad, hopeful, thoughtful. I'm interested that you're thinking of being a writer. It's one of those rare fields where everything depends on what you do, nothing on what you say that isn't in print. Nobody can even help you much, except with general advice: learn how to type well, read a lot, find out the things that you like and the things you hate, go off alone and find out what you already know about everything from angels to zebras, and what you think that's fun and different from what other people know, write it down and send it off to a publisher. Good grammar and punctuation are pretty basic, so you'll know which rules you'll be breaking when the time comes to break 'em. (Sometimes you might want one sentence to run on for 3,000 words, other times you might want a sentence: "m."

The most important thing in writing, I think, is not to pay attention to what anybody else has to say about your work . . . just to be true to what you honestly like to write and read. If you write for yourself—to surprise yourself, make yourself laugh and cry, amaze yourself with the things you notice, tiny details and huge canvases wrapped around planets, you'll be a success. The only thing you have to give as a writer is your own originality. If you copy what you think other people think you ought to write, and say it the way everybody else has had a safe time saying it, then your originality has remained untouched and the publisher says, "I've seen this before." On the other hand, if you are true to your inner original self, you'll never have any competition as a writer . . . others can imitate what you've already done, but no one can imitate the next thing you write. That way you'll always have a fresh unboring gift to give to the world, and people will always be eager to see the next idea that Jonathan Bach puts in print.

You do an excellent job of painting a picture and connecting it with feelings, and that is what writing is mostly about. Nearly every story is this simple: somebody wants something, something stands in their way, this is what they do about it. That is a huge simplification, but try it on any story and see if you can find it there. Luke Skywalker wants freedom for the people of the galaxy, Darth and the Empire stand in his way, this is what he does about it. Joe Pendleton wants to be a quarterback for the Rams, he is killed by mistake, this is what he does about it.

If you continue with your writing, now or ever, I'd be very happy to read your stories. The only string attached is that I only want to see the stories that you have written that you like most of all. If you don't like a story, or think it doesn't work somehow, then if I say, "I don't think it works," I'm not telling you anything you don't already know. If you think it's terrific, I can tell you where and maybe why it's terrific, where it impresses me and where I don't understand it. There is no reason why you can't write and sell things right away . . . publishers don't care how old somebody is, or what they look like; all that matters is what they say and how they say it.

For more practice, you might try writing about the first thing that meets your eye, or the first thought that meets your mind after you settle yourself at the typewriter. What do you know about that leaf, for instance, or that bird, or that cloud or raindrop? Why should your reader care about them? To practice writing about thoughts, let me know why you're depressed, and what you plan to do to become happy again. You might practice with an interview with Beth or Erica or Jim, find out what they believe, what makes them happy and sad, and write a story about them using accurate quotes of what they say. Your job as a writer in that case would not be to make them happy with what you write, but to say something true about who they are. If you do this well, they will tend to be happy with what you write. If you would like an assignment, consider it this: I commission you to write a story at least 2,000 words long about The Incredible Young Bachs (or whatever better title you have), based on interviews with Erica and Jim or Beth, that has a viewpoint and comes to some definite conclusions about why these people are different from any others in the world. No help allowed, except of course you are free to ask them any question for the interview that they feel like answering. Maybe in the course of the story you'll find something surprising about them, and about you, too.

What do you think?

Love,
Richard

I started reading the letter again, slowly—scanning for something I might have missed, never forgetting that these were the first words I'd ever heard from that man in the wheelchair.

There was nothing about going out to see him. Maybe that would come later, in response to my next letter.

I read the letter a second, then a third time, trying to let his philosophy about writing sink into me.

"What's he say?" Erica asked.

"Oh, stuff about writing . . . " I said, scanning paragraphs, "and how he'd like to see whatever I write and . . . he says I do a good job of painting a picture for a reader . . . that kind of stuff."

She gave a slightly interested "hm" as I thought of what I was going to send him next.

I put a new piece of paper in the typewriter.

The Bachs
by Jonathan Bach
September 15, 1980

In writing today at school we did something called a brainstorm. It's just like letting your mind go crazy about anything and writing it down. The first things that come to mind right now is the family:

Kris: 22, tall, smart, nice, likes purple things, lives in Colorado and goes to school there, went to a private high school in Michigan and played the flute and danced ballet. She always calls me Jonathane.

Rob: 19, knows how to fly a plane, is really funny, went to that same school as Kris, played bassoon and did some acting in a play there, and draws cartoons for me. He works in a deli in the town where we used to live.

Erica: 16, reddish hair, freckles, is nice, but can be mean sometimes like Jim—but not so much anymore. She worked at a golf course last summer and made lots of tips. She's funny sometimes too.

Jim: 14, really smart, brainy, likes dinosaurs and planets, computers, and got all mad at Jon for making him do the work we all do. He's just lazy, but he really gets mad too about it. He hates the work. So do I, but he's more bold than me.

Beth: 11, a good skater with all kinds of patches and stuff, blonde hair, blue eyes, lots of boyfriends who are really bad I think. We get along okay, but we fight sometimes. She's in the fourth grade at my school.

Mom is just the best. There's too much to tell. She raised us all by herself and doesn't yell at us or hit us or anything like that. She gave me Captain's typewriter he used to write *Jonathan Livingston Seagull* on for my birthday. It really feels like it's important.

There was nothing else to write about the family. I knew a lot about flying and it occurred to me I had never written a brainstorm about it.

Flying: free, fun, high, exhilarating, instruments, ratings, fast, scenic, up into the wild blue yonder, sometimes silent, useful purposes, career, airshows, need gas, push throttle . . .

I cheated. Took a second or two to think.

Scenic is seeing the houses, cars, etc., below like tiny toys. Green Mountains, green everything. On the lake, sailboats, scattered like spilled pepper. Ferries going across, cars traveling on the roads.

Nothing else came. I read what I had written and decided I'd captured the basic elements of flying.

I'll try to write more later.

But when later came, I read the brainstorm writing again and decided there wasn't any way to make it into a story I felt good about sending. I decided that even though I had been "commissioned" by Richard to write it, *The Incredible Young Bachs* wasn't something I wanted to write.

In an hour, I had finished a story about playing soccer.

September 15, 1980
Dear Captain,

Your letter was a relief to receive!! I've written another story about soccer season. It's okay, but it could be better. I'll try to keep you up to date on my stories. We (the English class) have been working on leads for future stories.

I've often thought about writing a book but I can't seem to develop a good topic that pleases me and the reader too. One technique I like to use for writing is humor. I like to make the reader laugh. The second technique I like to use is imagery. Make the reader feel that he-she is in my shoes.

The graveyard story was true, by the way. It was flattering to read I had the right idea of what I was doing. Like a pro, huh? Well, I do my best. It's exciting to read about young authors writing books. I figure at the rate I'm going, by the time I'm 16 or 17, I oughta be pretty good at writing. I plan to take a writing course in high school. I'm going to be the best at the writing profession.

Hint: as quoted by Jonathan Bach: "A letter in the mail is very gratifying!"

Love,
Jonathan

Chapter Thirteen

A few letterless days later, Mom handed me the phone and looked away as I took it. All she had said to the caller was "Hello," "Fine," and, "Yes, he's right here."

She told me it was my father.

I felt tingles of excitement for a flash second and took a deep breath. "Hello?"

"Jonathan, my son!"

His voice was slightly gravelly and genuinely warm. Hearing the soft long-distance whine in the background made him seem omniscient. It was the first time I heard a man call me "son." It might as well have been said by any one of those male pilots at Sugarbush.

"Hey! How are you?" I asked.

"I'm great! I just got your last letter!" he said.

"Oh, good! So you really think I'm good at writing, huh?"

"Good? You make my stuff seem utterly booooring!"

"Yeah, right . . . "

"No, really, I'm serious! That's some impressive stuff you've got there and I guarantee you'll be a success if you keep going the way you are."

I took a pen from the jar near the phone and began writing on the back of the phone book: *guarantee success if keep going.*

"Well, I just write what I like—my experiences and things like that. Maybe I'll even write about this or something."

"Oh, that would be great! Sounds like you're finding that anything, any experience, any feeling, any thought or emotion can fit in any paragraph you create, and that's wonderful to see. Have fun with those crazy sentences only you understand. Spin them around, backward, forward. If you write what you see, what you feel, you'll take your reader down the same path you took and a lot of them might say, 'Yeah, I know what that's like, too,' and you'll speak for those who don't find writing as much fun as you."

"Wow . . . " I said. I had abandoned my note-taking and was just as spellbound as when I'd started reading *Nothing by Chance*.

"So write those stories about graveyards and mower blades and soccer games. You'll only get better. There are bits and pieces, minor elements of your soccer story that could stand a little practice in smoothing out, but you have an astonishing gift of theme, of overall impact to your stories, that I've never seen in any young writer anywhere. Your final sentence, in every story I've read, has the kick of a practiced field-goaler. You do not explain too much, you do not talk down to your reader, and those are things so many people never learn. What they learn and you miss is to type all stories double space and to replace bad ribbons!"

He laughed a little bit and I joined him.

"Sorry, I'll try to watch out for that."

"Great, then you'll have this writing business sewn up. My, you have a future in this business if you want it! What fun it will be to get together one day and have a chance to discuss this in detail! Until then, though, show what you live and what you love, write what you see as clearly as you can, as excitedly as you can, and let your destiny take you from there."

"I could write a whole book about this place," I said, "but sometimes there's just too much to do."

I talked about the chores I was doing around the house, mentioned how Jon had helped me buy a motorcycle, which was running better since he'd taught me how the carburetor worked. I even mentioned a little about the drudgery of cutting wood, but didn't get into the specifics of the ax incident or anything else about Big Jon.

He listened patiently as I talked.

Five minutes later, I had told him all the interesting stuff. There was a moment of silence and I asked him if he was writing anything new.

He said he was dealing with something called the IRS and how that was intense work that left little time for writing.

"I know the feeling," I said, thinking of how badly I wanted to get out of doing the small list of things Mom wanted me to do that day.

"So, my son, I just called to see how you were doing. Let me reiterate that I'd be glad to see any writing you want to send me, provided you like it."

"Okay. Thanks for calling. I'll probably send you something when I get it done."

We said goodbye and I hung up the phone.

Richard hadn't asked to speak to anyone but me and it felt great. There was something in his voice, his vocabulary, his tone, that immediately inspired me to write. I didn't think of him as anything else but a man who was famous for writing.

A minute later, I was at the typewriter.

I figured since Richard had already seen my first-person nonfiction style, he might like some fiction.

The paper was canvas and I saw the pictures I wanted to write. They came fast, as if I were watching it: there was a guy named Stu and he was trying to get out of town with his pet goldfish Herman who was in a fishbowl on the passenger's seat as he drove and it was a tornado they were escaping, no, wind and rain and clouds so dark they were night . . .

CHAPTER FOURTEEN

I hadn't read many books at age twelve, but *Nothing by Chance* was my instant favorite.

It was a story about Richard's adventures when he was barnstorming with two friends in the late '60's. One of those friends, like Mom had said, was parachutist Stu MacPherson, and the other was a guy named Paul Hansen who flew a Luscombe. Richard flew a 1929 biplane as the trio traveled the midwest of America, surviving on the money they made flying three-dollar rides out of hayfields.

The book was full of stories: the mouse that ate through a clothes bag and got to some cheese and chocolate; the time when Stu's parachute failed, but he landed without injury in thick, tall grass; the time Richard let Paul fly his biplane and Paul smashed it up when he landed; and yet another time it was smashed.

The images were so vivid, I felt like I could easily tell Richard, "Thanks for letting me come along on the trip."

Mom was mentioned once or twice, but not us kids, so I puzzled where we must have been while he was doing this barnstorming stuff.

I guess it didn't really matter. Richard was my favorite author. His writing made me glad that flying, an activity no one else in school had experienced, was my culture. And like having a secret stack of candy bars under my bed, I was excited to read the rest of his books.

Chapter Fifteen

In the living room one night a few weeks later, Jim had center stage in front of the TV. Erica and I watched him from the couch as he harassed Beth with "mousies"—a cast of hand characters he had invented.

I was only half watching because I was trying to read another of Richard's books, *Biplane,* about why people don't fly antique biplanes from coast to coast. *A Gift of Wings* and *Stranger to the Ground* waited in a pile next to me.

I was nearing the final chapter when Big Jon came through the front door. He'd just come from Erica's and Jim's bedrooms in the apartment over the garage.

He stopped where the kitchen linoleum met living room carpet. Conner had been sleeping there, but he sprang up quickly and walked sleepily away, surrendering his warm place on the floor to Big Jon's muddy boots.

"Jim, would you like to sleep in the barn tonight?" he said nonchalantly.

I felt a chill, gulped, surprised I wasn't used to these situations by now.

"What?" Jim asked, looking straight at Big Jon.

"Would you like to sleep outside in the barn, which is cleaner than your room?"

Beth turned down the TV slightly. Erica looked at Jim from the couch.

"What difference does it make if my room is clean?" Jim asked bravely.

"Because I won't have a pig living under my roof, that's why. Pigs live outside. I didn't build that place for you so you could keep it looking like that. I used my blood, my sweat, to build that place and . . . "

"That's stupid," Jim said sullenly. Erica sat uneasily next to him, staring at the floor.

Jim was right. That was stupid. We'd all helped build the annex.

"Stupid? Listen, I don't owe you a house, food, I don't owe you a damn anything." Jon punctuated every word with a finger point.

Mom was washing dishes right next to him.

"Jimmy." She sighed, turning toward us. "All we want is for you to volunteer to do some things around the house instead of us always having to drag you to do them."

Jim nodded, got up, and went toward the kitchen.

"We all have to do our share of the work," Mom said. "Nobody likes it, but it has to be done."

Jim walked past Big Jon and into the kitchen. For a moment I thought he wasn't going to let Jim walk by, but he must have figured Jim was going out to clean his room like he was told. Jim sat on the boot bench in the entryway, putting on his shoes.

"I do my share," he said quietly.

"Listen, it's your attitude," Mom said. "We don't want you around here if you're going to be brooding all the time! We don't want grunts in the morning from you. A civil 'good morning' and a willing helping hand wouldn't kill you."

Jim sat silent. He'd heard this before. We *all* had, but it had never been this intense.

"Understand that?" Jon asked.

"Yeah."

"You understand that I want your room to look like a human lives there and not a cow?"

"No, I don't," Jim said.

Big Jon stood and stared at Jim.

"You push me to the edge, Jim, you really do," he said with an unstable, threatening chuckle.

Nobody talked for a few heavy seconds. This new comment from Jon wasn't part of their normal disagreements.

"What. You gonna hit me?" Jim asked with a shaky voice. "Go

ahead. Maybe . . . maybe you might find some holes in your damn airplanes!"

Big Jon glowered. "You do that and maybe there'll be holes in you!"

Jim stood up, his face red. He was at his limit too. In his face I saw the same kind of aggravated frustration I'd seen when Astra died. It was as if Astra were being killed again—this time by Big Jon.

"If you touch me I'll kill you with the shotgun!" Jim hissed.

I knew Jim had a 20-gauge in his room. Big Jon had given it to him for his last birthday, and he'd taken it with him when he and Big Jon went hunting this fall.

The gun might just as well have fired from the kitchen. I couldn't believe what I'd heard.

Apparently, neither did Mom.

"Now stop it! Dammit, you guys! Stop it now! I won't have you two doing this, I just won't!"

Erica watched them as Beth turned the TV all the way down without taking her eyes off the confrontation. We were transfixed not just by the prospect of seeing a battle between Jim and Big Jon, but mainly because Mom never swore. Her "dammit" upgraded the argument to the seriousness of an impending nuclear attack. It sobered us more than the harsh words between Big Jon and Jim. It told us that this was it—this was the time for something major to happen.

They stayed quiet.

It seemed to be up to Mom.

"Jim, I think it's best if you leave. Not to your room, but out. It's clear you guys can't be in the same house. I won't have this anymore!"

"Fine," he said quietly and went out to his room.

Erica, Beth, and I breathed uneasy relief from the living room a few feet away. Uncertainty surrounded us. Anything could happen. Big Jon could suddenly decide to hit Jim anyway, lash out at Mom or at us, or maybe just leave and not come back.

Beth stared at the silent TV, Erica stared at the coffee table, I stared at my closed book. Big Jon went out the door and headed to the garage. Mom followed him.

When the door closed, Conner returned to his sleep at the edge of the kitchen linoleum and the rest of us were silent.

CHAPTER SIXTEEN

Lucky guy, he's outta here.

I was happy for my fourteen-year-old brother, who, that next day, was in his room packing boxes to move into a place Mom had found for him a mile away called, ironically enough, Mother's Motel.

I was excited for him because I knew he was smart enough to live by himself. I was also glad that his leaving would lessen the tension there had been around the house every time Big Jon and Jim had a discussion about his attitude. The icing on the cake for me was that as soon as he was gone, I could have his annex room.

Mom had called Richard, told him whatever, and things had been put in motion for Jim to leave. Jim told me he talked with Richard too.

"What'd he say?" I asked Jim as he spilled parts of a computer into a box of books.

"He's going to be sending me my part of the child support money— two hundred and eighty dollars a month. I guess a hundred and fifty of that will be for rent at the motel."

He threw clothes into the box as Beth and Erica watched from the doorway of his room.

"You mad?" Erica asked, sitting on his floor.

"No way! I'm glad to be outta here, man!"

"Yeah, I'll bet."

None of us doubted him. Big Jon's directness and laws were a wall to Jim's aspirations and we all knew he'd have to get past that wall to survive. But just when all of us were expecting him to dig under it, he crashed through it.

He was free of the chores and the rules now, but whatever jealousy we had melted into an easy support for him. We all knew it had to be this way. We all knew Jim was a special case. The rest of us could put up with the military discipline.

I helped him throw the rest of his stuff into four empty boxes. His intelligence covered the floor: a microscope, an old chemistry set, electronic parts, a *Dungeons and Dragons* game, another military strategy board game I had tried to play with him but never understood, a few maps of the solar system, assorted wires, rocks, and fossils.

We took the boxes over to the motel and left him to settle in.

Two days later, I went over to see him.

When he answered the door to his dark room, there was a faint smell of bug killer, frozen pizza, and propane from the gas stove. The room was stuffy, and the blinds were drawn. Dead ants littered the kitchen counter.

Jim was shrouded in the glow from the Apple computer Richard had bought him a few months before. It was the only uncluttered part of the room.

The place scared me. Even though he was there, I felt alone and uneasy, as if I were hundreds of miles from home. I hoped I would never have to have my own place at age fourteen. Home was fine with me, even with Big Jon's rules.

I kept my shoes on when I entered, just in case there were any live ants still roaming around.

"So this is your pad, huh?" I asked my brother.

"Yep."

The room was perfect for him. The darkness fit his brooding, gloomily pensive character. Any room seemed to be perfect where he was away from Big Jon. But it wasn't just Big Jon that Jim defied. In school, he reacted to rules by breaking them. He got into fights, never did homework, skipped a lot of days because he stayed up so late working with his computer that he often slept through his alarm.

But he never drank or smoked or did drugs or committed any crimes. He was unpopular even with the kids that were unpopular.

And now that Jim was out of the house, he had regular conversations with Richard. At a pay phone down the road from the motel, he'd tell Richard about computer programs he was working on, or the problems he had with school.

He said Richard supported his absences because it was clear to him that school wasn't making Jim happy. I wished Richard could give me the same endorsement, but the way Big Jon talked about the "real world," I knew school was the better plan for me in the long term, no matter how bad I wanted out.

I figured that Jim didn't need a dad, just a fellow philosopher-scientist-thinker-reader. I thought about Richard's letters and suddenly understood why they got along so well.

Every time Jim talked with Richard, magical things happened—Jim's usual calm, brooding attitude turned perky, optimistic, energized, inventive, and creative.

He was all of these one day.

"Guess who's thinking about flying out to see us?" he asked me, taking my right arm and shaking it excitedly.

"Uh . . . Kris?"

"No, man! Richard! Can you believe that?"

I couldn't believe it.

"Wow, that's cool," I said apprehensively.

I thought of his books about flying—the ones I could easily understand. But those were the books by "Dick" Bach, not this philosophical Richard guy. Mom told me they were two different people and I could see that very clearly. I knew *Jonathan Livingston Seagull* or *Illusions* might help me understand who he'd become, but after reading the first few pages of each book, I found it too hard.

Richard and I couldn't talk about the flying books, I thought. *I'll bet he doesn't like to talk about such practical things. We could talk about writing, of course, although I haven't done much lately . . .*

Jim whistled as he waited for his computer to come to life. I sat on his bed, a few loose corn chips next to me, scanning for ants as I usually did.

I suspected Jim would soon be out of this place, zooming off somewhere, probably with Richard. Unlike me. He was a superglider, able to be launched with only a whisper of air. And while Jim rose above the clouds to the rest of his life, I would stay on the ground because it was safer.

Now that he was out of the house, Jim had the world at his disposal. I saw his life in motion picture frames:

Jim smashes wall and finds himself in an endless, open field. Circling above him in a bright yellow airplane is Richard Bach and a mysterious woman that is his wife, Leslie Parrish.

Strangely enough, Jim doesn't wave for help. He looks around, gets his bearing, sets his sights on building some type of structure for himself. All he has are his clothes and a computer. That's all he seems to need.

As Jim looks around, Richard and Leslie land nearby and taxi over.

Brother Jonathan watches them from within walls of transparent steel, but he's content there. It is frightening to him to think of breaking through those walls. He doesn't think he'd be able to survive. Jim's grassy field would be a hot, scorched, brutal desert to him—a place where survival was everything. Forget trying to build a house. If it came right down to it, Jonathan thinks he would die if he had to be on his own. For him, it's safer in the walls.

Jim, Richard, and Leslie are still in the field, its soil fertile enough to grow rocks. But fertile soil or not, Jim is a seed that can grow in any climate. Richard and Leslie have their plane, allowing them to bridge any distance and land where the best climates are. Together, they seem like an unconquerable team.

Jonathan watches them, but to his surprise, Richard and Leslie do not load Jim in the plane. After they circle and land, they just talk to him. After a short while, Richard and Leslie take off, but stay circling above. Jim trudges off into a nearby forest, cuts wood with his bare hands, brings it out to the field and starts building his house.

Jonathan keeps watching as the picture fades.

Richard asked me if I wanted to try. I lay there as Richard sat peacefully in a chair. He said the same things about relaxation to me and I did the best I could to listen. He said to tell him the kinds of images I was having. It was like dreaming while I was awake.

I flew over clouds and down into a huge field. I saw a big, white farmhouse, with hardwood floors inside and big windows facing east. The sun was up and the day was clear blue, but it was snowing. The snow covered the ground and disappeared at first, but then it piled up an inch a second as I watched from inside the house. It covered the house and as I went to the top floors and above the snow it melted just as quickly as it rose.

It was weird.

"Snow on a sunny day in a big house," I told him.

Just saying that much was spooky.

I opened my eyes and said, "Is it supposed to mean something?"

"Hm," Richard said. "Could be a lot of things. You'll know in time, I think. Hard to say for now."

He looked down on the floor for a half second and looked up again, raising his eyebrows at me. It was as if he knew exactly what my visions meant, but couldn't tell me about it. Either it was so weird he really didn't know what to make of it, or he knew and didn't want to get into it.

Beth and Erica didn't want to try. Maybe because of something they saw in Richard's face or mine, but I was the last and that seemed a good time to end. I spent the rest of the day listening to everybody else. We went in a bookstore and he told us that we each had $100 to get any books we wanted. A hundred dollars! It was a better treat than going to a toy store. I picked only two science fiction books and stood by the counter and waited for everybody else.

"Only two books?" Jim said. "Geez, man, you should get more than that! Look at my pile." He must have had twenty books of varying sizes: seven about computers, two science fiction, and a mess of others. Erica and Beth were busy picking. Their piles were also bigger than mine.

I looked around and strained to find another science fiction story I liked. I returned to the counter with it. It was the same size and price as the other two in my hand.

"That's all you want, Jon?" Richard asked.

"Yeah, really. This is it."

Beth and Erica looked at me. Erica had six books, Beth had five.

I felt good for staying low. They didn't say anything to me. We all thanked him and Leslie, then headed over for lunch at Carbur's, that restaurant famous for its 26-page menu describing meals in funny detail.

While Beth and Erica were having a great time drawing pictures on their paper placemats, and Jim and Leslie talked, Richard touched me on my left shoulder and commented to me that I had been so quiet.

"Yeah. I guess I don't have much to say, that's all," I said.

"You don't have to have anything to say."

"I guess I'm still thinking of that hypnosis thing."

"Ooooh . . . and what about it?"

"It just came to me and I didn't do anything. Like a dream when I was awake. That's pretty weird."

"What do you think about what you saw?"

"I want a house in a field?"

"Maybe," Richard said, "but a house might represent stability or comfort, the field might represent your own space or freedom."

Leslie touched his left shoulder. "Richie," she said. "Sorry to interrupt, but what are you ordering?" He answered her and I thought about something philosophical to say to him. I couldn't think clearly. I was nervous about trying to come up with something so quickly.

"So anyway," he said to me, "it may take some time before you figure out what the images mean, but that's okay."

Dinner came and went, with everybody talking except for me. I didn't know what to say, but it was more fun to listen to everyone else anyway.

After that, we went over to a small ice cream place. Richard somehow knew about the little place, but couldn't remember the name. It was something like Bill & Jeff's or Biff & Joe's or Benson-meier & Jedediah's. He must have come up with another five or six name combinations. He got us all trying to help him remember and we came up with some real doozies in the process.

"No, those are too wild," he said. "It's two basic names . . . "

We pulled into the parking lot of the ice cream parlor, a former gas station, a little place now known as Ben & Jerry's Homemade. Even though we found the place, we didn't stop coming up with name combinations. That was the joke for the rest of the day. Richard had a sense of humor I liked.

At the very end of the day, right before it was time for Erica to drive us home again, we spent the last hour talking as we walked down Church Street marketplace. Leslie walked with Erica and Beth, Jim walked behind them and read one of his new books, Richard and I walked ahead of them and talked about writing. He handed me this red felt-tip pen and this notebook with a green leather cover.

"This might come in handy when you write those images."

I took the little notebook from him and said thanks.

"I guarantee you that ideas will come without notice. This will make it easier for you to keep track so they don't slip away. Any ideas that strike you are fair game. Any observation, anything you hear, taste, smell, touch. It's all good stuff. Consider yourself armed and dangerous now," he said. He said "armed" and "dangerous" in a huskier voice.

"Armed and dangerous. I like that," I said. I stopped right there, sitting on the ground in the marketplace as Richard laughed from above.

CHAPTER NINETEEN

Months after Richard and Leslie went back to the Washington State island where they lived, it was time for a lot of transitions in the family.

Just before I started high school, Jim dropped out. Another wall smashed and he was barely sixteen.

While I stayed in school and played by the rules, Jim was out in what teachers called the "real world," where billions of people went to work, paid bills and taxes, had babies, killed each other, killed themselves. I'd think of Jim as I stared out the classroom windows and out onto the sidewalk watching "real people" who didn't have to be in school.

Mom worried about his seemingly limited and bleak future. She didn't talk much to Jim, and there wasn't much she could have done to persuade him to stay in school. Once Jim got a taste of his new freedom, he was more independent than ever before.

Erica was starting her independence too. I watched her pack to go off to college, glad that she didn't have to deal with woodmares anymore. She said she felt bad for me and Beth, who had to bear the brunt of the chores now, but she'd try to get home as much as she could to help us.

I asked her how much it cost to go to college. She said, "Richard is paying for it."

But after her first semester, Erica was having trouble with grades. I heard her talking to Big Jon about how Richard had told her he couldn't support her anymore. Something about how Richard had gone bankrupt the year before.

How could a guy with so much money go bankrupt? I thought. *The computer he bought for Jim, all those planes Mom said he owned, all*

those books he's written, buying Mom the Tiger Moth, buying all
those books for us in Burlington, the child support checks I see on the
counter.

I knew whenever any of us kids played Monopoly, "bankrupt"
meant you were out of money—right down to the dollar.

I suspected he meant a different kind of bankrupt—that he was just
being philosophical.

But Erica was really distressed. She needed to do something to pay
for college. Without a degree, there was no hope of fulfilling her desire
to be an engineer at IBM like Big Jon. To add to her dismay, Richard
and Leslie sent her a gruff note about how they could only give so much
and to just leave them alone.

I couldn't believe a distant father had the right to be so abrupt.

In January 1983, she enlisted in the National Guard to get the
money for tuition. Then Richard sent her another gruff letter after
she enlisted, remarking coldly that the military was the worst way to
pay for college and that she was ruining any chances for success
because of it.

The letter upset Erica, who, in my opinion, was the gentlest and
most sensitive member of the family.

I was confused.

But Richard had been in the military . . .

I asked Kris what she thought of it and she said Richard did a lot
of strange things like that. She told me a friend of hers had heard him
on a radio talk show and called to ask why he never mentioned Kris
or any other members of his family in any of his books. She said he
gave a terse answer, saying that he wouldn't accept questions about
family. That was that.

I figured it made sense for him to say that because he wanted no part
of being in a family. But if he wanted no part, why had he bought Jim
a computer and written to me about writing and why had he been
paying Erica's tuition?

Weeks later, Mom said he had cut the child support checks he
was sending. He sent the minimum amount he could get away with
by law.

Maybe he *was* bankrupt.

I reminded myself about the nine planes Mom said he had, the few million dollars he had made. Now it was all gone, and for what? So much for setting up security for us. That was the least he could have done after deserting the family.

Soon after that, Beth and I started to get monthly interest statements from a bank in Washington. Sometimes we'd even get short notes from Richard telling us what it was about. Apparently, money for me and Beth was being funneled to two accounts. One of his short notes said we could have access to the accounts when we were eighteen. I didn't understand why the accounts had been set up, but I figured Mom knew why and that was good enough for me.

There were no more letters about writing. He sent short notes along with financial statements.

Dear Jonathan,

Thought you might like an update on all your accounts! We shift the funds from time to time in order to get the best interest rates. Hope all goes well and happily for you.

Love, L&R

Some of the short notes helped to make sense of the official-looking jargon on the lined paper that accompanied them:

Deposits debits totaling service charge money market deposit account interest paid to date in effect today $.00 transaction description 13.68 + interest credit no check activity balance summary 6.5% federal taxes withheld . . . interest paid state taxes withheld this period Y.T.D. ——— balance forward ——— direct purchase distribution since 8/3/82 exchange/liquidation services for which no certificates have been issued shares held by you capital gains 0.00 reinvestment annualized yield 7.90% . . . Checking statement summary: balance $2,082

Wow . . . I thought. *Two thousand! He definitely isn't bankrupt.*

I didn't know what to think of Richard Bach anymore. Nice guy? Indifferent guy? Did he care at all?

I put the financial statement in an envelope with about five others in a bigger envelope in my closet. That same envelope held the few philosophical letters Richard had sent about writing.

Chapter Twenty

Even though it was just Beth and me left at the house, it was business as usual: chores, school, homework. But in the family, changes were occurring with everyone.

Kris had married a guy named Brian, and they lived in Iowa. She wrote me occasionally about her adventures as a student at a place in Iowa called Maharishi International University, but never said much about Richard.

Rob was engaged to Cami, an artist and former professional downhill skier. They headed out to Iowa for reasons I didn't know. Jim went with them because there was more opportunity to work in computers.

Erica was at Vermont Technical College a hundred miles away, trying with renewed effort to fulfill requirements for an associate's degree in electrical engineering.

Richard hadn't called or written in the two years since his visit. I presumed he was busy trying to recover from bankruptcy. I still couldn't believe anyone could blow a few *million* dollars.

In school, a few teachers on learning my name joked about a connection with Johann Sebastian Bach. Three or four asked about a connection with Richard Bach, the author, and I told them what I knew.

I wasn't sure if they were surprised by what I told them or by how readily I spoke.

"Yeah, that's my father, but he left when I was two and I haven't seen him very much since then except for one time when he came to Burlington to spend the day. . . . Yep, I was named after the book, but the book's not written about me or anything, it was just what they decided to name me. . . . No, I'm not the only one, I have two brothers and three sisters, all of them older except my little sister . . . my mom

raised us all by herself until she married my stepfather in 1978. . . .
Time magazine even published a picture of us in 1972 . . . he was the
cover story. . . . My father made a few million dollars and had nine
planes, including a small jet, but now he's bankrupt. . . . He also
remarried in 1978 or thereabouts to this actress named Leslie Parrish,
which was funny because he vowed he would never marry again. . . ."

I always looked at the ground and tried not to sound like a braggart.
I pretended it was just trivia—game show answers.

I couldn't tell them the probing, important information they wanted
to know: what kind of fruit he put on his cereal or his favorite color,
or his age, birthday, what he did on the weekends, or about the first
story he ever wrote.

In autumn 1983, I was starting my second year in high school.
Whenever the subject of parents came up in conversations with my
friends, I complained with the rest of them, but I never mentioned
Richard. I mentioned Big Jon. Most of my closest friends knew he was
just my stepfather, knew about Richard Bach too, but only because
they asked why Big Jon's name was Fineman and mine was Bach.

"This is Jon Bach," friends would say when I met their parents.
Some would add, "His father wrote *Jonathan Livingston Seagull*," and
I'd explain as much of the story as I thought they wanted to hear or
until awkward silence from my lack of information about him eventually stopped the conversation.

They seemed to understand as I stood there, sorting feelings that
swirled like snowflakes.

If they had time, they could go to any library, research some interviews or a biography, do something as effortless as that and they'd be
more informed about him than I.

Most of my friends' parents had heard of *Jonathan Livingston
Seagull*. Most said it was an inspiring book. Some of my friends had
even read it.

I still hadn't. It lay with the others on the den bookshelf, just like
the manila envelope in my closet which contained Richard's letters.

CHAPTER TWENTY-ONE

Erica didn't seem nervous when she told me Rob was planning a family reunion with Richard that 1984 summer in Vermont. I assumed Richard and Erica had resolved whatever bad feelings she'd had about him.

But a reunion. That was interesting. It'd be the first time the entire family was together with Richard since the divorce.

Mom didn't want to go. Not a chance. She didn't give an ounce of indication that she wanted to see him. So Rob planned another gathering upstate in Alburg the next day so Mom could be treated to seeing all us "kids" in one place for the first time since her wedding in 1978.

The reunion with Richard took place at a cabin a hundred miles south of Alburg—Richard and Leslie; Kris and her husband, Brian; Rob and his wife, Cami; Erica, joined by her boyfriend, Dan; and Jim, Beth, and me.

Kris seemed shorter, Rob had a little bit of a beard, Cami was pregnant, Erica was more muscular from military training, Jim was taller and more bulky.

Richard and Leslie looked the same.

Everybody was excited and friendly. We were too old to squabble about who got to sit in the front seat of the car or who got the plastic submarine in the cereal box. We talked about ambitions, school, careers, activities.

We took group pictures: one with just "the guys," one with just "the girls," Richard alone with the guys, Richard alone with the girls, all of us together.

Inside, then, we gathered around a huge couch in front of a fireplace. Rob opened the discussion by thanking everyone for coming, expressing his hope that it was going to be a really cool time, and then turned it over to Richard, who sat next to Leslie by the fire.

I sat between Beth and Erica as I listened to my father. He held Leslie's hand as he spoke.

"To explain what this feels like is almost impossible," he said. "To sit here and see who you've become and who you want to be after years apart is just unexplainable. I thought when I left in 1970 that I'd forgone whatever rights I had to be a part of your lives; that in my leaving, I wasn't entitled to be experiencing what I am now.

"I think a few of you know why I left, but let me make it clear. Bette and I had a good marriage for a long time, but it was a strain on me after a while, and my impulse was to escape. I found myself using my writing as an escape from the responsibility of taking care of all of you. It was hard for me to have a nonintellectual relationship; it was hard for me to relate to you all as children. I knew if I stayed, I might become violent; my temper was becoming shorter, so I knew escaping was the right thing to do. I knew I couldn't be a father. I started to see the reality I had created for myself and knew I couldn't survive there."

It was like Mom had told me. He wasn't cut out to be a dad.

"But you were just a small part of it," he said. "The real problem was between me and Bette."

I looked into my father's eyes. He wasn't Captain anymore, he was Richard. And I wasn't sixteen anymore, I was sixty-six, ready and willing to hear something important and serious.

"Bette and I had a mutual friend named Pauline. She was a true friend to both of us in good and bad times. There was voluminous correspondence between us—representative of a level where things are happening in an exciting, creative world. We had a meeting of the minds that was wonderful. I can only speculate that the kind of communication I was having with Pauline, which Bette was part of as well, began to be threatening to your mother. She probably felt she and I weren't having that kind of intense communication, and her jealousy started a fairly quick downward spiral in our marriage. Bette became less and less a happy participant in that communication. She probably thought, 'Richard likes to talk with Pauline more than he does with me.' When she backed away, I sensed she was jealous. But part of me said, 'I'm not going to ruin a friendship because she chooses to be jealous.' "

Rob looked at the carpet as he sat next to Richard. Kris supported her chin with her hand. Erica stared straight ahead into the fireplace. Jim looked sideways at Richard, past Rob's concentration. Beth looked at the three or four rings on her fingers. Cami, Brian, and Dan watched Richard. I wondered what they thought of it all.

Richard paused, looked down.

"Bette began criticizing my communication with Pauline and then my specific responses to her letters. It made me feel more locked in chains than ever. There was nothing romantic going on at all. So I told Bette, 'If you're going to pick at this communication, don't read our letters. I enjoy it and I'm going to do it.'

"Bette made some kind of critical comment of something that happened in a letter. I had asked her not to read those letters. I felt really ... wow ... a breach of trust! I remember putting a thread across the top of the file drawer where I kept the letters. I was sad that I didn't trust her. But as I feared, the thread was gone one morning. I questioned her about it and she said she hadn't read the letters. She even started to get upset. The trust between us dissolved and the marriage began dissolving with it."

Over and over in my mind: *Did Mom really do that?*

No answer.

"I had once told Pauline if she ever needed me, back there on the East Coast, just call and I'll be there. It was a statement of friendship. But wouldn't you know, Pauline *did* call one day saying she needed my help with something. I told Bette I was going to go, and she was quite distressed about it. Instead of calling Pauline and saying this was going to be a real problem with Bette, I said, 'A promise is a promise.' I had given my word to Pauline.

"I told Bette there was nothing to be jealous about. I remember being very happy that I could have this wonderful friend in New York and I just took for granted that she would understand that happiness. It shattered when I got home. Bette was really upset and really distrustful. I think she was convinced that something romantic had gone on. I remember her words exactly: 'No husband of mine is going to act the way you're acting!' I said, 'You're absolutely right.'

"For me, the marriage ended right there. I remember fragments of a conversation in the kitchen, where we said we no longer loved each other, but that was basically it."

What Richard said made sense, but there was no way *I* would leave to see a woman friend in New York if I had a wife and six kids in Iowa. *Any* wife would get jealous. Any normal husband wouldn't dare do such a thing.

At least he was man enough to face all of us with it. I had to give him credit for that.

"It's like seeing hydraulic pressure pull and pull and pull apart a steel bar. The gauge is going up . . . three thousand pounds, four thousand pounds, nothing happens to the bar. But then . . . WHOK! Very abruptly the steel stretches and snaps. It echoes through the whole laboratory. There is a jagged fracture between the two pieces— no possible way to put them back together."

He paused.

"And during all that time, the airplane was there like a patient friend. I knew I could just walk out that door one day, get in the airplane and fly away. And, at last, that's exactly what I did.

"I regret terribly the pain it caused you all, and had I known a better way I would have chosen it. But if I had stayed with Bette, I would have been destroyed. For better or worse, I could not have become the person you see in front of you now."

Leslie squeezed his hand as he spoke and I realized again that Mom was right when she said he was a different person than Dick Bach. He'd just admitted it. He admitted his mistakes, expressed his guilt, wanted forgiveness. He didn't want to be an abusive father or a mistrusted husband. I was beginning to see his humanness. I even felt sorry for him.

I could handle that. Mom had done a good job raising me to that point and I figured I'd grown out of my need for someone to call dad. He still seemed too philosophical to be a dad anyway.

He told us that after he left it was painful to see Mom build walls to shield him from the six of us, but that was a consequence of his own act. So he paid the child support, bought us the Michigan house, bought Mom the airplane.

"It'd be easier now to answer any of your concerns," he said to his laced hands.

There was a brief silence. Then Beth asked him why he never sent presents or birthday cards.

"That's a fair question," he said. "When you believe that we are never born and we can never die, it doesn't make much sense to celebrate years, to celebrate make-believe limits. We choose life in space-time because we need to learn, because we love to learn. Birthdays are hooks to mortality, baited with cake and candles."

He added that he felt so guilty for leaving, he didn't think he had a right to know what was going on in our lives. Mom had told him it made her sick even to see Richard's postmark, so he stayed distant, communicating only when we communicated with him.

Hmm, so it wasn't just him . . .

He talked about the IRS problems, the friend he had trusted to invest his millions, and how the investments mysteriously vaporized. He admitted his ineptitude with money, told us the shock of trust betrayed, which led to the problems, which led to bankruptcy.

While he talked, *The Bridge Across Forever,* his love story with Leslie, sat on the coffee table. There was a copy for each of us.

We were all getting chances to know him collectively and privately. We took turns talking with him in the next room about anything and everything.

As I waited for Erica to finish with Richard, Jim taught me how to play harmonica. In the two years since he quit school, he'd covered a lot of ground. He'd taught himself computer programming and was now developing educational computer software in California. His fortunes were soaring, he was self-educated, always hungry for knowledge, and exhibited his energy through his harmonica playing. But as he was teaching me to play some easy blues riffs, I was busy thinking about what I was going to say to Richard.

There was no writing to speak about. I had written only a few pages in the two years since he gave me the little green book. School was fine, and there wasn't much else to say. Everybody else seemed to have volumes to talk with him about. I was glad they had so much in common, but it put pressure on me. He would probably notice I was too quiet and ask me questions the way he had in Burlington.

I let the rest take as much time with him as they wanted.

Erica came out with Dan and Richard. Jim immediately stopped his playing and headed over to him.

"See ya', bro. Gotta go rap with Richard," he said briskly.

Nearby, Rob teased Beth about the twenty-five ice-skating merit patches on her jacket, and she loved it. Cami talked with Dan as they cleaned the kitchen; Brian talked quietly with Kris.

I interviewed Erica.

"What'd you guys say?" I asked, sitting next to her as she took her seat with Dan on the couch.

"We talked about college a little bit . . . and the military . . . and IBM a little bit. Not all that much, really."

"Oh," I said, looking at the carpet. "But you guys have talked a lot before though, right?"

"Yeah, pretty much. He knew a lot from the time I went out to see him."

"Oh."

Now I was sure Erica and Richard must have patched whatever disagreements they'd had about money. But Erica still seemed a little distant.

"But I bet *you* guys will have a lot to talk about," she said.

"Yeah. That's a safe bet."

That moment, I missed Mom. My loyalty was to her. She supported our reunion with Richard, but I could sense her real joy would come the next day when we gathered at home. I hoped she wasn't threatened by this gathering, but I made a promise to myself right there to make sure she knew she was more valuable to me than Richard.

I let Erica talk with Dan, decided to pay my reverence to Mom by escaping just a little from this reunion with Richard.

More thoughts as I walked out to the deck and watched the sun sink like a leaky helium balloon.

He'd like that: "Oh, I was just out on the deck, Richard, watching the sun sink down like a leaky helium balloon . . . "

I wondered what writing advice he'd give me this time.

Chapter Twenty-two

Jim came out on the deck ten minutes later.

"Hey, bro, you're next."

As I walked inside, I felt some chills which shortened my next breath.

"Thanks, man."

Richard stood at the kitchen counter at the far end of the living room. He was talking to Beth when he saw me.

"Ready, my son?"

I smiled and said, "Let's cruise."

He laughed and repeated my statement as he closed the door to the bedroom. Leslie sat on the edge of a bed.

We talked about Big Jon and I didn't hold back about how scared he made me sometimes. Richard and Leslie sighed occasionally, shook their heads in disbelief when I told them about times he had threatened things like making us sleep out with the cows to prompt us to be disciplined.

I smiled when I talked about him. After six years with Big Jon, I was an experienced professional in How to Live with Discipline. Talking to Richard made me feel used to Jon's way of teaching responsibility. The lessons didn't seem as harsh as they used to. This is what it meant to be grown-up. Control.

I wanted to tell them other things that had scared me about Jon, so I told them about how he had grabbed my wrist the time he came to dinner when he was dating Mom, told them about the day in the woods with the ax, told them about leaving the cupboard doors open and the fines. Telling them made me feel I had survived them, surmounted the biggest obstacle to growth—fear.

As I talked, they grew more shocked with each story.

Too shocked, I thought. I didn't want them to feel it was so bad that they had to take some kind of court action against him.

Like a trained reporter, I started to balance my stories.

As many times as Jim, my sisters, and I would joke uneasily about how we were privates in basic training, Big Jon taught us practical, easy-to-understand skills.

I told Richard and Leslie that Big Jon had taught me how to level a sight on a .35 Remington hunting rifle, how to change the oil filter on the car, how to grease the bearings on the cutter bar on the back of the tractor, how to mix two-stroke oil with the proper amount of gas for the outboard motor, how to strip paint off an old wooden sailboat, how to put a new piston in my motorcycle, how to tie a necktie.

Big Jon encouraged me to join the Alburg Volunteer Fire Department, of which he was a member, and we spent Monday nights helping to sell cards and food at the weekly bingo game.

He was patient when I mistakenly put kerosene in the tractor gas tank, when I was having problems filing a nick out of the mower blade, when I broke the kitchen window with a rubber ball.

"Oh, it's not like he hits us or anything," I said to a much-too-concerned Richard and Leslie. "He never has. He just threatens sometimes. He's never made anyone sleep in the barn with the cows, but I guess that's just his way of making us learn. He's never yelled at anyone either. He just gets real calm. It's no big deal now. I'm not as scared as I used to be."

Richard spoke. "Jonathan, that's amazing. To stand an environment like that, at least to us, is just phenomenal. I'm baffled. How do you survive?"

I'd never thought of it as "surviving."

"I don't know . . . I just do, I guess. Now that I've thought about it, it's not so bad living there."

Leslie spoke. "We were so worried about you when we heard stories from Erica about fines and threats from Big Jon. But it's not like we can just call, because your mom doesn't like to hear from us. Still, you and Beth really seem to be coping extraordinarily well in spite of it."

I thought of Beth, told them how I felt about her and me being the last ones at home, told them a bunch of other things about the two of us. I told them how the few adolescent battles I'd had with her were well in the past.

I told them Beth was in my high school now and had quickly become popular. She had lots of friends and stunned art teachers with her abilities, stunned the guys with her evolving femininity: her pure blond hair, crystal-blue eyes, Barbie-doll figure. She made friends easily with her honesty and good nature.

I told them the work around the house was the same, even with only the two of us to do it, and she and I seemed to bond because of it. We'd made a kind of unspoken treaty to end our hostilities and focus on paying our dues and sharing the work until we could get out on our own like everybody else.

We liked school and I helped her with the same freshman classes I'd had. Her boyfriend didn't live far from my girlfriend and we'd coordinate trips to see them to save mileage on the car. We both hated chores and had the same fear of Big Jon, but we were a lot less afraid of him than we had been.

As I was telling them about Beth, I realized that even though we'd grown up, neither she nor I mentioned Richard very much. I didn't know how she felt about him. I didn't know if she was getting or sending any more letters than I was. I never had the urge to ask her what she really felt about him and she never volunteered the information to me.

I wondered what she talked about when she was in here. . . .

" . . . so we think she's destined for something wonderful if she stays interested in art," Leslie said.

"Oh, yeah. *Big* time. She's really getting good," I said.

There was a brief silence, quiet enough to hear conversations in the next room.

Richard broke the silence, asked me about school. School was fine, I told him, not much to tell, I didn't hate it as much as Jim had.

And a few brief silences later, there was nothing to talk about. We'd covered school, the family, Big Jon, and a little about how I hadn't done much writing but that was okay, Richard said.

The three of us walked out into the living room, toward the coffee table and the few first-edition copies of Richard's new book.

As they talked with Rob about flying, I collapsed on the couch and started to skim through my copy to see if the family was mentioned in it.

The first few pages didn't appear to be philosophical. It was pretty straight stuff about how he'd given up barnstorming and was looking for a woman.

But around page 50, a few short paragraphs whacked me back into disillusionment with my father. My understanding of his humanness dissolved like ice in hot tea.

On that page, he had written about a woman he had met, a stranger he had found interesting and attractive. Met her at an airshow. Gave her a ride in his biplane. They had talked, had dinner, and:

> Two hours later I was stretched out in bed, imagining what she would look like when I saw her next.
>
> I didn't have long to wait. She would look delicious, a tanned, curving body covered for a moment by terrycloth.
>
> Then the towel fell away, she slipped under the covers, leaned to kiss me. Not I-know-who-you-are-and-I-love-you did that kiss say, but let's be lovers tonight and see what happens.

I closed the book, tossed it onto the coffee table. From jealousy or confusion or hollow disillusionment, I threw it a little harder than I meant to. The book missed the coffee table and fell dramatically to the floor, setting itself tentlike on green carpet.

Kris and Rob looked to see what the noise was about. I was afraid they'd see my face red, my heart hollow if I didn't pick up the book fast and act like nothing was wrong.

I tried to block out the vacuum in my chest, fought to remember that Richard Bach was a different guy than what my friends would call Dad, that he was not only a strange philosopher, but a human too, complete with frailties, fears, regrets.

"Oops," I said casually to any onlookers, that iron ball in my throat. "Didn't mean to do that."

I quickly got up to retrieve the book, clamped my right thumb and fingers around the cover and sat back down with it. If I put it on the coffee table now, they'd see I was disgusted with whatever I'd just read.

I opened the book to pretend to resume reading it, and the pages fluttered again. I caught sight of black markings on the first blank page. It was from one of Richard's trademark black felt-tip pens.

Jonathan! the markings said triumphantly. *So happy for who you are! Love, Richard and Leslie.*

The part of me trained to say please and thank you told me I should be cordial and loving in return. I should be happy for who they are, I should love them back.

I couldn't.

Chapter Twenty-three

We called it the "chain letter." It was a package of letters designed after the reunion, like a treaty of communication, to keep each of us posted about events in the others' lives.

Richard and Leslie would write the first letter and send it to Kris, who would include her letter after reading theirs, then send it to Rob, who would read Kris's, Richard's, and Leslie's and include his own, then would send it to Erica, and then it would go to Jim and his new wife, Kim, and then to me and Beth. After Beth and I wrote our messages, we'd send it back to Richard and Leslie, who would update the news with a new letter and start the cycle again.

I didn't know whose idea it was, but it worked well to keep communication open and current.

For a while.

A few months after the reunion, something happened between Rob and Richard—something about lending Rob money. Now they weren't talking very much. The chain letter took longer and longer to make the cycle and soon miscommunication seeped into it. Something had happened between Kris and Richard too, and they weren't communicating. I told myself I was still too young to know what was going on.

But the chain kept going.

Beth seemed to like it more than anyone else. It might have been something she felt about being the youngest, but she couldn't wait to write her letters to everybody. When the most recent chain came, she wrote excitedly at Mom's electric typewriter. She, like me, wrote friendly words to Richard. But while mine were just polite, hers seemed to be genuine.

I wouldn't have been surprised if she had no problems accepting

Richard. She seemed to be more mature than I, she was a better artist than I, even her letters were better written.

I sat in the living room on a January day after school, listening to Beth type her part of the chain. The reunion had been six months ago.

Christmas had come and gone as usual, but this time Richard and Leslie sent Beth and me each a hundred dollars. I was surprised that he was celebrating a holiday, but I didn't question it too much. Even though a hundred dollars didn't seem to be all the money in the world, as it had in the Burlington bookstore in 1982, it was still plenty of money.

Beth and I wrote him thank-you postcards at Mom's urging, but I sensed Beth didn't feel like I did—that there was still something not quite right about Richard.

Had Beth read that part about the woman Richard had slept with? I wondered how she really felt about him, but I didn't want to ask and the noise of her letter-tapping upstairs in Mom's room didn't give any answers.

Chapter Twenty-four

February 1, 1985

The noise was incredibly loud, even for me. I got its full blast with a rush of hot air when I opened one of the double doors to the school gymnasium.

It wasn't just the noise that assaulted me, it was the whole scene: wall-to-wall kids, the smell of cheap perfume and cologne, old basketballs and new sweat. Dizzying colored light shrouded everyone and everything. I didn't mind the ninety-degree heat at all. It must have been two or three degrees outside.

I pushed through kids necking, kids standing in tight, sloppy circles as they shouted to each other, kids dancing violently, kids just taking up space. I was surprised how bothered I was by it all, considering I was the same age as these people, but I was on a mission. My little sister was somewhere in that teenage soup.

There she was, dancing with her boyfriend and three other guys over by a speaker an inch taller than she. It was easy to spot her with the cowboy hat she always wore—blue felt adorned with two feathers dangling from leather strands. I yelled to her.

"Beth!"

I pushed through more kids. Some gave me cold stares as I vigilantly pursued my target. They knew who I was, they knew who she was, and they knew what was about to happen. They'd seen this scene before, probably experienced it for themselves a few times: big brother telling little sister it's time to go home.

The song everyone was dancing to started to fade. The lights stopped blinking. Beth spotted me five feet from her, her blue eyes accidentally meeting mine.

She looked scared for a second. I was midnight to Cinderella.

Three guys surrounded her—an adolescent fortress. Her boyfriend held her hand tightly.

I yelled more softly to her over the fading music.

"Beth, c'mon, let's cruise!"

I didn't mean to be rough, I was just nervous.

"It's starting to snow, we gotta cruise," I said, less threateningly.

"Oh," she said and looked at her bare wrist. "Okay. Uh . . . what time is it? It's ten already?"

The guys, all taller than I was, gave me a look that could have hardened the snow outside. I was the villain, come to steal their princess. They were big, sure enough, but they couldn't touch me. She and I were related. I had a right to act powerful. I had diplomatic immunity. If they tried to intervene, they would violate all kinds of sacred, unspoken, universal laws about family.

She avoided an international incident by plowing through them without saying a word, heading for the far wall. Her boyfriend and I followed.

We got across the gym and stopped next to a pile of coats. It was half as tall as I was. Almost three feet. Her coat was buried in this mess.

Oh, man! This is going to take all night!

We started digging.

I looked up at Beth for a second. She was feverishly trying to find her coat. Her expression told me volumes: she knew I was impatient, she knew it was snowing because she'd heard me say it three times, she knew I wouldn't compromise about leaving.

I sighed after feeling her feelings—apologized silently for pressuring her. But the snow was piling up outside. It was pressuring *me*.

"Beth, geez . . . what coat did you wear?"

"The maroon-and-white one."

She has so many these days.

After five minutes of throwing other people's coats uncaringly aside, we found hers.

"Wait," she said, as her boyfriend helped her put it on. "I gotta tell people I'm going."

"Okay, but don't be too long," I sighed. "It's snowing. I'll be out in the car."

She went with her boyfriend toward the speaker where she'd been dancing. I pushed again through people on my way out, getting a few boos from her friends.

Double doors opened as kids came in and I went out. I forgot to prepare myself for the cold.

It numbed my face instantly, but I was too nervous to care. When I reached the car, it was still as toasty as I'd left it. I was glad I'd left it running—even more pleased that no one had stolen it while I was gone.

I fastened my seat belt and watched the snow come down harder. The wind had picked up since I'd pulled into the parking lot.

Damn.

If it's possible for butterflies to swarm, that was what they were doing inside me. I took a deep breath to settle them, tapped my fingers on the steering wheel to release nervous energy.

C'mon, Beth . . .

She came out a few minutes later and tried to open her locked door.

Oops.

I reached over and unlocked it, felt the butterflies quicken a little.

"Oooooffff! It's cold, cold, cold!" she said, sitting down, closing her door and rubbing her mittens on her face.

No argument about me being so brotherly? Hmm. That's weird.

"Take your mittens off, that'll work better. I doubt your hands got cold enough to freeze from here to the gym anyway."

She did as she was told. She placed her mittens between our seats. Fifteen miles to go.

I looked both ways for traffic. Not many people were on the road.

Good.

"You looked funny trying to open your door with those big things on," I said with an uneasy half-laugh.

She laughed a little too.

"I know. They're kinda big for me."

Snow blew across the road violently. Streetlights swayed, signs waved, drifts started to form between buildings.

Beth fastened her seat belt and settled into her seat.

"How was the dance?" I asked.

"Okay . . . good . . . before you yanked me away."

"Yeah, I'm sorry. A deal's a deal, though. I said ten. It was ten."

She nodded and put her hands up to the warm air coming out the dashboard vents.

"The flakes aren't big now, but a while ago, they were really big, like half-dollar-sized. They fell really slow too. I mean, reaaallly slow. It was so weird."

She gave another "hmm" as we crossed the bridge from New York to Vermont. Right after that, she unlatched her seat belt and lay back, more relaxed in her seat.

She took a sip from a can of root beer.

"Want some?" she asked.

I took the can from her.

"Thanks, dude," I said to her, handing it back after I took a sip. "So, anyway . . . "

A hundred yards ahead of us, just before the first curve past the border, I saw headlights that didn't make the curve, went straight instead, bounced around a little and stopped.

"Beth, did you see that?" I said as we rounded the curve.

"What?"

She sat up on the edge of her seat and stared in front of us, her head up close to the windshield.

I slowed the car down and looked in the rearview mirror to see what we'd just passed in the darkness.

Three people emerged from a pickup truck.

"A truck just went into the ditch back there."

Our car was almost at a dead stop in the road. I was fascinated by what I'd just seen, but I knew that it required a decision. We were already past it by a hundred yards or so, it was snowing harder, we had to get home, Mom was probably worried.

The people appeared to be fine. I stared into the mirror as Beth craned her neck around to look out the back window.

"Should we go back and check?" I asked.

"Not if they're getting out, I guess. We should just go," she said, sounding more nervous than I was.

Two people in the truck started to push it out of the ditch while one of them steered. I saw the driver illuminated by the dome light. He kept the driver's door open as the other two passengers pushed. In another few seconds, the truck was almost on the road again.

The butterflies danced in me like the kids we'd just left in the gym. Beth faced forward.

"I think they're on the road again. Let's just go."

She sounded kind of uneasy. I was too.

"That was wild," I said, trying to make myself feel less anxious about driving in this mess.

Beth took a sip from the root beer and gave another "hmm."

For that second, I felt younger than she was. I realized I hadn't debated her decision to proceed home.

I asked her again how the dance was.

"Okay," she said. "Loud."

"Understandable, since you were living in that speaker, just about."

She smiled, but didn't answer, sipped the root beer.

Where'd that root beer come from, anyway?

I was about to ask her for some when she offered it to me again.

"No, Beth, don't you know drinking and driving is bad?"

She smiled again and closed her eyes.

"You're such a dude," she said.

"So the dance was good, eh? I saw you there with Peter. He's quite the dancer. Who were those other three?"

She answered without opening her eyes.

"Just other guys," she said unemphatically. "I only knew one of them, really."

A few miles later, we rounded a corner to the left, and started down a long stretch of road. Nine miles to go.

Another corner, this one to the right. Headlights appeared from it.

Geez, they're awful close to the center line . . .

As the car tried to move more into its own lane, I knew I was about to see yet another car bounce off the road and into a ditch. The car made too much of a swerve. Such a sudden lane correction in weather like this meant a sure crash.

I couldn't believe the coincidence. I had never seen an accident, and I was sure I was about to see two in the same night.

In the next second, I saw the car try to correct to get back into its lane. In another second, my instinct told me the driver wasn't going into the ditch. It swerved to the right. Into the road. Into my lane.

In that last second before the headlights veered into our path, head-on and out of control, Beth gasped in a kind of half-second squeak.

I held on to the wheel.

CHAPTER TWENTY-FIVE

Black, ear-shattering silence.

Then cold.

No slow motion like accident victims described in those driver's education movies. It happened in real time. Seconds were seconds.

I didn't feel an impact, but the weight of this silence was incredible. It was louder than the dance.

Another moment of black, then restored sight—a dark dashboard, a cracked speedometer showing zero.

No pain, just sudden cold, like walking into an air-conditioned bank on a hundred-degree summer day.

What the hell happened? We aren't moving.

Beth was huddled in the front part of the passenger side, almost totally off her seat. Above her, a cobweb design on the windshield.

Beth was snoring, heavy breathing, like a saw slowly cutting wood—put to immediate sleep, I figured, by the shock of collision. She didn't appear to have even the slightest scratch. No blood on the windshield, but I didn't dare touch her.

Her white mittens were on the top of the dashboard.

I felt pressure. There were a million things to do and thirty seconds to do them.

The stopwatch started.

First item: Beth.

Nothing I can do. Can't touch her. Shouldn't touch her. At least she's breathing. Good.

Next item: the other driver.

Tick, tick, tick . . .

I knew I had to get out of the car.

Just like in the movies, the door wouldn't open.

With adrenaline surging, I tried to smash the door open with my elbow. The door didn't give. The window was my only way, but something held me in—a force against my shoulder and across my lap.

What am I, paralyzed?

A tinge of panic. My feet could still move, but the top of me wouldn't. My arms were at my sides.

I made a huge try to move, powered by frustration and determination. A force pressed across me in a diagonal line from my right hip to my left shoulder, like a tight seat belt when you lean into it.

Discovery.

Click, unbuckle, release.

Snowflakes poured in the window.

I felt incredibly smart, discovering the window would be a great way to get out of the car.

I spilled onto the cold, snowy pavement and went over to the other car. Its dome light was on and two very old ladies were bleeding from facial cuts. Both were moaning.

"Help . . . " one of them said softly.

Damn . . . help. I need help.

In a second, a car appeared, slowed down. A jeep.

Two people got out, a man and a woman, young, thirty-ish.

"My God, are you okay? You're a mess. Stay calm," they said.

Their words punched me.

It was instant pain and I felt the wetness of blood. My nose was shattered and throbbing, my wrist and collarbone were broken and tingling, and I was extremely cold.

I was getting lighter. Gravity leaked away from me and I fell to my knees as one of them tried to support me.

Another car slowed down as it approached the curve.

"Help's coming," someone said.

My mental stopwatch had one second left before it exploded and there seemed to be only one thing to do.

I saw lights on the horizon. Pretty lights: flashing red, yellow, white, red, yellow, white. They flashed safety, help, comfort, safety, help, comfort. I wanted to watch them for hours.

Twenty minutes had passed, must have passed, for that ambulance to be on the horizon. I tried to figure out how twenty minutes could pass in twenty seconds when time seemed normal.

The battery of Mom's car lay on its side, making a pool of acid-slush on the snowy road. The engine was a smoldering, hissing, steaming, oily pile of dark metal. The old ladies' car had been knocked back ten feet after impact.

I held my forehead and cupped my shattered nose as I marveled at the awesome damage. As the people who had stopped tended to the women in the other car, I hunched down for a brief second and saw what laws of physics could do to a 1978 Honda Civic.

The ambulance lights got closer on the horizon. They were as peaceful as my unconscious sister had looked . . .

Beth.

I hadn't been thinking about her after I left her. Someone told me she was fine, but I heard no voice say it. I knew she needed help. Maybe she was awake by now.

I went to the driver's window of what used to be Mom's car, and the bystanders let me. The mental stopwatch had hit thirty seconds long ago. I didn't know if I had failed or succeeded in doing everything I was supposed to do. Neither Beth nor the old ladies could help themselves, and the bystanders didn't seem to be a factor in the help equation. I was certain I still had something important to do.

Beth was still snoring, still crouched in the lower part of the passenger side, almost off her seat. I wanted to make her more comfortable, but I didn't dare touch her.

Beth. Sleeping still. Good. She's not bleeding. Good, good, good signs.

I felt at peace with Beth and she returned peace. There wasn't a scratch on her. Not a cut.

I tried to think. There was everything and nothing to think about.

The ambulance arrived and some familiar men guided me into it while they tried to get Beth out of the car. There were Tim Richardson, James Kernstock, Keith Bellows, and Mike McCormick, the fire department's senior members. I trusted them to get her out, to save her.

"Don't worry about me, I'll be fine, just get my sister out, just get her out," I said to Keith as he walked me into the ambulance and helped me lie down on one of the two beds.

But Beth, shouldn't she be awake by now? She has to be awake, especially now. Who can sleep through that noise of the cutting tools, the siren, the men shouting? Yes, she's probably conscious and disoriented. Poor Beth. She's probably confused as hell.

They loaded her in after what seemed like years later, put her on the floor six inches below me, closed the doors, and after a quick siren blast, we started rolling.

She was still snoring. I offered to trade places with her, but they said it wouldn't be necessary.

"Just stay calm, Jon," Keith said.

"It's cool, Keith, I'm fine. Just get her conscious, okay?"

She still snored.

"Okay, Jon, okay, we're doing it."

He kept trying to calm me down, which was strange because I felt perfectly calm. I just wanted to be sure Beth got more attention. I was so intent that I insisted that I not be touched until she was awake.

Then I realized Keith wasn't trying to calm me down for the way I was acting, but for what I was *about* to see.

Mike started CPR on Beth.

No. Not CPR. Not my sister. Something's wrong. They said she'd be fine. They were telling me this even now. Why CPR? She's breathing, she's just asleep, right? Why do CPR when she's making such a racket with that breathing? Can't they hear the snores?

But I hadn't heard her snore for at least a minute, maybe longer.

The radio clacked with traffic. Tim was trying to get the hospital to understand that no names were going to be revealed. Some kind of policy not to reveal the names of the injured so people couldn't hear it on their home scanners. I knew the routine, had heard it from other runs the crew had made while I stayed in the station and listened to the radio.

I thought about Mom. When was she going to be told?

If she's coming to the hospital, she'd better drive carefully.

"One, two, three, four, five—breathe."

I closed my eyes.

"Pulse. Got it. Got a pulse," said the big man named Mike, leaning over my sister.

I concentrated on her, sent mental signals to keep her alive. I had a strange feeling that she knew what was going to happen, that she knew I was by her side and that it was great fun for her and me to be on the same team, fighting this newest challenge in both our lives.

I thought of Mom, how I wished she could feel the easy peace I was feeling.

I concentrated on the growling tires beneath me for the next twenty minutes.

Hospital.

Unloading.

Warm ambulance air to cold air to warm hospital air.

They wheeled me over the sounds of squeaky sneakers on linoleum, under humming fluorescent lights, past two people talking, two other nurses standing, others clearing space on tables while instruments hissed and beeped and a different life-saving gadget was prepared each second.

I was taken to one room, Beth to another. I wanted to be with her, but I knew she needed special treatment. She went to some obscure room reserved for what I figured to be top-secret, very serious and complex operations.

I lay in the emergency room and looked at the clock. 11:35 P.M. This was not a scheduled stop on our way home. A mental joke was born.

Where do I get humor now?

Mom and Big Jon appeared from nowhere.

A wave of warmth passed over me and I felt like crying.

I didn't.

"I'm not going to look at you, but I'm going to hold your hand," Mom said, starting to cry, taking a seat next to my gurney.

She fought the tears.

I didn't look at her either as I took her cold, soft hand.

"Okay . . . that's okay. You wouldn't want to look at me anyway. I bet I'm a mess," I said to Mom, now sitting at the side of my gurney. I spoke nasally to her.

Beth retreated to the back of my mind again, out of the way.

Why am I so calm? Did they shoot me up with something without my knowing?

Mom said Beth might be transferred to Burlington—to a hospital fifty miles south.

Nurses came in and wheeled me into a little room.

They took X-rays of my face and arm under more humming fluorescent light. It sounded the way a school sounds after all the kids have left for the day.

Back in the emergency room, Mom held my hand again as a nurse ran water over a cloth.

"Let's just get you cleaned up here," the nurse said, pressing hard and wiping quickly. She disregarded what little pain I allowed myself to show her.

"Guess I won't be winning any beauty contests, huh?" I said, trying to take my mind off the feel of the tepid cloth, growing sticky with clotted blood.

She laughed a little.

"Not for a while, I think," she said.

They took me away from Mom again, wheeling me into a little room with about eight sinks and a million printed-label bottles on pristine white counters.

A doctor came in.

"Let's see if we can get a cast on here."

He wetted some gauze under warm water and dipped it in some paste.

A nurse warned me that I was going to feel pressure.

A needle came from somewhere and I felt chilling anesthetic or whatever go up my arm. I started to feel heavy. I was losing consciousness. I didn't need anesthetic. I was just about to lose it anyway.

"It's a sedative," the doctor said.

A sedative for a broken wrist?

I was already calm.

Mom was in the other room. I wondered what she was thinking.

Two more nurses came in.

They were crying, but their sniffles were barely noticeable.

Crying nurses.

I had a feeling they weren't crying about my broken wrist.

"Jon, your sister . . . " one of them tried to say. Another nurse broke out into soft sobs. Both of them tried to mask their tears with smiles as they prepared things from cupboards.

That explains the sedative.

As induced exhaustion from the injection took effect, I felt tears welling up in my eyes.

I didn't think. My mind was blank. They made sure of that, injected me with that potion that robbed me of feeling. All I felt was warm fatigue from every muscle in my body, cool tears in my eyes that ran down my tingling face.

I didn't know if the tears were new or if they were left over from the pain of my wrist.

As I turned my head to the side, they left my eyes and streamed onto the gurney's sanitary paper coating.

A nurse smoothed my hair.

Tingles traveled up my right arm, into my shoulder, got lost in my neck.

I wanted to comfort her; she was still sobbing slightly and her hand was warm on my forehead. But I was sleepy and fatigued and confused and numb and I cried tears I couldn't feel.

My sister is dead.

Chapter Twenty-six

Somewhere in the darkness, a phone rang.

I opened my eyes and saw faint features of a hospital room lit by fluorescent light leaking under the door.

Ring!

Its volume scared me in this dark, foreign room.

Ring!

Over my left shoulder. I tried to move my right arm. It reminded me that my wrist was broken.

Damn!

Ring!

I scooched up on the bed and felt the vertigolike effects of postsedation.

I picked up the phone with my left hand.

"Hello?"

I didn't have much of a voice.

"Hello, my son, this is your father calling."

"Hey . . . " I said politely, clearing my throat. "Hey. How are you?"

"I was hoping you'd tell me how *you* were. Do you feel like talking?"

His voice was very calm, but warm. Here we were, just like every time we had talked; he very nice, me very nice.

"Talking? Uh, yeah, I guess."

In one long sentence, I told him what had happened in the last five hours.

I was calm when I talked.

Richard sighed, gave a few whews and I took a breath, giving him the first opportunity to speak.

"Whuf! Jonathan! When Leslie and I got the call, we just couldn't believe it. And here you are in the middle of it all."

"Yeah."

"Well, there are a lot of things Beth knew that we will never know. She's chosen a different form of consciousness for her own very good reasons, but we'll miss her."

"Yeah," I said, staring at the fluorescence of my white cast in the hospital darkness.

"I'll bet you're tired, though," he said. "I'll let you get your rest."

"Thanks."

I tried to think of something to say. There was nothing.

"Well, I'll talk to you later," I said sleepily, not caring when or if he called back. "Thanks for calling."

"You gonna be okay?"

"Yeah, I bet Mom will be a good nurse."

He and I said good-bye.

I hung up the phone and the room seemed alive, having just heard our conversation. The walls seemed to wait for my reaction.

"I don't know," I said to them.

I moved my leg and my whole body tingled. I was dead weight. I couldn't read the clock on the wall, but it must have been well into early morning.

Beth is gone, I sighed in the predawn darkness.

Chills came and went in a breath.

I'm too practical to think about Beth choosing to die, I thought. *All I know for sure is that she's dead, Mom's car is totaled, I'm beaten up. Simple physics. She impacted the windshield and died from medical complications, internal injuries, or a concussion. She didn't choose a different realm of consciousness as Richard says. He didn't know Beth like I did. She wasn't a philosopher. How could someone who's never talked about choosing to die choose to die?*

I wondered how Richard could take a tragedy and reduce it to antiseptic, indifferent philosophy. In the six months since the reunion, he had talked with Beth as much as he'd talked with me. That wasn't much. It hadn't been much before the reunion either.

He didn't have a right to call me. Dick Bach had helped to create her, he had a right to know, but the Richard Bach who'd left her a year after she was born certainly didn't.

But if Richard Bach wanted no part of being a father, why did he call?

There were too many other things to think about besides Richard. Beth was gone.

I couldn't manage to force tears. I felt only the throbbing of my broken nose, wrist, and collarbone. I juggled a lot of "if only" and "what now?" thoughts and wondered if Richard was going to start acting like a dad to make up for his mistakes.

CHAPTER TWENTY-SEVEN

There was a gathering at the house the following Saturday. No funeral, no wake, just a gathering of a hundred friends and lots of food, lots of cards, only a few people in black. Mom had insisted that it not be a depressing gathering. Kris flew in from Iowa, Erica drove the one hundred miles from Randolph, Vermont, Rob and Cami drove the fifty miles from Burlington. I didn't know why Jim couldn't be there. Richard stayed on his Washington island a continent away.

I sat next to the buffet on the dinner table, my casted right arm resting near all kinds of food I couldn't smell or taste. My nose was still patched with tape that stretched up and around over my eyebrows.

Friends came up to me and hugged me as best they could. Some cried. I felt sorry for them, wished there was something I could do for them. I wished I could've forced tears, but nothing came.

Big Jon stayed distant and quiet. He stood in a circle of family friends, mostly male, but he wasn't his usual loud, boisterous self. For a second, I wondered how he felt. He was calm, like me. Maybe he didn't know her well enough. Maybe he felt he wasn't close enough to act like a real dad.

A while later, after almost everyone had left, Mom mentioned something about going up in the airplane, flying to Mount Ellen in Sugarbush Valley and sprinkling Beth's ashes there over the mountain she had climbed once with Jim. Two other pilot friends were going to fly formation with them.

The lake outside had been frozen over for the past month and a half and was thick enough to serve as a runway. The three family friends who had flown in went out to their planes parked a few feet out from the beach.

I watched three planes and our little Aeronca Champ takeoff into

105

the sunny late afternoon. I watched them disappear to the southwest, silhouetted by the setting sun as they flew toward Beth's favorite mountain.

Beth seemed to stay with me, as if we both watched the planes fly away.

Behind my back as I stared out the window, Kris asked me if I wanted anything. I told her no, I was fine. I was almost too fine.

I went up to Beth's room to think. Beth's room was where Mom had wanted me to stay while I recuperated. It was right next to Mom's bedroom, and since it was in the main house, it made it easier for her to take care of me. I didn't mind.

I lay in Beth's bed and thought about her.

Some of her sketches hung on the wall; her felt cowboy hat with the two feathers on leather strands rested on the nightstand. The room was clean, except for my textbooks and lots of cards of support for me lying on the floor, but my sister still lived and breathed around me. This was still her room.

I looked at Beth's artwork on the walls. There was a charcoal sketch of a cougar, a pencil and ink mosaic, another charcoal sketch of a figure skater, and a colorful something wedged in the darkest corner of an already dark room.

All the times I'd been in her room, playing with Legos, sitting on the edge of her bed while waking her up to split wood, cracking the door open to call her down to dinner from her sketching or homework, I never remembered that colorful something being in that corner.

I sat up, squinted my eyes.

It was a drawing of a scene I had just seen outside: our Champ, flying silhouette against an orange sunset.

Chapter Twenty-eight

I had been interviewed by the police and the insurance people. My story matched their measurements of skid distance and relative position on the road. It was a rare thing, they told me, for a young male driver to be in an accident like that and not be responsible for causing it.

The police said the accident was nobody's fault. They blamed it on the weather. They called it an act of God.

There was money available for me from the insurance settlement—enough to think about going to college just when I thought I would have to join the military to get the money as Erica had. I was glad not to have the problems she'd had when she asked Richard for support.

The chain letter had made the rounds to the family and came to me that day. In it was Beth's last letter from the previous chain she'd written two weeks before the accident.

I read it slowly.

January 16, 1985
Hello all!!

Wow! Those reunion pictures are GREAT! I love them! All those different personalities joined together to make a strong, loving family. I am very happy to be able to communicate to you all.

Well, gosh! This little piggy certainly is busy! I would really like to write a lengthy letter to everyone, but Jonny and I wish to have this chain completed before 1986! Anyway. These past few weeks have been occupied by that ever-popular strain—MIDTERMS!! The studying, checking, reading, and re-reading have definitely affected my concentration on more important things, such as the chain. Relief has been found, though in the form of a person. This person is named Peter Leary, and lately he has been providing my doorway to reality within midterm week. We are going on three months now, and are closer than ever. Just a little info, he is a sophomore in high school, an excellent runner, chef, tennis player, paperboy, etc. He is ambitious, smart, caring, helpful, and (wait . . . there's still more!) he is very excited about the family and wishes to meet all of you someday! Peter has made me very happy and it seems this happiness does not want to expire.

FAMILY NOTES

Richard and Leslie: Those articles you sent were fantastic! I greatly admire you two for going through all this alive. Thanks for keeping our spirits alive too. My spirits are still soaring from that shining $100 you sent! It handled my phone bill and my ego . . . (you really know you're an adult when you have a hidden $20!) Thank you, thank you, thank you!

Kris: my art is dying to get to you, but the teacher won't give it up!! I may end up sending you one of my latest sketches or even a block print which I am currently working on. Whatever I find I'll send!

Brian: YES!! I have a dream! It is a little far from now, but with the help of Cami, Rob, and a little improvement of basic skills, I wish to be a part of an art college. Once I get out, I'll decide on a job suited for my talent. (sigh) Only a dream . . . but slowly my mind is capturing reality as well as fantasy in oil, pen & ink, or maybe just a plain old #2 pencil! SURPRISED???

Rob & Cami: Your helpfulness toward my art future is greatly appreciated! Anything you can pick up that you think might be interesting to me, please send it!! I really enjoyed the chat on the different schools and their surroundings that would be best for me! Thanks! Are you guys coming to see the skating show in February?? If you do, can you get hold of a video camera? It seems my only cheering crowd this year will be Jonny, you, and maybe the janitor who knows my last name! Just look for the Pink Panther, or the Ghostbuster, or the dancer to "Footloose." It will be a show to remember!

Erica and Dan: Hey, like, Erica . . . thanks again for that, like, gnarly calligraphy set! It is sooooo tubular! I can do many different styles with my writing now! Thanks! And to Dan . . . I wish you all the best with your dream! Just reach out and go for it! You'll do great in whatever you do! Best of luck and happiness!

Jim and Kim: Welcome to the family, Kim! My first chance to write you and I wish you well in your guitar playing! Jammin' Jim will be the best person to jam with! I'm just happy he has taught you the art of "mouse-ing." It's great to have someone new to carry on the tradition.

Well, I have to wrap it up so the webs on this envelope don't spread all over the house! One last thing to Richard—Please . . . keep the spirit of the envelope going! I may not have all the time in the world to write these letters, but I crave hearing the family's tales, and I always want to be a part of it!

LOVE TO EVERYONE!
Beth

I felt chills, but I didn't cry. I hadn't cried since they'd injected me with whatever chemical the night of the accident. If Erica or Kris or Rob or Big Jon or Mom cried, I never saw them. Maybe they did and I was thinking too much to notice.

Two weeks after the gathering, Jim called.

I asked him why he hadn't come back East. He told me Mom had said there wasn't going to *be* a gathering. I was surprised at that, but not surprised that he didn't sound happy.

I told him it wasn't worth coming all the way home.

We listened to some static on the line for a brief moment, we talked about how I felt, and how he felt. He was calm, like me. He actually seemed less depressed than when Astra died.

He asked if I had seen Beth's last letter to the family.

"Yeah, I got it," I said with a sigh, made difficult by the bandages on my nose.

"Did you read it?"

"I didn't have to. I was there when she typed it. But yeah, I read it again, just for . . . yeah, I read it."

"Did you notice anything weird about it?"

"No," I said.

"Well, go get it."

"Wait, it's around here somewhere."

I found the letter.

"Yeah?" I asked without the slightest clue of what was about to happen.

"Look how many times she refers to life and death."

I felt a chill and started to scan it, read aloud to Jim the parts about life and death as I went.

" . . . seems this happiness does not want to expire . . . greatly admire you two for going through all this alive . . . thanks for keeping our spirits alive too. My spirits are still soaring . . . "

More waves of chills.

" . . . my art is dying to get to you . . . it's great to have someone new to carry on the tradition . . . keep the spirit of the envelope going . . . I may not have all the time in the world . . . "

"Geez, Jim."

"I know. It's creepy."

"Maybe it's just a coincidence."

"Right! It's definitely a coincidence, but it's a *meaningful* coincidence. Like Dad talks about—nothing by chance."

"Well . . . "

"Jon, don't you see? She knew the accident was going to happen on some subliminal level!"

"Wow. I guess."

"That part about passing the Mousies on to Kim? Why would she say that? Mousies are just hand puppets. That really gets me. It's just weird how she put it that way," he said.

"Yeah, that's really way out there," I said, not knowing what to think of it all.

"But that's not the weirdest part," Jim continued.

I braced for more chills. I hoped he would stop talking, but I knew I should listen. I'd always wanted to be as smart as he was, so I told myself that anything he had to say was good for me.

"Beth was killed on Saturday," he said. "I got her letter on Monday, the *following* Monday. So she must have sent that letter the day before the accident."

I didn't know what to say, so I said nothing.

"Jon, this is a letter from our *dead sister*."

"Oh . . . " I said, sitting down on the floor. I felt the chills and I told myself I should be crying upon hearing words like this, but I could feel Beth right there. She wasn't gone, so why cry?

We hung up a few minutes later, after I told him I had to go. I started to think more about the choice-to-ascend theory. I read Beth's letter three more times, felt more chills, saw her premonitions more pronounced each time.

Back in Beth's room, I started to write. There was a pen and one of her notebooks underneath her biology textbook from school. I turned on my stomach, careful not to crush the cast on my right wrist, reached for the stationery and wrote sloppily with my left hand.

> Why don't I cry like her friends? We had never got along better than that night. I could easily say I loved her, and I know I'll miss her, but I stay calm. It must be shock. It just hasn't set in yet.
>
> She didn't choose to die. That's so stupid. Jim calls it Beth's "ascension to another consciousness." Sounds familiar. That's Jim, all the way. So like Richard. But why does Jim seem normal to me? Sure, he's always been smart, but never so smart that I couldn't relate to him. If he says she ascen

Something passed through me that made me instantly tired, as if I'd been awake for three days. I didn't want to write or think another word about mystical anything.

> Damn, I don't know.
>
> I do know that Richard isn't here. He didn't care after all. He called me that night in the hospital just to be polite. He wouldn't know what to do here if he did come. He'd have to face his mistake

of never getting to know Beth. He'd have to face me, face Mom, face everybody. More cowardice. Another problem he's running from.

I don't run from my problems. I stick it out with working around the house, I've stuck it out with Mom as she tried to raise us, I'm sticking it out here. There's no running for me. I deal with my problems.

For a second I thought about calling Richard and talking about it, but I remembered that he wanted no part of being a father.

That day he wrote me a brief letter.

Dear Jonathan,

Just a note to tell you that we've shifted the funds from Bethy's trust account into yours. We felt sure she'd want it that way.

It brings the total in your account, at the moment, to $7,466. With our further deposits and interest through the coming year, you'll have around $10,500 by next April 2. That ought to give you a few options—a good start in college, or you can spend it for travel or business or play.

There's so much to say to you about so many things, but it's difficult to communicate clearly at such long distance. I was always sure that we'd have time to talk at length someday—a time when you and Beth would have some little chance to make up your own minds about who we all are to each other. Though Beth's conscious-ness is at a level where she knows without the talking, we missed the fun of earthside communications with her. You're such a charm— we very much look forward to those times with you.

Meanwhile, we hope you're healing nicely and that life has begun to return to normal.

Love,
Dad

Anger masked my slight desire to explore any further this stuff about ascension.

How does he know what she "would have wanted"? He didn't know anything about her! And who is he to say he's "Dad"?

CHAPTER TWENTY-NINE

A year passed and I didn't call or write to Richard.

I was making plans to start an adult life of my own. All the tests they put in front of my high-school-senior eyes sobered me to the decision I had to make about my career. I knew my only real talent lay in a writing career of some sort, but I knew I wanted a steady paycheck. I didn't want to live the stories Mom told about how the car was repossessed when Dick Bach was a struggling writer. Seven years with Big Jon had made me very practical and very attuned to fiscal responsibilities. I made it my policy to live within my income.

Mom suggested journalism.

It was perfect. Writing, and with steady money.

I applied to a few colleges, but set my sights on the University of Maine because it was close to our Vermont home, it was affordable, and it had a decent daily newspaper.

A letter from the university waited for me one March day after school.

March 16, 1986
Dear Mr. Bach:

Congratulations! Blah, blah, blah . . .

"Yes!" I cheered.

I thought of Beth. If she were alive, she'd be happy for me, would brag to her friends about me going to college.

"Mom, I'm in!" I yelled from the kitchen to her bedroom upstairs.

I had a fleeting urge to write Richard, just to tell him I was going to make it as a journalist—on my own, without having to ask him for money as Erica had.

I didn't want to get involved with him about college or anything else in my life, because I knew it would only cause problems.

I learned that Erica had recently received a letter from Richard expressing his disapproval at her plan to be confirmed as a Catholic before she got married in three months to a fellow engineering student named John Roy. I knew that there was still some kind of rift between Richard and Rob, and one still with Richard and Kris. I didn't ask them why; all I needed to know was that when it came to family, Richard got disappointed too easily. I didn't need that.

A day after my eighteenth birthday, I received the check from the bank where he'd been sending the child support money. No more notes and statements. One check for ten thousand, money he had to pay Mom, money he had to pay for fathering us then leaving, and I was free from ever having to deal with the confusing Richard Bach.

Chapter Thirty

Six months later, I collapsed on a bed 360 miles from home, soaking up my first day of true freedom as a first-year student at the University of Maine. No more woodmares, no more lawns to mow, no more chores, intimidation, anything. I was free at last from the chilling sound of Big Jon's truck tires on our gravel driveway.

I stared at the stucco-moonscape ceiling.

College.

On the other side of the country, on that mysterious island in Puget Sound, Washington, my father didn't know what was happening. I thought of him for a second and wondered if he would care, if he would be excited for me.

The door opened and roommate Todd Chambers entered with his family. They had just met Mom and Big Jon after I said good-bye to them in the hall.

Mr. Chambers said my parents were nice.

In high school, that term, parents, was fine for describing Mom and Jon. Here, in college, it didn't seem to fit.

I had a compulsion to tell him, "Mom is my *parent*—the man with her is my stepfather." But it was easier, for the sake of keeping the conversation brief, to pretend they were both my parents.

"Yep," I said, sitting up, starting to unpack one of the five boxes I had brought.

"It's not hard to see from your dad there where you get your height," Mrs. Chambers said to me.

Arrggh.

A compulsion to tell them the whole, sordid family history lingered in me a bit longer than a silver-white strobe flash. I didn't want to get into it.

"Yeah, I guess I'm the tallest of the family except for him," I said, unrolling a Lamborghini poster.

One of Todd's younger brothers, his right arm in a cast, spoke next.

"Dad, can we go to the video arcade we saw in the student union building before we leave?"

"Now how in the world are you going to zap aliens with a cast on?"

I looked out of the corner of my eye. The boy held up his encased right arm.

"You'll press the buttons while I steer the ship!"

Mr. Chambers laughed with his wife and older sons.

"Well, okay then! That sounds fair."

It sounded like something you'd hear from those happy families on the backs of cereal boxes.

The father spoke again.

"Todd, make sure you get set up with those Air Force ROTC folks as soon as possible. You might want to go over there tomorrow."

"Okay, Dad."

As I put up my poster, Todd got a hug from his father first. It lasted four seconds.

"Okay, son. Aim high and all that. I love you."

"I love you too, Dad."

He got a brief hug from his mother. That lasted two seconds. He gave playful punches to his two brothers.

A few more good-byes later, they left Todd and me in our new room.

All this syrup in the room is making me ill, I thought. *And if he makes another reference to my stepfather, I'll have to tell him the whole story. Get it out of the way for good.*

"Did your father say something about flying home?" Todd asked.

I gave a frustrated sigh.

"Yep. He's a pilot. So's my mom," I said.

He looked amazed.

"Your mom too? Wow . . . that's what I hope to do someday—fly airplanes. . . . " He stopped, corrected himself. "Oops, not just airplanes. Jets! F-16s!"

"Wow, that's cool," I said flatly, separating Styrofoam packing from a box.

"Your dad's a lucky guy. Do you fly too?"

My back faced him as I started to connect one of the wires to the computer I had just bought.

"A little bit." Strange that I was raised around airplanes and never learned how to fly. "I know how to land if something happened to my parents in the air."

"Wow, that's neat. I have a lot of books about flying. There's this really neat one in particular . . . "

I turned my head to see him searching through one of eight boxes on the floor on his side of the room.

He pulled out a book called *Wings.* It was one of those coffee-table productions with big pictures and few words.

I turned back to the computer, connected another cable.

Those books are a dime a dozen, I thought. *He ought to read the good stuff.*

I wanted to scold myself for giving mental praise to Richard's writing, but I honestly had never read better writing about flying. I also wanted to show Todd that I was aeronautically literate.

"Have you ever heard of *Biplane* or *Nothing by Chance?*"

I turned around again, rested against the counter to see his reaction.

He looked at the ceiling for a brief second as he unpacked.

"Mmmm. No. I don't think so."

"They're pretty good." I paused for a second, debating how much to tell him about those books. "They're real descriptive—the writing makes you feel like you're right there with him when he's flying."

"Who's 'he'?"

A second of silence.

"Uh . . . " I said, thinking lightning fast of what to say next. He could find out the next time he was in the library, see *by Richard Bach* on the cover, notice the surname. There was no way around it.

"My father."

"Really?"

"That guy who was just in here, that's my *step*father. My *real* father is on the other side of the country. He divorced my mom in 1970. . . . "

He listened to the family story as we both unpacked our stuff. Ten minutes later, he knew the abridged version. He listened passively, didn't seem impressed or amazed, didn't ask many questions about Richard or the family. Maybe telling him about the accident shocked him too deeply into sympathy for him to able to talk about anything.

Telling him the story reminded me of all the things that contributed to who I was.

All kinds of family friends had told me college would be a great experience—a chance to find myself, meet all types of people, learn all kinds of things that had nothing to do with classes. And maybe I'd meet more people like me, the ones with ghost-dads and bitter moms, the ones who knew the difference between "dad" and "father," the ones who felt incomplete not knowing their other parent.

All the stuff I knew about Richard clouded my thoughts, but I dismissed my agitation as first-year-student jitters.

CHAPTER THIRTY-ONE

College wasn't as hard as I'd thought. The teachers spoke English I could understand, and the assignments didn't seem too challenging. But there were plenty of assignments to keep me busy. I balanced the work by shooting pool with Todd and hanging out with some other guys I met across the hall.

By the end of the first week, I'd established myself as an eager-to-learn production assistant at the college's newspaper, *The Daily Maine Campus*. I had also joined the university's volunteer fire department because I thought my experience as a junior member of the Alburg fire department would come in handy.

That saying "I wasn't born yesterday" doesn't really seem true, I wrote one night after not doing my homework. *I do feel like I was born yesterday. This is a new everything. If only I had someone to share it with, that'd top everything.*

In the second month of college, I met Rachel Naughton.

She was an attractive sophomore who made college seem like true freedom. No curfews or driving tens of miles to see her. She lived in the all-girls dormitory right across the big lawn they called the "quad."

The next evening after classes, I went over to her dorm with my new friend Peter Chase, who lived down the hall. Pete's girlfriend was Rachel's roommate, Tania Chadbourne.

Eventually conversation shifted to the subject of family. I let everybody go before me.

Then Rachel asked me about mine.

I told her about Kris and Rob and everybody and . . . here goes . . .

" . . . my father's a writer too."

"Oh, really? What does he write?" she asked as we sat on the floor, her back against my knees.

"He wrote . . . "

Bombs away.

" . . . *Jonathan Livingston Seagull,* and . . . "

"Oh, really?! You're kidding!" she said.

I smiled a bit.

"No, ma'am."

Pete believed me right away, Tania didn't.

I told them about *Time* magazine, the stories Mom had told about him, the letters about writing, the day in Burlington, the reunion. I made sure not to get into too much detail about the night of the accident.

The spotlight shone on me a little brighter and hotter than I liked, but it was bearable. I didn't have to tell them as much as I did, but at least it was out of the way.

Pete sympathized and seemed to be overwhelmed by the story, Tania talked about her parents' separation, Rachel had one of those cereal-box families and she stayed quiet.

They all felt bad about Beth, and their comments about Richard sounded like a tune I'd heard a few times in high school: "I didn't know Richard Bach had kids!" "That's neat that you're named after the book." "He really had a few million dollars and then went bankrupt?"

I answered all of their questions, responded to their comments as best I could, all the while looking at the white carpet on the floor of room 422.

It was another time the "family story" reminded me that having a famous father can be fun and agonizing.

I loved the attention, I loved telling a good story, I loved making people feel amazed.

I didn't like the incomplete information I had about him, I didn't like wondering if the listener would feel sorry for me, I didn't like feeling guilty for not knowing more.

A few hours later, I opened the door to 111 Gannett. All the lights were on and Todd was writing a letter.

"Hey, Todd."

"Hey."

"Getting some writing done? That's a good idea."

"Just something for the family. Kind of a two-month progress report. A report card that isn't bad news for once!"

"Yeah, right," I said with a polite laugh, as if Todd were ever a guy to get bad grades.

I took my journal from the bookshelf on my side of the room.

"Okay if I turn off the main light? It's really bright," I said.

"Uh, okay, I guess. I'm just about to bag it for the night anyway."

I turned it off in favor of my own little nightstand light. It was harder to write by, but I liked the somber mood it created.

November 11, 1986
12:30 a.m.

Just left Rachel's, told her, Pete and Tania about Richard.

Dad. Father. Some father I have. Purely biological. I don't want someone who says great things. I just want a dad. I want someone to say, "That's my son." A mom I've got—so very loving and caring. The one who raised me, who loved me, who shaped me. But no dad. Lost dreams, dreams never there. No call to come out to see him, no sadness in a loss. Beth died without a dad. Am I going to die without one too? I want to. But I don't. No one knows the real story. But I am a Bach. I take his name.

So why don't I change my name? Pretend I'm not related to Richard Bach? I don't know. I am his son. I don't want to lie to people. It'd be nice if people knew that the Great Richard Bach had children. Nobody knows. I want to carry around that picture in *Time* magazine, remind people that he's not the guru of soulmates that people say he is. He divorced mom, abandoned Beth and

My eyes watered and a few tears silently fell, smearing the ink and smearing my vision of the dimly lit journal. It seemed so futile, so hopeless a situation—my father on one side, me on the other, no way we would ever meet on common ground. No way. There was nothing I could do.

That's just the way it is. For the rest of my life. Face it. Accept it. He doesn't care, never has; not about Beth, not about you. Mom was right. His daddy-part died a long, long time ago. There's no bringing him back.

I let the tears come, fought hard not to gasp or heave so Todd could hear me crying.

Screw Richard Bach. Lots of people don't have dads. You're just one of the many. Big deal. Lots of people have it worse. Chill out. Get a grip. Are you going to let it wreck your life? You don't need him anyway.

I sighed and wiped my eyes with my bedsheet.

ANYWAY, Rachel's upstairs over across the quad, in bed now. Her light's still on. The ballet's tomorrow. Wish she would've told me she liked ballet earlier than tonight. Would've got tickets. Rats.

I closed the journal. Todd settled into his bed and I figured I better bag it for the night too.

I turned off my nightstand light and lay, still fully clothed, under my covers. As I melted into the increasing warmth of the mattress, I played with the idea of sending him the thoughts I had just written about him.

I closed my eyes and thought about it.

I had nothing to lose.

CHAPTER THIRTY-TWO

NEXT DAY
12:27 p.m.

Just woke up. Warm. Rested. Peaceful. Writing mood. Thinking about family. Letter-writing mood. Don't know what to say.
Dear Richard,
This is Jonathan. If I came to see you, would you be afraid? Would you cower under the strain of awkwardness? There have been a lot of things I've been wanting to know about you. Do you want to know me? You've made attempts to know everyone else throughout the years, but never called me and Beth out to visit you. Why, Richard? Why when there's so much you don't know about me, yet I've been waiting. I like to write too . . .
Your son,
Jonathan

I read the paragraph again five more times.

No. Not my style. Too sappy. It goes against the vow I made never to get to know him after Beth died. He has to make the first move. Not me.

Chapter Thirty-three

Six months passed of a relationship with Rachel that involved disagreements about all kinds of little things. Rachel always seemed to have a lot on her mind. She was increasingly depressed and wanted less and less to spend time with me. I tried to respect her space, but felt more and more helpless about her moods. Perhaps I was too intense, seeing her too much, or perhaps I was a novelty that was wearing off.

On Valentine's Day, 1987, she gave me an I-hope-we-can-still-be-friends speech in the basement of Gannett Hall.

And with that, we looked at each other for a second, Rachel's eyes wet, mine dry. I didn't know why she was crying. She was the one who didn't want the relationship. I couldn't figure it out. I had too much on my mind about Richard to want to figure it out. Rachel's speech was easy to tack on to my life as just another rejection. I filed it at the back of my mind partly because I didn't have a choice.

No final hug, no lingering gazes of remorse. She went to her dorm and I went to the only place I knew for sure needed me—*The Daily Maine Campus*.

For the next three days I worked every hour of each production shift. I could depend on the newspaper. Every day on its front page it had the words "The University of Maine Newspaper Since 1875."

I had a feeling it wasn't going to fold up and leave anytime soon.

The paper was my church, and like a reverend welcomes a faithful churchgoer, the paper was glad to have me.

I didn't need anything else. I figured the less I needed, the less could dissolve and leave me stranded. So on the third straight day of a twelve-hour voluntary production shift at the newspaper, I decided to put my energy into becoming the best editor the paper ever had.

CHAPTER THIRTY-FOUR

By the start of my second year of college, I was established in what I figured to be two of the most worthwhile jobs on campus: crew chief on the fire department, responsible for a crew of three of my fellow firefighters, and Magazine page editor on the newspaper, responsible for administration and paste-up of a two-page section of arts and entertainment articles.

I liked my accomplishments, I liked my confidence, I liked my independence. Nothing and nobody threatened those. Even writing about feelings was no chore because there was nothing to tell. My journal turned into a diary: *Today I did my laundry, studied for economics test, played pool with Todd . . .* and things were pretty uneventful. That's the way I liked it.

Then I met Tempest: an ambitious, boldly independent young broadcasting student and a production assistant at the *Campus* who had been assigned by my managing editor to cover the Portland Symphony Orchestra's performance at the campus arts center. I learned this after going to the concert with my notebook and rushing into the newsroom afterward, my lead paragraph ready to be fed into a computer file. The managing editor asked me what I was working on for deadline and I told him. When he told me he'd assigned this Tempest Farley character to the concert, I knew what I had to do.

Had the assignment not been on deadline, I would have had the patience to work with her writing, but no volunteer writer I knew managed to turn in acceptable copy on deadline without needing major revisions.

So I called Tempest. She had taken twenty-six pages of notes and was busy trying to make an article out of them. As I held the three pages of notes I had taken, I told her, with as much politeness as I could

125

muster, that it wouldn't be necessary to do her review.

She came down to the the paper ten minutes later to, in her words, "see who was showing her up."

Even in blue sweatpants, she was gorgeous. Still madeup from the concert, her eyes were seductively shadowed. Not a blemish on her round face, not too much foundation to cover her dimples. Five-foot-four, I figured, long brown hair corralled by a yellow bandanna.

We talked about the mechanics of deadline writing as I typed the three-hundred-word review. I put the final period on the last paragraph and offered to help her with her next review when and if she wanted to do one.

It was a stab in the dark, a chance in a million, but I added, "I could even go with you if you wanted."

She agreed.

A week later, we went to the Zurich Chamber Orchestra—had a great time talking about music.

A day after that, we went dancing.

An hour after that, we were in the basement lounge of Gannett Hall involved in a conversation that lasted until the dawn of the next day when she sleepily walked over to her room in the adjacent dorm. It was the first of four marathon talks that week.

She was only a year younger than I, but she made me feel much older. She went wild on the dance floor and had a spirit of independence that sometimes made me feel uncomfortable. She had many close male friends and she saw them regularly. She always had lots of homework to do and put great energy into making it better than best. She loved Madonna's music, loved to dress in sexy clothes now and then, had an extremely willing and open mind, never compromised an inch on her beliefs.

In the first week I knew her, I told her the long family story.

Her eyes watered and she held my hand when I told her, with a hardened journalist's stoicism, about Beth.

To me, the story would have no theme or purpose unless I told her that Richard Bach was my father. So I did.

"Richard who?" she asked.

"He wrote a book called *Jonathan Livingston Seagull*."

"What's it about?"

I smiled.

Her reaction exposed something in me I rarely had a chance explore: I was *glad* not to get a surprised "You're Richard Bach's son?" reaction.

At the same time, though, I was disappointed.

Strange.

As I tried to remember what *Jonathan* was about, I realized I had never read the book! I remembered reading the first few pages during the time I was reading his other flying books, but that's as far as I got. It was something about a seagull who tried to teach himself to do spins and stalls.

"It's about a seagull who learns to fly aerobatics."

"Oh. And you're named after it, of course."

It was easier to forget about it.

"Yeah. Anyway, he caused a lot of stress to my family, he's hypocritical and he's done some other things I'm not too thrilled about."

She picked up on my reluctance, started talking about *her* father.

I wanted to listen to her. If I focused enough, I could forget the whole Richard mess. I could get back to feeling my everyday feeling, that I had one parent and always would. I would be able to listen to and care about what Tempest was saying about her father.

Why does it take so much effort to control the things that make us angry, frustrated, embittered? Why do we have to be a slave to our emotions?

Because he doesn't want to be a dad.

CHAPTER THIRTY-FIVE

In the following weeks, Tempest became a motivating part of my firefighting and newspaper life. I had more energy to do the things I did, knowing that someone cared about me intimately.

I found strength in her ambition and her energy. When her batteries ran down, I was there to recharge her. I took care of little things like washing her dishes, maintaining her car, helping her with her tougher journalism assignments.

I met her parents a month later.

Rita, her mother, seemed just as direct and honest as Tempest. She spoke her mind, told me what she thought of Tempest's other boyfriends, lectured expertly about the trials of raising children as if she were a war veteran. I listened respectfully to anything she had to say.

Her dad, Tim, was on the quiet, easy-going side. Of all the dads I'd met in my life, I felt most comfortable with him. He made the difference between a father and a dad clearer for me: calling Tempest when he was at work sometimes just to say, "Hi, how's it going?", making me feel like a welcome part of the family, and he had a neat sense of humor which made him very nonthreatening. He wasn't inconsistent or confusing, and the few times I was at the Farley house before he got home from work, I never got nervous when he pulled into the driveway.

This proof of the difference between a father and a dad made it easier to write Richard and tell him what was on my mind on December 16, 1987.

Beth would have been eighteen that day.

I looked back on the old entries in my journal about Rachel and discovered how much help it was to write about how I felt. I remembered how badly I wanted Rachel to read my entries about her, but I never showed them to her.

I didn't want to have the same regret about Richard. I decided to send him a letter to end all letters. I reminded myself I had nothing to lose by telling him what I thought of him. I wanted to tell him that Beth's birthday meant a lot to me, that she had died without really knowing him and how that didn't have to happen. I wanted to reject him, plain and simple—tell him I could make it without his money and without being known as the son of Richard Bach. Mostly, I couldn't wait to tell him he was a failure as a dad.

I sent the letter, ignoring the part of me that wanted to edit it for its harshness.

December 16, 1987
Richard -

I don't fully understand the reason for this note, but I only think of the fact that I have nothing to lose by it. You see, it's Beth's birthday today. That fact has me thinking about a lot of things. One of the most predominant thoughts on my mind this day is of you.

How strange a thought that is for me. I feel angry, helpless, and bitter. Beth died at the tender age of fifteen, but I was told once that age doesn't make a whole lot of difference to you and I can tell that very well from your actions (or more appropriately, non-actions).

My gist is that as I write this on her birthday, I think that you had a chance to develop a beautiful relationship with your daughter. Now you have no chance. She is gone, not in spirit, of course, but in body. I wish you could have known her, Richard. She was the most talented and attractive human being I have ever known. I envied her in a lot of ways.

But now she is gone—without knowing who you are or you knowing her. I find it incredibly puzzling that someone would create a human, and then not pursue any chance for a relationship.

I remember a time when you were living in Los Angeles and my older brothers and sisters got to come out and see you. They did, two by two. Rob and Kris, Erica and Jim, then it stopped as if you had no wish to see the last two.

You speak of soulmates, those who are "appropriate others," as Milton Mayeroff puts it. Beth was mine in a way. Being the two youngest members of the Bach family and being so close in age, we had a lot in common growing up.

The reunion in 1984 was an interesting event for me. Yes, it allowed me to see a little more of who you are. But Beth and I felt out of touch with everything that was expressed by the older members of the family. They could remember special times with you, we couldn't. To describe such feelings is almost impossible. But Beth felt the same as I did. We just looked at each other and shared a language that only she and I could understand.

Now I am the keeper of that language and forever will be. You had the chance to develop a language that only a father and a daughter could understand. You can never know what kind of language you two could have spoken. It may have been one that defies all characteristics of speech, hand signals, or written communication. We had our own language because we could not speak yours.

I used to hope that someday I would overcome my bitterness and develop a relationship with you. I thought that maybe Beth's death would make you realize how precious life is and how easily it can be taken away. But you made no effort to establish a relationship with me even though my life is just as precious. I can't be the one who initiates a relationship.

Jim established a very successful relationship with you. For him, though, it was a matter of circumstance. Jon pushed him out of the house, but I managed to stick it out and pay my dues. Now I'm a college sophomore with my own life, dreams, ambitions, talents, and belief system.

This is me writing, not Jon or Mom or any other member of the family. In that sense, I feel lucky. I am my own person and unlike the rest of the family, am more detached from you. I am biased only by your actions (or like I said before, non-actions) that I have experienced throughout my life.

I doubt anything will come of this letter. I don't seek anything from you. I know what kinds of miscommunication can be produced from letters. From Erica's experience, I can say that you will probably read too much into this. You have a tendency not to see the forest because the trees are blocking your view.

Money means very little to me. I look forward to making it on my own without your help. I am fortunate that I am in college, but I am here only because of Beth's death and the insurance money. So this letter can't be misconstrued as wanting money. Nor can it be taken as wanting anything else, for that matter. It is an airing of grievances, anger and confusion. Take it as you will. Like I said, you have made it so that I have nothing to lose.

I have always wanted someone to call "dad." Jon is not my dad and he never will be. A dad is someone who shapes you to your liking and guides you and who you may even revere. But I have no dad. Rob is a dad to his son. You are my father, not my dad. Rob refers to you as Dad often, but he can only use that term through his experiences with you and the language you and he can speak because of that.

There is a statistic that says that if one's parents are divorced, there is a 50 percent chance that the children produced from that marriage will also become divorced after they get married. I can't wait to disprove that statistic. Like Rob, I will be the best father I can be. I thank you for showing me what not to do. In that respect, by knowing my current feelings and experiences of being "dad"less, I can get married and have children knowing that I wouldn't want my kids to have the same feelings and experiences I have right now regarding you.

I hope that if I ever become as famous as you, that I am not known as the son of Richard Bach. I've had to live with people asking if I'm related to you and upon answering yes, I've had to explain to them that while I am related to you, I don't know you at all. I wonder how many people know that you have a family.

I used to want to know you, but I've always been intimidated by your isolation. Even your letters are usually sent on note-pad paper. They are brief, hasty and denote how busy you are.

So I conclude this with a spirit of pride that I have finally written the feelings I have had since my early teens and especially since February 1, 1985. You may not believe in birthdays, but this one I think you ought to remember. It is of my little sister and your biological daughter, Bethany Jeanne Bach, born December 16, 1969.

Jonathan

There! I thought. *We'll see how he likes that! Just one last stab before I never talk to him again. Let him chew on that for a while. No way he's going to respond to that.*

In the next flash of feeling that followed that thought, I sensed that if Beth had been alive, she wouldn't know what to make of my letter. The feeling lasted for little more than a second and it came with a slight chill—a tinge of regret before I ignited a gasoline-soaked bridge.

I shivered away the mood. I was too mad to think.

Chapter Thirty-six

Christmas break came and went. It was a new year, and a new semester was starting. After greeting my buddies and settling back into room 111, I found a letter in my Gannett lobby mailbox. A letter from Richard.

I couldn't believe he'd actually responded.

I opened the letter, an iron ball in my throat like the one that came whenever Big Jon pulled in the driveway. I tried to convince myself there were going to be all kinds of apologies in the envelope.

December 25, 1987
Hi, dear Jonathan,

What a pleasure to hear from you at last!

I stopped reading. A pleasure to hear from me!?! What letter did he get?

A pleasure because as an adult you've chosen on your own to open a line of communication between us. As you've been without me for a dad, so have I been without you for a son.

The iron ball grew bigger.

He misses having me as a son? He's got Jim, who's more his type anyway. Why would he miss me for a son? Probably saying it because it's polite.

There's much we could have learned from each other lost to date, but if we wish, there's the delight of getting to know each other still ahead.

Delight? Uh . . . I don't think so.

So much to say! Round about this paragraph in the first draft of this letter I got off into trying to say too much at once.

I read the first paragraph again. I didn't know what he meant.

Please know that I welcome the chance to get to know you, and to let you know a bit about your dad, though it's not the work one letter can do. Given a channel has been opened by your letter and that I'd like to keep that open, what's the best way for us to go from here, what would you like to see happen now?

"I have no idea, Richard," I said aloud, smiling at how he could actually think I wanted to start a relationship with a letter of such anger. And he wanted to keep this channel open—it wasn't my plan to open anything. Why was he asking me what should happen?

Even under the best conditions, 2500 miles is a challenging obstacle to close communication. Is your computer tied into CompuServe?

Now he's talking CompuServe? What the hell is this guy thinking? He's so weird he doesn't even understand hate!

Our subscription has lapsed as all priorities here turned to book-writing, but if you were on the network, we'd renew.

You're right, it's a busy time for us. We had been working non-stop against a hard deadline on this book, got sixty thousand words into it, threw the whole thing out and started over. Another false start took 30,000 words. Those made things a little tighter, but this version is what we want, and we're determined to deliver the first draft on February 1. Then we're into editing and so on to a publication date of October '88. After this book, for the first time in years, we can ease back into a normal life!

I didn't care.

I'm encouraged by your letter, too, because Leslie and I have had a wonderful relationship with Jim, and more lately with Jim and his wife, Kim, though between striving to recover from the bankruptcy and writing the books, we haven't talked with them nearly as much as we wish. The times we have spent together have been enormous fun. Jim and we don't always agree with each other, but he runs his mind with such ruthless integrity that we love the guy, we're honored to know him.

No surprise there.

I had the same feeling about you, the few times we saw each other.

The iron ball welled higher in my throat. I knew he wasn't lying. He had no reason to.

In those days you weren't living on your own, though, and I saw the walls behind your eyes, your recognition that I was with you for a moment while others around were permanent.

His perception was right on the mark. How did he know?

I understood that those were the ones you had to deal with daily, not me. So I crossed my fingers and hoped someday we'd find a way to say hello.

Who says he just had to cross his fingers? Why didn't he just make the move?

Sure enough, there's a lot in the past that we need to talk about. If we start with a rehearsal of misunderstanding, though, is it likely that it will lead to where we'd like to go? I lean on your guidance and direction here. What kind of relationship would you like to have?

The iron ball shrank a bit. He was giving me power, control. He needed *my* guidance, of all things. My *guidance* after my impetuous letter?

> There is a great deal of misunderstanding damming the channel you've opened, but I sure don't see anything there that would shut down communications unless we want them to be shut.

I was still deciding if I wanted them shut. It was tempting to keep communications closed, not admit my misunderstanding or my ignorance. It was tempting to forget I'd written the letter in the first place.

> Before I get to your letter, some elements and assumptions I'll take for granted unless you tell me otherwise. I assume:
> That we both want straight communications, for the purpose of understanding and enjoying each other. (If you haven't read it, there's a little book called *I'm OK, You're OK,* with an excellent description of straight and crossed communications).

Not interested.

> I assume we don't have to communicate at all. If you're uncomfortable with me or with your perception of me, you're free unilaterally to say not another word. Same for me.

That's more like it.

His invitation not to communicate was the perfect rationale for denying my ignorance and impetuousness. He was making it easy for me not to respond.

> I assume we're both doing our best, to be the best people we know how to be. Though there was a lot of pain in your letter, I assume that you're not opening communications to advise me just that you think I'm a son of a bitch on my way straight to hell.

Hmm.

Again, you're free to say that I'm a son of a bitch and I'll accept that from you for a while, but if we don't move on from there, things get a little pointless.

No problem, I decided. Things weren't going to go anywhere from here.

I assume we're entitled to our misunderstandings until we've talked them out. If I drag mine in again after you've addressed them clearly, I owe you an apology, and vice versa.

Please don't think that I intend this letter to be an answer to any more than the intent of yours. I'll bet that feeling as you do it took a lot of courage for you to write, and I'm proud of you for writing.

Wow.

The ball swelled again and my eyes watered quickly. I was hot and nervous.

If we go on, I'll talk a lot more about the points you made so well.

You have a fair idea of my values from the books I've written. I'd love to learn a little about your values, about what path you're choosing for yourself this time, about who you are.

Hi, Jonathan!

Love,
Dad

More thoughts and feelings came. I grabbed my psychology notebook and headed down into the basement study lounge to write. "Love, Dad."

Just like the letter that said he felt "Beth would have wanted it that way." Why again does he assume he is "Dad" to me? And why does he again think he can use the word "love"?

And he gives a diagram for a relationship. I don't want to be in an equation, I just want him to be a normal dad. Dads don't give diagrams, they're supposed to make the first move to plant the seed of a relationship. No plans for what our roles will be, no assumptions, no typed proposals for hope. Just father and son shootin' the breeze. That's the way it is with all my friends' dads.

I stopped writing. I admitted to myself that Richard's letter made sense. It sounded a lot like something out of the textbook for my Interpersonal Communications class. It was sensible, direct, honest.

I'm not going to write him. He'll understand if I don't. He said so.

I folded the letter and put it neatly in its envelope. In another minute, I was back in my room. I opened the door to my dorm-room closet and put the letter in the manila envelope with all the others he had ever sent me.

CHAPTER THIRTY-SEVEN

Summer break 1988 came a few months later and I felt like a real adult. My home wasn't Vermont anymore. For the first time, my home wasn't in whatever state Mom lived.

Home was Maine.

My friends were there, I was becoming established as a pretty fair journalist, and I was excited to explore this new independence.

I had money to get me through the remaining two years of college and enough to live in Freeport for the summer. It was two hours south of the university and close to Tempest, who was working at the famous L. L. Bean store.

She moved in with me soon after the summer started. Her parents lived three or four miles down the road, and though they were reluctant about their daughter living with a guy, they liked me well enough to tolerate it.

I was in heaven. Clinching this stage of what I perceived to be "adulthood" meant I was powerful, responsible enough to myself that I wouldn't need to think about needing Richard to be a dad.

I was riding the crest of that adult wave, but to keep riding it, I needed a good job.

I applied for journalism internships at the local papers in southern Maine and my best hope was with the *Brunswick Times Record*. I had a great interview with the editor, a burly man who radiated professionalism, but seemed to be easy-going with the rest of his staff. He gave me the "I'll be in touch" line and I trusted he would. I called every week after that to see if he'd reached a decision. By the fifth week, and the fifth "not yet," it was time to get serious about finding a job. No other papers were hiring.

Tempest encouraged me to apply at L. L. Bean. Her father worked there too, and that could be helpful to mention in an interview. Whether or not it helped, I was hired the first week in June and started orientation for summer cashiers a week later. Two days after that, I was running my own cash register in the campware department.

I was lucky, I was told, to work there. I made sure I earned the honor by being the most productive, courteous summer temporary employee the store ever hired.

It felt great wearing an apron and name tag with the L. L. Bean logo. Some cashiers had their first name, some had their nickname. My co-workers told me I didn't have to put my full name on the tag, but it was part of my journalist ethic to tell the whole truth.

But that tag, that icon of pride and identity, was, at times, a bright red beacon.

"Hey," one customer asked me that first week, "you ever hear of a book about a seagull named Jonathan?"

Questions like that set my mind on fire.

There were thirty or so other customers that summer who asked about my name. Half of them noted that I had the same last name as the famous composer and I was delighted to tell them I even had the middle initial S.

For the other customers who commented about Jonathan Seagull, I tried not to give any hint that Richard was a father I didn't know and didn't respect. It was too complicated to get into. For the most part, I kept it general, never lying, but not telling everything I could tell. I'd just say I hadn't seen him in a while, he lived on the other side of the country, he stayed pretty busy.

When I mentioned I was in Maine getting my journalism degree, some commented that it was natural that I be a writer. It prompted me to tell them the difference between a writer and a journalist. I wanted to emphasize that journalism was a very practical and nonphilosophical writing career. Writers were introverted, arrogant, eccentric people who starved as they tried to convince tough-as-nails editors to accept their masterpieces. I wanted them to see how different I was from Richard, understand he had nothing to do with my being a journalism major.

Their comments seemed reasonable enough: there are sons of actors who become actors, sons of baseball players who become baseball players, sons of horse breeders, etc.

Was it inevitable that I'd sought a writing career?

Coincidence, I thought. *Just coincidence.*

But I had to do something—something permanent about this Richard stuff. Otherwise I'll always hear that side of me saying: *"Shake me, ask me about Richard Bach, watch the snow swirl and fall around a son who tries to figure out what to say, how to act, what to feel about a father he can't call Dad. And he'll stand there, that son, and will do nothing. He has tried to run and he can't and he will suffocate and die from that plastic snow unless he does something tremendous, masses an incredible burst of energy that melts the stuff once and for all."*

There's so much I don't know! And shouldn't I know? Shouldn't I be able to tell people a complete story of who he is and what he's up to?

What's my role? Ambassador? Dutiful son? Hateful son? Just a guy with a first name Jonathan and a last name Bach?

Would it be all that bad if I called him for answers? He seemed sensible in that letter, in all his letters to me, but . . .

The plastic snow stopped and I heard and saw nothing but cloudy white. All the other times, these clouds would mean peace from the storm. Now, in achieving adulthood, they filled me with emptiness.

Chapter Thirty-eight

Summer 1988 ended.

Tempest and I had been through a roller-coaster four months of living together. There were times both of us felt trapped by the other, her wanting to spend time with her friends, who all seemed to be male, me having no friends, but feeling like I'd better allow Tempest to live whatever lifestyle she wanted or I'd lose her. Her need for independence and my need to keep her led to the compromise of having separate bedrooms.

Just like with Rachel and Richard, I told myself that being an adult meant accepting things I couldn't change.

I was trying to break my bad habit of wanting to be romantic with Tempest, but it wasn't easy. Sometimes she'd consent and we'd talk about our lives over a candlelit dinner, sometimes she'd be out with her male friends and I wouldn't see her until she got in late.

But I figured I would eventually get the hang of this "go with the flow and let Tempest be Tempest" stuff. She was my first serious sexual experience and I was hers. I was sure that would enable us to accommodate any change in our personalities, any new vector in our career goals, lifestyle, anything.

Living together could be fun if I could learn not to be so dependent.

And with those words, I persuaded her to join me in a new apartment in Orono just a mile from the university.

When the fall semester started, I still hadn't learned not to be so dependent.

September 11, 1988

Missing Tempest a little although I'm not on her good side today. Attracted to her more than she knows because I'm able to subdue my emotions up here in Orono. Went to a concert on the quad with her Friday and she looked awesome all made up and I was really proud to be with her. She even treated me kind of like a boyfriend. She actually followed me around where I went and hung around with me by choice. I was amazed. We both have our independence, though I know she wants hers more than I want mine. My weakness is intimacy. It seems the more I act independent and uncaring about what she does with her day, the more she wants to be with me. The more I act dependent, the less she wants to be with me.

I have this feeling that when she's ready to make a real commitment, I'll definitely be there, but part of being in relationships is patience. So far so good. I've been able to keep my emotions in check, managed not to show her any major jealousies.

But by the middle of the new fall semester, I couldn't manage it anymore. It was too hard to hold back the tide of impulses that told me it wasn't wrong of me to want emotional commitment from her. After a few arguments about whether expectations are fair in a relationship, she finally told me what I knew anyway: she was too independent to want an intimate relationship.

I knew that a lot of women complained about how unromantic their boyfriends were. There were all kinds of articles and lectures and TV shows for women about how to deal with uncommitted men. The more I heard women complain, the madder I got, especially because of what was about to happen.

November 27, 1988

Start of a new chapter in my life. Nothing is hitting home with me more than pulling nails out of blank walls where Tempest's posters used to hang. I came home from November break to an apartment with only my stuff in it. No trace of Tempest, yet her presence is everywhere. The apartment echoes now and I feel empty too. She left with a part of me. Life goes on, pulling me by the hands, my heels making big ruts in the ground. What does it all mean? I'm clueless. The void is there and I try to mask it over, not fill it, hoping it fills in, heals itself.

The message on the answering machine says she's living with friends in Bangor.

I wanted to tell her that NO ONE does this to me and gets away with it. After all the sacrifices I made to try to live her way, go with the flow.

My fault. I wasn't selfish enough. Just like Rachel, I got too dependent. She's got the right to live whatever way she pleases. I should have made a better choice. I should have been just as selfish as her.

Fuck her. She wants to live like a damn honeybee going from flower to flower, she'll never find someone to treat her as well as I did! She'll be like Richard and that woman on page whatever. Empty relationships, no commitment, don't crowd my freedom, but don't be as carefree to me as I am to you. I don't need that attitude.

What's so wrong with commitment, anyway? Cripes! Women talk about how uncommitted men are, but it's women who have the problems! Look at me, Mr. Commitment. Look at me alone, guilty again of being too romantic or whatever.

I was pushed into my only sanctuary, the two things that had always been there: words and paper. They'd always accepted me. Now they were my career, or at least the makings of one.

The newspaper was it for me. It was my friend and my committed ally. It was there five days a week, seven days if I just wanted to do my homework down there. It was there even when I put it second priority to girlfriends, the fire department, homework. Journalism wasn't philosophical, it was as down-to-earth and realistic as I was. It was straight, honest, concise, and as easy to understand as a story about a bank robbery. It was a steady paycheck, even a bit glamorous. There was "Good column today, Jon," from friends, and "I called you because I knew you could do a good job with this story idea I have" from a few professors, and even a "Way to fucking go!" from a journalism teacher.

There were interviews to do, deadlines to meet, melodramatic quotes from irate student senators to joke about in the newsroom, the rush at one o'clock in the morning to finish the layout of the paper and meet the truck that delivered the page proofs to be printed forty miles away.

Journalism reminded me how valuable it was. By the end of the fall semester 1988, great things started happening in my career.

I applied for a summer internship at the *Ellsworth American,* a weekly newspaper on the Maine coast, and I was hired to start working there when the 1989 spring semester ended.

Meanwhile, I was assistant editor at the *Campus.* Though the job was mostly keeping the production department running smoothly when the editor wasn't there, the title was fantastic! Near the end of that spring term, I felt I could be a competent editor.

A week after I applied, I got the job.

After three years of pleasure-pain work, following, respecting whoever was in charge, I was at the top. I was the editor who was going to really listen to staff problems, keep communication open among all departments of the paper. I knew the problems that could occur, I'd done every production job except advertising. This was gonna be cool!

Spring semester ended a week later and my internship at the *American* started. This was the real thing—no advice from professors or problems getting sources to talk because I was only working for the *student* paper.

I wasn't in the internship long before I got a real sense of my destiny as a reporter.

"Take a camera to Mount Desert Island and see what the brush fire is about," the managing editor said after hearing reports on the office police scanner.

Who better qualified than a firefighter? I knew the right people to ask which questions and when not to ask.

I drove the ten miles to the site and discovered it was no brush fire. It was the fire of the twentieth century, at least in this area. The Jackson Laboratory, one of the most prominent research facilities in the country for breeding genetically pure strains of mice for experimentation, was burning to the ground.

I took pictures, made notes, and managed to get statements from spokespeople before they had formally prepared what they were going to say to the media. I had beaten the three major television crews to the site, I had taken two rolls of film before the fire reached its full stage. I had the start to a fantastic internship and the success of my future career. All by being in the right place at the right time. Destiny whacked me so hard it was difficult to stay conscious.

I rushed back to the newspaper and was told that a senior reporter had gone to the fire, so my notes and pictures weren't necessary.

So much for Destiny.

But I was kind of glad. To get a story that big during the first week of the internship was a daunting responsibility. A misquote or some other major mistake on the front page with my name on the by-line wouldn't be a great way to start.

The editors did want some of the pictures I'd taken, and that was fine with me. If they published any of them, I could take those pictures anywhere, to any job interview in the future, and let my work speak for itself. There was no erasing that. Those pictures were locked down, with my name below them, in the permanent record of the *American*. They printed three.

I was honored to be a part of such a noble occupation. I took great pride in being a member of Sigma Delta Chi, a journalism organization at the university, even signed my name under the pledge: *I intend to undertake journalism as my profession. . . . I believe in the ideas of the Society and agree to abide by the By-laws of the Society as they affect me either as a student member or as a professional member after I am graduated or leave school.*

But the excitement of having my photos published by the *American* wasn't much without someone to share it with. Mom seemed glad for me, as did the rest of the family. Part of me wished I could tell Richard, but I told myself it wouldn't be interesting to him anyway.

I thought of Tempest's dad, Tim. I knew he'd make me feel like a real professional. He'd probably say something like, "The *Portland Press Herald* better not let you get away when you graduate!"

Now, that's a real dad, I thought.

CHAPTER THIRTY-NINE

I drove the two hours down to the Farleys' Freeport home the day after the laboratory fire had made the front page of the *American*.

Tim wasn't home, but I was just as excited to talk to Tempest's mother, Rita.

"Did you tell your father?" she asked.

"I probably won't. He's just too distant and disinterested to care."

"Why do you say that?"

I started to tell her the family story as she prepared dinner, shelling lobster meat and collecting it in a big bowl in front of us at the dining room table. With her left hand, Rita took a new lobster body from the pile on her left and began to coax the meat from it with a small pick. The meat joined the last half hour's accumulation in the large stainless-steel bowl. The empty shell she dropped into a large bowl to her right.

"You called him Captain?"

She threw another lobster shell into the bowl.

"Yeah."

I thought of that old image of the man, the wheelchair, and the captain's hat. I twirled my paper napkin, tearing off pieces every few seconds, herding them into a perfect round pile.

Rita suddenly looked up from her work and stared out the bay window facing the driveway. She lost interest in my story in favor of something that had activated her radarlike senses.

I looked behind me where she seemed to be staring. An old Plymouth drove by.

"Nope, that's not Tim," she said.

"What was I saying?" I asked Rita as she emptied the gutted lobster shells into a bigger bowl on the floor.

"Something about knowing Tim better than your dad because you never saw him much."

"Yeah . . . "

I fought hard to remember something. I thought of hypnosis, Ben & Jerry's, a little green book to write in, going into a bookstore.

"I swear, I have the worst memory. I'm trying really hard to remember."

I stared at the neat pile of napkin shreds in front me while I took a few minutes to describe the time Richard and Leslie came to Burlington.

Then I paused.

"This is boring, though," I said, waiting for some kind of reaction.

"Not at all," she said. "There's just a lot of it. Doesn't sound like you've ever sorted it out before."

"Yeah, I guess. I just talk as it comes."

"So keep it coming. Maybe you'll find something out. It's really interesting to hear about your family. I've known you all this time and you've never told me before. You always seem to be listening to me talk about my family."

"Well, it's your house, Rita. I just try to be a polite guest."

"Oh, that's bull—'polite guest.' Jon, you're family. You were here more than Tempest was last summer! But I thought we'd seen the last of you when you and Temp broke up," Rita said, revealing her surprise that I continued to visit her and Tim.

"Well, Rita, family doesn't have to necessarily be related, right?"

"So I see."

I continued my story, told her about the reunion, the chain letter.

"You know what the clincher is about Richard and me, though? With all this stuff about the family, it was Beth that really made me hate the guy."

Rita was almost done with her project. She sat between a diminished pile of lobster bodies on her left, the brimming bowl of meat in front of her, and the shells on her right. She sat back, wiped her brow with a napkin, wrinkled her eyebrows, and looked really confused.

"Beth, your sister?"

"Yeah. You know. Beth and 1985 and everything."

She still looked confused.

"How I got this broken nose?"

"I didn't know your nose was broken!"

"I've never told you this?"

She shook her head.

"Sure I have."

She shook her head.

"How long have I known you?"

We both counted the months.

Eighteen.

She smiled for a second, then her radar went off again.

"There he is," she said, her eyes focused on a shiny white Oldsmobile pulling into the driveway.

I left Rita at the table with her lobstering and watched Tim Farley get out of his car. He carried a newspaper.

"Has he got the paper?" she asked.

"Yep."

Door chimes banged music as he walked in. He turned to me as he put the paper on the table.

"Hey! I thought that was your vehicle taking up perfectly good space in my driveway!"

He stepped over to hug me. He was solid and strong, but I was taller.

"Yeah, well, you know . . . whenever there's a free dinner, I'll be around."

"Doesn't surprise me," he said.

He gave his wife a kiss hello and a two-second shoulder rub.

"Ah, lobsters!" he said, preparing to dive into the biggest bowl on the table, brimming with lobster meat.

"Wait!" Rita warned. "I'll start dinner after Jon finishes."

Jon finishes . . .

"No, that's okay, really. It doesn't really matter," I said.

Talking to Rita was one thing. Being on stage, having an audience, this spotlight, was another.

Tim returned from the kitchen with a wooden bowl filled with pistachios and sat at his usual seat.

"Jon is going to finish something?" he said, loosening his tie and removing his shoes.

"He was just starting a story about his sister and his father."

Tim began to shell the first pistachio, leaned back in his chair as he did so. Rita dropped her picking tool on the table and leaned back in hers.

I sighed.

I can't believe I let it get this far, I thought.

And as Tim shelled the first pistachio, I started telling them about the night I watched my sister die.

CHAPTER FORTY

Fifteen minutes later, my story was done.

Tim supported his head with his elbows on the table and stared into pink pistachio dust in the empty bowl. Rita dried her hands.

"That's quite a story," she said.

Tim nodded his head, still staring into the bowl.

"More stuff to include in that book you'll write," Rita said.

Writing a book was the last thing on my mind.

I turned to Tim.

"She thinks I should write a book about this stuff," I said. "She told me that before you got home."

He picked a piece of lobster meat from the bowl.

"Mmm. Sounds like a fair idea."

"You guys . . . " I said, shaking my head, not wanting to take them seriously.

"Well, why not?" Rita asked. "Sounds like a book to me."

I softly mashed the pile of napkin I had shredded in front of me.

Would more of my friends think the same? Maybe. But there's no way I can just abandon college. All that progress, all these accomplishments. No way I want to be a free-lance writer and starve like Mom did with Dick Bach.

But if I did write something, people would know about the "real" Richard Bach, the one who let his daughter die without knowing her, the one that alienated Kris, Rob, Erica, and me, refused to talk about the family on radio talk shows, never mentioned us anywhere else, carelessly spent millions on planes instead of us, talked about never marrying again and then married again . . .

I was loaded with powerful artillery to blow the Richard Bach fans

151

into reality. He was no guru. He was a deserter, a coward, plain and simple.

With one book, I could sweep away the foundation of my father's mystical success. His fans would curse him, never buying his books again, seeing what a hypocrite this guy is. If it was interesting to Rita and Tim, it'd be interesting to others.

It's time Richard Bach came down to earth with the rest of us.

A book!

CHAPTER FORTY-ONE

I didn't remember a single scene of the two-hour drive from Free-port to Orono.

A book.

I didn't know I was carrying so much around.

I needed a reality check. Would this idea work?

I thought of Jim as I opened the door to my dark, lonely apartment. After all he'd gone through, he'd never had a problem with Richard. And no one in the family seemed to understand Richard better. Since the accident, since that talk with Jim about the weird prophecies in Beth's last letter to the family, he and I had had a strong feeling of brotherhood.

Who better than he to tell me whether this idea was possible?

Jim was in California now, working in the heart of Silicon Valley as a software quality assurance manager for Apple Computer. I was prouder of Jim than I ever had been about anything. No high school diploma and he was making forty thousand dollars a year at one of the biggest computer firms in the country. He was hiring people older than he, people who had just graduated from Cal Tech.

Since he'd left Vermont, he'd called me every ten days or so to fill me in about life in the "real world." He'd tell me his managing strategies at work and I'd tell him my managing strategies at the newspaper. He'd call me when he was excited about a new action-packed computer game, when he'd just seen the latest blockbuster adventure movie, or to see if there were any new romances in my life.

Now that Jim was married, he'd razz me about being the only Bach who was single. I'd tell him it wasn't like I wasn't trying, and he'd always see my side when I speculated why Rachel and Tempest had broken off their relationships with me.

Jim would also talk about what great people Richard and Leslie were. He said they called him often, just to see how he was doing. It was hard to believe they could do such an uncomplicated, down-to-earth thing, but Jim never lied.

He told me they were extremely supportive, energized him when he was depressed or uncertain about his future. It was clear they were valuable to Jim, but I suspected that was only because he was still mad at Mom for not defending him when he had that climactic argument with Big Jon.

I figured again that his relationship with Richard was filled with philosophical talk.

As much as he talked about what a great guy Richard was, he never put major pressure on me to get to know him. He knew I was very reluctant. Maybe he even knew I had a list of strikes against Richard that he couldn't defend.

At 1:30 A.M. East Coast time, 10:30 P.M. California time, I dialed Jim's number.

"Hey!" I said when he answered. "I've got this crazy idea and I want to bounce it off you."

"Cool!" he said. "What is it, man?"

"I think I want to write a book about Richard."

"Really? Good!"

I spoke fast, hoping his enthusiasm wouldn't fade faster than I could tell him what I meant by a "book about Richard."

"Well, not all right for him. See, I've got a lot of ammunition. Y'know, things like Beth and Mom and Kris and everybody and all that's happened."

"What do you mean? You're going to slam him?"

He spoke aggressively now, almost angrily. His enthusiasm was gone. It made me nervous.

"Well, yes and no. Kind of."

I was hoping he'd see how excited I was.

"Well, Jon, that's pretty stupid."

I gulped.

"Wha . . . what do you mean st . . . "

"I mean stupid! You know, ignorant?"

His words hit me like Big Jon's had when I'd done something wrong. It was tough to swallow, and I stayed quiet.

"How are you going to write a book about someone you don't know?" he asked aggressively. "You'd better call him."

"What more is there to know? I know what happened."

"Do you?"

I thought I did, but now that he mentioned it, I was kind of fuzzy on the details about what had happened between Richard and Kris, Rob, and Erica.

"Well, kind of. All I have to do is call everybody to get their stories and that'll do it."

"Then you should call Richard too."

I was about to tell him no, but it occurred to me that if I didn't get Richard's side, writing a book about him would violate a journalism ethic to tell the whole truth. That meant calling Richard.

"Well, maybe," I said. "I don't know."

If I paused, I knew he'd start telling me loudly that I better get Richard's side.

I hurriedly continued.

"But I *do* know he didn't try very hard to know Beth!" I said.

I was charged with anger. Jim wouldn't dare question my feelings about Beth, just as no one questioned whether or not Astra had been *his* dog.

"So you're angry that he denied Beth and you're going to avenge that by denying Dad and writing this book."

It was too simple.

For the next hour, Jim went on about his relationship with Richard and the difference Richard made in his life, how supportive he was of anything Jim was excited about, how eager to share Jim's successes and how valuable he was to Jim in helping him to understand his failures.

"And what if he dies before you speak to him again?" Jim asked. "What if you never get the chance to know what kind of man he really is? Could you live with that?"

As stupid as it seemed, my answer was yes. But there was no way I was going to tell him that. I didn't want to sound any more stupid than I already felt, so I said nothing in hope it was a rhetorical question. It must have been, because he spoke too quickly for me to answer.

"That's just so stupid, Jon! If you had a bit of sense in you, you'd call him. Right now, okay? Right now. 'Bye."

Jim hung up and I let stunned chills freeze me into the muffled static on the line.

Direct. That's Jim. I could handle it usually. I even thrived on it. But not tonight.

Tonight I cried.

I searched for some aftertaste of logic.

I might as well forget the whole idea. That's easier than calling him. It's easier to live without him. I'll forget the book just as long as Jim forgets I had this idea in the first place.

Call him? That's not my job, it's his. That goes against all my convictions. He left, I didn't.

Geez, I don't have Richard's number—even if I did want to call.

That makes the decision easy.

The phone rang.

I cleared my throat and prepared to talk calmly to whoever this was.

Long-distance static for half a second. It was Jim.

Okay, that's more like it. He's calling to say he's sorry and to go ahead and write the book because it's what I have to do.

"By the way, this is Richard's number," he said quickly. "Get a pen."

I did as I was told, wrote the number.

He hung up after he told me the last digit. I'd never heard him more direct, abrupt, serious.

I fought hard for an excuse not to call. I knew the right thing to do was call him, but I also knew the right thing to do was stand my ground.

Damn.

The receiver buzzed a dull tone in my ear.

Decision.

Now.

Call or don't call.

The embarrassment of getting Jim's reaction to my book idea set in and tears came again. Then more and more.

I was still holding the phone. The line was still silent and it made me cry more. All this after a few direct words.

What a wimp I am!

There didn't seem to be any alternatives.

"Be a fucking man, Jon!" said Jim's silent and unsympathetic voice.

Beth stood in the shadows of my mind, waiting for me to do something.

I don't know . . .

I can't make the first move! Not me! He's the one that left, he's the one that bailed out, he's the one that hurt the family then preaches love and soulmates! Him, him, him! Richard fucking Bach!

But then, out of the cloud of anger came an unmistakable figure. It took the form of a feeling and it was contrast to the clouds like the silhouette of a biplane in a dark orange sky.

Just call him, Jon, said the feeling.

CHAPTER FORTY-TWO

Two hours passed. Two hours of dialing and hanging up before the call could go through. Two hours of questioning: what if I get rejected all over again?

I thought back to how warm he always sounded whenever I talked with him.

Do I trust him? He's never been mad at me.

Like a novice cliff-diver on his first hundred-foot dive, I jumped, part of me hoping my death would be quick on the jagged rocks below.

I dialed his number again, daring myself to wait another second longer before I hung up.

I was drunk with confusion, but I managed to let the phone ring more than once in a house clear across the continent.

The dive starts. I jump.

Freefall.

What a traitor! So much for loyalty to Mom and Kris and Rob and Erica and Beth . . . right, Jonathan? So much for being part of the family.

The phone rang and rang again.

Water coming up fast to meet me now. *If you worry about the pain upon impact, there will be pain.*

1989. Nineteen years after he left, eight since Burlington, five since the reunion. I'm twenty-one, I've seen him three times I can remember, seen pictures of him in photo albums, still have his letters somewhere around here. I can't believe I'm doing this.

The phone rang and rang again. It was 1:45 A.M. his time. I expected an answering machine at that hour.

Fifty feet gone, eyes closed now, I could hear the surf against the rocks and one spectator say to another, "I can't believe he jumped!"

If I got Richard's answering machine as I expected to, that would be an excuse to hang up. I didn't want to just leave a message. What could I say? "Richard, this is Jonathan. Obviously you're not in. Well, I was going to write a book about how much I disrespect you, but I bounced the idea off Jim and he crunched me with a few sentences. I thought maybe you'd help me make sense of this mess. Just tell Jim I called you and make like everything's fine between us, okay? This is just a state of rash stupidity anyway. I don't know why I called. I vowed never to make the first move. Uh . . . don't bother to call back. I'll regret this in the morn—"

"Hello?" said a low, soft, sleepy voice.

"Richard?" I said with my cracking voice, bringing the phone up to my ear, but holding it slightly away as if it were white hot.

Jon, the cliff diver, hit the water at a hundred miles an hour and it hurt like hell.

It had been four years since I'd last spoken to him.

I cleared my throat and sniffed, thought about the hate letter and how I hadn't written him since, so he must have thought I'd written just to call him a son of a bitch. He probably didn't like that.

I was swallowing cold salt water as I fought to get to the surface. It was hard to talk.

"This is Jonathan . . . "

I hadn't hit the rocks, but I was drowning.

I sobbed and breathed, deep and hard on the phone, fighting for air. I felt a strong fatigue, too. The two-hour drive I'd just made from Freeport, stunned embarrassment with Jim, and now this, weighted my chest.

"Jonathan? What's wrong?" Richard asked nervously and with a bit of fear, as if I might be calling with news that somebody else in the family had died.

I couldn't inhale enough to form the words to answer him and I was afraid he'd be so scared he'd have a heart attack or something unless he got an answer.

I managed to say, "Nothing . . . "

Then, after a few seconds of crying, I said, "I just talked with Jim . . ."

Naturally, he was hanging on the completion of my sentence, trying to figure out what I was going to say to him after four years.

Something about Jim.

"Is something wrong with Jim?" he asked.

I kept him waiting between sobs. I managed to say no, then, "This is so hard for me . . ."

More sobs.

"Take your time," he said softly. "It's all right."

What's all right, Richard? Geez! Do you know what I'm doing here?

Inhale.

Maybe you do. According to Mom, Jim, according to all your fans I've met, you're magically perceptive.

He communicated a few sympathetic "oh"s while I fought for my voice.

Like that night in 1985, like all the other times I had spoken with him, his voice was warm, comfortable, easy, supportive. It wasn't what I'd expected. I'd expected abruptness and business. Something like, "I don't want to talk to you, Jonathan. Good-bye." Or something like he would say in a letter: "Jonathan, if you have something to say, we can go from there. If not, we have the option not to go anywhere, but that's not the way to have a relationship."

Jon the diver streaked upward like an air bubble in twenty feet of water.

In one long breath, I managed to explain the book I was going to write and how I'd called Jim and he told me I'd better get Richard's side of the story and I'd felt that it wasn't my job to get his side because *he* was the one that left because he didn't want to be a father and I couldn't do anything about that, yet if I *didn't* call Richard, Jim would know I was having a hard time dealing with this whole father-son thing and he probably wouldn't talk to me again unless I did something about it once and for all and called Richard, so here I am calling you to say *I don't know what,* but it's just as well because you wouldn't understand what I've been feeling all these years and I don't expect you to because I'm not sure I understand either, so just ignore the fact that I called because I don't really know what to say right now because I'm still young and stupid and obviously confused, but hey, I know it's late for you out there and I'm sorry to wake you and like I said, I don't know why, I mean. . . .

Then I breathed.

I breathed air instead of water, heard the spectators watching me on the cliff wall saying how stupid I was for diving so far.

Richard hadn't said a word while I spoke.

I felt immediate regret. I was realizing the magnitude of what I had just done, the depth of the Pandora's box I had rashly opened.

I waited for Richard's rational voice to tell me if I wrote the book I wanted to write, he'd sue me for sure. I waited for him to tell me what a bad idea it would be and how we both had better talk about it with our lawyers.

Then he spoke—calmly, warmly, genuinely, just as he always had spoken to me before.

"Write your book, Jonathan," he said. "Write every word."

CHAPTER FORTY-THREE

"Write every word?" I said with a sniff.

"Absolutely. I'll write you a release statement giving you full legal rights."

"Yeah."

"I'm serious! I'll send you a consent form. Do you have access to a fax machine?"

"Uh . . . "

Okay, Jon, you got your wish. Now what?

"No . . . uh . . . I don't know," I told him. "It's a stupid idea. I'm just having a bad night, that's all."

"Well, we all have those at times, Jon. But I think you may be on to something. Writing what moves you, what shakes you, that's what'll lead to amazing discoveries. Harness that energy and it'll take you anywhere."

Familiar words from years ago.

"Anywhere. Well, that's just it. I don't want to go anywhere. I like my life the way it is. I mean, this journalism career here in college and the internship at the *American* and now the editorship of the *Campus* in the fall. I mean, that's fine for me. I'm not a philosopher, I'm just one of those down-to-earth kinda guys."

"Nothing wrong with that at all."

"But I want to be able to tell people something when they ask about you. I've tried to just write you off, you know, just forget about you, try to do fine without a father, but it keeps coming back to me, you know, but you're . . . " I paused, sniffed again. "You're inconsistent and you want to be isolated but then you want to communicate . . . "

"I didn't want to push myself on you," he said. "But I didn't want to be so distant that you'd think I didn't care. I wanted you to make

162

the choice whether you wanted me in your life or not."

I wondered what Beth would say to him now.

"What about Beth?" I asked coldly.

"Beth? If you mean how did I feel, I was crushed when Beth died."

"It didn't seem like it."

"What could I have said to you to show I cared? I knew Beth chose that time in her life to leave. I called you in the hospital because I thought you must be in terrible pain and I wanted you to know I was there for you. I realized how little I knew about Beth and I was hoping you'd want to talk about her. I hoped that would lead to something between us. But I couldn't make the choice for a relationship by myself. You had to want it too."

He sounded too logical, too right.

I didn't want to think about it. I changed the subject, talked about the hassles of wearing the name tag at Bean's.

He apologized for the questions people asked me, apologized for making me deal with all those questions to which I had no answers. He asked me if I could have put something different on the name tag.

"I suppose I could have just put 'Jon.'"

"Sure, but that wouldn't have been any fun."

"Fun?"

"Sure. The deeper level of yourself who *wanted* people to ask about me wanted to play. Sounds to me like it's a good thing you *did* put your full name because it got you to think about what it means to be Jonathan Bach."

It made sense—sounded like something I had read in my *Theories of Personality* textbook for psychology class.

"Why would I want them to ask when I don't know anything about you?"

"That's exactly why! This conversation is evidence of that, right? It sounds to me like it pushed you to make this decision to call me. Correct me if I'm wrong, please!"

"No, no . . . you're right, I guess."

"Now don't be afraid to tell me I'm wrong."

I angrily told him that at this point, I wasn't afraid to tell him anything.

"That's fantastic!" he said.

His enthusiasm was so out of place it made me laugh. Wasn't this supposed to be a serious phone call?

"What's so funny?" he asked.

"Just your attitude. Do you have to be so positive?"

Now Richard laughed.

"Oh, I'm sorry," he said soulfully. "Let me be less positive." In a deeper voice he thundered, "Jonathan, you're supposed to be afraid to tell me things! Do you hear me? You have no right to speak unless it is to say, 'Yes sir, father'!"

"Okay, okay," I said. "You don't have to go overboard."

He laughed and said he was glad to hear I wasn't giving consent to let him dominate me.

I thought of something else to say. We were getting along and it bothered me. It was like those times I would throw snowballs as hard as I could at Jim and he'd catch and disintegrate them like they were balls of talcum powder.

"It's hard to be mad at someone who's being rational," I said.

"I'm sorry," he said. "Would you like to stay mad for a while?"

The conversation stopped.

What was I supposed to say? "Yes, Richard, I would like to stay mad for about twenty more minutes, please"?

That's what I said.

"Go for it. Give me your worst anger," he said, like a veteran baseball catcher pounding his fist in his open glove, ready to see how strong the rookie pitcher is.

I said I was doing my best, which didn't seem to be very good.

"Nonsense. It's fine. It's crystal clear that you're quite passionate about how you feel. 'Your best' sounds like it'll be a bedrock foundation for clear communication between us."

He suggested I read *The Bridge Across Forever* and his latest book, *One*—they would tell me about who he was and help eliminate misunderstanding. He invited me to call him whenever I wanted, just to talk my feelings out or to ask questions. He asked if it would be okay if he did the same.

I said that was probably a good idea. It sounded like the "right" thing to do.

"Well, I guess I need to really think of what I want to say to you next," I said. "I'm fuzzy on what I'm feeling now . . . I mean, I really didn't think you'd pick up the phone."

"Neither did I," he said. "But I'm so glad I did."

"Yeah."

Just like that day hearing Todd's parents tell him they loved him, I started to choke on the syrup between me and Richard. I didn't want him to have any doubt that I had good reason to be angry.

"I'll talk to you when I get a better grip on what's going on with me."

"If that's what you need to do, fine. Don't hang up because you think I don't want to hear what you have to say."

"I'm not. I'm just not sure what it is I have to say yet."

"Okay. . . . Remember. I'm here."

"Yeah, okay. I'll talk with you later, I guess."

After we hung up, I sat on the edge of my bed while the sun rose. I had trouble remembering what we had talked about. It wasn't clear, but there was a hint of feeling which told me that calling him was a good thing. A good, adult thing.

The crowd of spectators applauded as I swam to the sandy beach in front of the rocks. It was neat to be alive. And the spectators weren't saying how stupid I was for diving, they seemed to be impressed.

But reading *Bridge* and *One* meant having an open mind. I couldn't see myself reading them because part of me was still loyal to the old Jonathan Bach. He didn't want an open mind. He sat and looked at me, the Jonathan who had just called Richard, wondering how the hell I had the nerve to do it.

How could you betray me like this? he said. *How could you go back on my word? How could you let Richard get away with abandoning, neglecting, and ignoring me and Beth? And what would Mom think? How could you betray my loyalty to her? She raised me, he didn't. Now you're going to let him experience the twenty-one-year-old Jon, the product of all her hard work? And what if you get to know him and get just as burned as Kris, Rob, and Erica?*

No answers. I felt guilty for betraying that part of me.

I talked to myself about the consequences of this call, hoping my own voice would sober me up. There was a chance it could have been a dream I was just waking from—an exciting dream about a spectacular dive.

The door seems to be open after all this time, I thought. *And I don't feel frozen the way I did last night.*

How the hell did I manage that? What happened? And how did it happen so fast?

I still didn't have any answers, but as I lay back on the covers of my bed, I admitted I felt pretty good.

So what happens now?

Chapter Forty-four

Morning shone through the curtain and highlighted the dust particles that hung weightlessly in the apartment's stale air.

I opened my eyes to find I was still in my clothes, lying on a bed slightly rumpled, but made. I was sure I was hung over, and I'd had some kind of dream about diving off a cliff.

The phone cord was draped over my right wrist.

Oh, man, what have I done?

On the floor by my bed, my *Theories of Personality* textbook waited for me to study it for an upcoming final exam.

I ignored the book, squinted my sleepy, watery, sore eyes.

Outside, the day didn't care about last night. The Saturday sun was high and hot in a royal-blue May 8 sky, baking a quarter mile of cars waiting impatiently at the stoplight on the corner. It was the end of another semester.

I went outside, leaned against the balcony and watched the exodus.

Slowly the line moved as cars took their turn at the green light. Like aircraft ready to takeoff, they went, all those students and their possessions, back to other towns in Maine, New Hampshire, Vermont, Rhode Island, Massachusetts, Connecticut, New York, New Jersey, the few from as far away as California and Alaska.

They were the lucky ones—the ones who'd had classes with no final exams, or with teachers who'd given the exams early.

Everybody seemed to be going somewhere except me.

Orono would be my home for the summer while I commuted to the Ellsworth internship an hour away. This was life in the real world. And despite whatever happened to me the night before, the world kept spinning.

Again the question: what happens now?

I didn't have a deep, thoughtful ounce of an answer. I *did* have a down-to-earth answer: Forget about it for now and go to my new office.

My fluorescent-orange Subaru station wagon with the fake wood paneling sat alone in the Orono Apartments parking lot, which was usually packed to capacity.

I got in the car and cruised fifty miles an hour in the twenty-five-mile-an-hour zone in my northward travel to the university while cars in the other lane moved one or two miles an hour to the south.

A mile and a half later, I arrived at Lord Hall—home of the *Campus,* site of all my practice for a great career that would surely take me to inevitable heights.

There weren't any cars in the parking lot. It was a sight prayed for on any college campus. All those letters to the editor complaining about the scarcity of parking space, all those statements issued by the administration to appease angry students, all those open forums with ad hoc task forces established to deal with the problem—they all meant nothing now. I could've had any space on campus.

It was a short walk down the stairs to the basement. I wondered who'd be down there that day, who'd be sticking around for finals.

The light in the editor's office was on, the door open. Inside, former editor Jack Anthony had his elbows propped up on his desk and was reading one of his columns. He was a dark, good-looking Italian, always dressed in expensive clothes, shirt sleeves always rolled up to his forearms in typical editor fashion.

The edition in front of him was one of the fancier ones printed with color. The box to his right was full of other papers and documents. He appeared to be reminiscing over each object before he put it into the box. He took his time, savoring his last day as editor.

He looked up as I passed through his office and into the newsroom. "Hi, Jon."

"Hey, Jack. Moving out, I see."

Aside from a pile of papers on his desk, his office was bare. It didn't look much different than it had earlier that semester.

"You have a wild night or something?" he asked. "Your eyes are wicked red."

I wiped them quickly.

"It's the sun. Can you believe how bright it is out there? It really hurts my eyes. Makes 'em tear up real bad."

"Huh," he said. "I didn't notice it was any brighter than usual." He went back to his silent reminiscing.

I leaned against the entrance to the newsroom, a few feet from his office.

"Glad to be outta here?"

He thought for a second as he stopped shifting papers.

"Yeah, it's nice to be done. But I'll kinda miss this place."

I left him to his packing and headed into the newsroom to get my stuff ready to be moved out of my old desk and into the "promised land" of the editor's office.

"Uh, Jon . . . some guy called you."

I turned around to face him.

"Some guy?"

"Actually, no. Not some guy. It was your dad."

My dad.

Surprisingly, I didn't cringe at the word. Still, I wished Jack knew the difference between fathers and dads. There was no way he could have known what had happened between me and Richard. I had a slight impulse to tell him that it was an extraordinary thing for my father to call me, but it was too early to talk about it with anyone. They'd probably be supportive, which would make me feel like I should have called him years ago. I didn't want to be reminded of my stubbornness.

I looked at the floor and thought.

Just because I'd called him last night and he'd been nice and supportive, that didn't make him "Dad."

I caught myself. No one said I *had* to call him Dad.

Good.

"What'd he say?"

"Something about calling to see how you were doing."

Butterflies of nerves.

Just great. Now I'll have to call him back.

I was sober now—rational, clear-minded, not drunk from impetuousness and emotion as I'd been last night. It would have been too weird to call him back. I wouldn't have known what to say.

"What time did he call?" I asked.

"Just a few minutes ago."

"Anything else?"

"He said he'd call you later."

"Okay, thanks," I said, walking into the newsroom.

Damn. What have I done? Now he's calling me. Is he ready to hear all the other gripes I have?

Am I ready?

On my desk, a phone sat on top of a huge pile of my notebooks, textbooks, stationery supplies. It rang.

Jack yelled from his office. "That's probably for you!"

CHAPTER FORTY-FIVE

"*Daily Maine Campus,* this is Jon, can I help you?" I said with tinges of nerves at each word.

"Yeah, new editor Bach, let's do lunch. You busy?"

It was Student Lieutenant Joe Cumberland, fellow firefighter, just one of the guys. He'd been my boss for a while, and my respect for him hadn't stopped when I quit the department because it started to conflict with my job at the newspaper.

"Well, I was just going to study some psych," I said, settling comfortably into my chair.

"That's a yes, then. Good, let's go. We're all at the station."

"Who's goin'?"

"Paul Estabrooke, Doug Bennett, Bill Stevens, and me."

"Where?"

"Pat's Pizza, I think."

He cupped the phone while he asked the other guys where they wanted to go. "Yeah, Pat's," he said.

"Wow. You guys still want to associate with me?"

"We forgive you for quitting the department . . . kind of. Just as long as you try to make the paper worth reading for a change."

"I'll try. I'm glad you guys understand that it just wouldn't look good for a firefighter to be taking notes for a fire story while he's trying to put the fire out. Who knows, though? I'll probably regret quitting. We'll see."

"Don't worry, you will."

"Yeah, well . . . "

"So what about pizza?"

"Well, I guess future campus leaders have to eat. Besides, I still can't move into my castle yet," I said with exaggerated arrogance, but hoping Jack wouldn't hear me.

"Okay, I'll be over there in a few."

I hung up.

"I'm going to lunch," I said loudly to Jack from the newsroom. "If my father calls again, tell him I'll call him back."

I heard me say "I'll call him back" as if someone else had said it. Did I really mean that? I wasn't sure. I just didn't want Jack to think I had anything less than a normal relationship with Richard.

I walked out the door, got into my car and started to drive.

"Tell him I'll call him back." Such a routine thing to say, a routine thing to do: a routine return-call, just as I'd do with a source who had called me about a story.

Did I really want Jack to say, "Oh, hi, Mr. Bach. No, your son's not in, but he said to tell you he'd call as soon as he got in."

I felt chills of regret and a sinking feeling like the time I broke the kitchen window with my super-bounce Incred-o-Ball.

I couldn't believe there wasn't a way out of calling him back if I didn't want to. Living up to my word was very important to me, so I was trapped.

I remembered Richard's response to my "hate letter" in 1987: "*. . . we don't have to communicate at all. If you're uncomfortable with me or with your perception of me, you're free unilaterally to say not another word.*"

That option not to communicate dissolved my regret as fast as it had appeared. It dissolved the aching in my back and neck, dissolved that sinking feeling.

Hm.

I felt good. I *wanted* to call him.

CHAPTER FORTY-SIX

At a pizza parlor table ten minutes later, Paul, Doug, Bill, and Joe talked about equipment inspections that had to be made at the station. When I was in the department, I had talked about the same thing. I could still speak their language if I wanted to, but I concentrated instead on what to do about Richard.

Joe looked across the table to me as I wrote on a napkin.

If he calls, tell him I'll call him back," I told Jack—easy as that—but started to think about Richard's response to the letter I sent in '87.

"Jon, you're not at work now," Joe said. "You can relax."

He'd already wolfed half his ten-inch pizza. The other three guys were halfway through theirs. I hadn't touched mine yet.

"Look at the guy!" Paul said with a mouthful of hot pizza. "Hope they give you overtime pay for that."

"Yeah, yeah," I said, trying to concentrate. "I just don't want to forget this thought."

The napkin ripped as I wrote.

"What is that, anyway? You doing a story on us?" Doug said.

I immediately started to fold the napkin, put it away for later. I was drawing more attention than I wanted.

"I don't know what it's for yet," I said. "I just feel like getting it down. Maybe it'll be something someday. At least I'll have it when I need it."

They didn't seem to understand.

I took the napkin back out of my pocket and wrote on it again.

I don't know why I feel like writing this. I don't know what it's for yet, I just feel like getting it down. Maybe it'll be something someday. At least I'll have it when I need it.

"What a geek!" Paul said, shaking his head.

"I don't know about you, Jon," Joe said.

I didn't expect them to understand and I wasn't about to try to explain it to them. The Jon who was "just one of the guys" knew that reconciling relationships was talk reserved for counselors' offices at Cutler Health Center, not something to discuss with buddies over pizza.

"I don't know about me either sometimes," I said.

They went on eating pizza.

I reached for a new napkin from the dispenser at the end of the table, ready to capture any new renegade thoughts I couldn't ignore. My pen was still in my hand, uncapped.

"Okay, Mr. Editor," Joe said. "If you're gonna be a journalist geek, can I have your pizza?"

Magically, there was a pizza in front of me. I touched the tip of the crust. It was cold.

"Sure."

"Hey, all right!" Paul said, reaching for my pizza.

Joe fought him off.

"Forget it, this is mine, man!"

When they'd finished fighting for slices, Joe asked why I was so devoted to my napkin.

"It's like this," I said. "You're at a fire. You think you've got it all knocked down. You wouldn't shut down Engine One and start rolling hose if you thought there might be some embers glowing, would you?"

Joe shrugged. "Probably if it's Neville Hall. I've got an electrical engineering final there tomorrow."

The guys laughed a bit, agreed it was a good plan for the buildings their finals were in, too.

"Yeah, well, anyway, it's just this: If I ignore some of my thoughts, it'd be like fighting fire without trying to make any necessary rescues. It's a matter of priorities. Ignoring a thought for me is like you guys ignoring a somebody on a burning thirty-story ledge."

I was afraid I was sounding too much like a writer.

"Or something like that . . ." I said, slowly twirling my pen.

Joe nodded with a mouthful of pizza, understanding me partially, but still baffled why I would give second priority to a pizza.

I wonder what these guys would do if they called their estranged fathers after years of confused emotions? I thought without writing. *Would they try to talk it out with someone? Would they try to act macho and pretend it was no big deal? What would they say if I tried to explain it to them?*

My journalist instinct was in high gear. If there was a *Bach Bugle*, this would be front page news.

I wrote:

> Wouldn't shut down Engine One if there was fire left to fight, so I'm trying to make sure I do this right, think this out, not ignore any thought that would help. Like a few feelings last night—to just call Richard, to chill out afterward.

A phantom feeling came that seemed to indicate a sense of subdued urgency. Richard Bach was more than alive now. He had awakened this morning as he probably did every morning, about to do business of some sort. Yet today he had put aside work for a minute or two to call me to see how I was feeling. To call me.

"Guys, I'm gonna scram," I said, getting up from the table. "I gotta call somebody."

CHAPTER FORTY-SEVEN

I drove back to the newsroom, checked the clock on the wall. No one else was in the office.

It was four in the afternoon on the West Coast when I dialed Richard's number.

"Alternate Futures, this is Stacy. Can I help you?" said a cheery voice.

I remembered seeing Alternate Futures Incorporated next to the copyright in *The Bridge Across Forever*. I figured Richard would be very busy with corporate stuff.

"Uh, hi. This is his son, Jonathan. I was just hoping to talk with my father if he isn't too busy."

"Oh, hi! Just a minute, Jonathan, I'll see if he's got a minute."

"Thanks."

I sighed a tingled sigh. I hoped he wasn't too busy with his corporation. Last night's catharsis seemed years ago.

I wondered if his secretary knew what happened.

"Hello, my son!"

I didn't understand how he stayed so enthusiastic.

"Hey," I said. "Just got down to my office and heard that you called. Something wrong?"

"No, not at all, I just called to see how you were doing."

"That's it?"

"Pretty much. I also called to see if there was anything else on your mind."

It seemed too easy.

"Uh, I don't know. It's hard to say. I think last night took it all out of me."

176

I was sure I was lying, but I had no idea what to say, what concern or problem to address with him.

"Nothing on your mind, huh? Okay . . . So, then . . . how 'bout them Seattle Mariners?"

The steel bars melted between me and Richard. It was pleasantly surprising that Richard knew something as down-to-earth as the name of a baseball team.

I laughed and said they had no chance this year, it was the Oakland A's who were looking pretty hot to take the pennant.

Richard joined me in another short laugh and whatever tension remained from last night faded. If Richard could share a silly moment like that and not be bothered by its simplicity, things were looking good that we'd hit it off this time.

"No, really," I said. "There's probably a lot I'm thinking of subconsciously, and I'm sure it'll all come up eventually. I just don't know if you'll be interested when it finally does."

With a leaky University of Maine ballpoint pen, I drew circles on a notepad.

"Oh, don't worry about that. If last night was any indication of what's to come, I'm in for a real ride," he said with a chuckle.

"Well, don't worry. I'll try not to make it a major trip on you or anything. I realize you're busy and everything, so I'll try to be as direct as possible."

"I appreciate that," he said. "But don't be direct because you think I'm busy. I want you to be direct because you want to and because you believe it makes communication easier for you."

"Yeah, I'm for that," I said.

"Good. I'm glad you play straight," he said.

"Yeah, well, straight communication is my business. You know, journalism and that whole deal."

"I'll bet. It sounds like an appropriate career for you."

"But I should say I'm no philosopher like you. I'm pretty down-to-earth."

"And what does that mean?"

Uh oh. Here it comes. He's going to tell me that down-to-earth is a stupid place to be. That's it's unchallenging, uninspiring, a waste of life.

"You know . . . practical. Subjects like choosing to die don't come up much at the newspaper or in daily life. I just don't see a need to be philosophical when there are bills to pay and deadlines to meet. I've felt that way all my life. Especially since Big Jon moved in. That's a big reason why I didn't get into your letters too much when I was younger. What you said just kind of went over my head, you know?"

I was talking fast.

"Yes, I understand," he said. "But at least for me, without philosophy, I can't cross the street. For me, philosophy is a way of thinking about the universe that guides me in daily life."

"I can understand that it works for you, but I'm just one of the guys."

"Uh huh. And what does that mean to you?"

The circles on my paper were deep blue-black.

"Mean to me?"

"Yeah. Why do you want to be 'just one of the guys'?"

"Uh, well, I think it's just easier to be the same than to be different. It's also a fear of rejection, I guess—if you want to get psychological about it. But, to be honest, I don't think about it much."

"Uh huh."

"I mean, sure, I think about it when I don't feel like drinking with the guys. For example, sometimes I'll have a soda while they drink their beer or whatever. Even though they razz me about it, I just tell them I'm on duty for the fire department or something like that. Then they chill out."

"Chill out? They get angry?"

"No, no. Chill out. They relax. They stop hassling me."

"Oh, I see," he said with a chuckle. "Chill out."

It was a reaction I'd seen a million times on TV: young, "with-it" son teaches his father about cultural slang. I'd always envied those sons. I tried to remember if I'd ever told Mom to chill out or that she was "cool" or "gnarly." Beth used those words more than I did. If Mom did know those words, she'd probably learned them from Beth.

"Speaking of drinking . . ." he said.

I remembered that Mom had told me he never drank. I figured he was about to give me a lecture, and I was afraid our new relationship was about to get its first major stress test.

"Do you like the taste of alcohol?" he asked.

"Uh . . . sometimes," I said, asking myself the same question. "I think I've really gotten used to it, though. I mean, it doesn't bother me as much as it used to. I guess I don't think about it."

"But you'll have a beer or a scotch-and-soda now and then for the taste."

"Uh, yeah, well, I prefer rum-and-cokes," I said nervously. I had a feeling I wasn't going to win whatever discussion we were having.

"What does it do for you?"

"Do for me? Uh . . . "

"Does it make you relaxed? Do you drink to get drunk? Escape problems? Or is it just the taste?"

"Relaxed? A little, I guess, but not much. After a while I feel more blurry than relaxed. And do I drink to get drunk? Uh . . . very rarely. I like to be in control in case an emergency happens. Do I do it to escape problems? Uh . . . stress, maybe, but not problems per se. For the taste . . . uh . . . pretty much."

"So why drink at all?"

"I've never really thought about it."

"Hm. That's interesting."

"Why do you ask?"

"I'm just curious about your decisions and why you've brought what you've brought to your life."

I wanted to think about it more. I felt stupid for never asking myself why I drank. I just did. The guys would come over when they were off duty and there was no question. We'd go drinking.

"Uh, I probably should think about it more."

"I'm not saying you should or shouldn't. I'm just trying to learn a little about your values."

My values. That was another subject I didn't think too much about.

For the next thirty minutes, we explored them. I told him about Rachel and Tempest and that I felt like the only guy willing to commit in a world of independent, uncommitted women.

I told him I believed that to get to the top, you had to work your way up and pay your dues.

I told him I believed in being frugal in the present to be financially secure in the future.

I told him that it was okay to read your notes back to a source you took them from, even though some reporters think it's prior censorship.

I told him that people my age and younger don't get enough respect from adults, so I try to let freshmen writers know what they're doing right more than what they're doing wrong.

I told him that trust was my strongest criterion for friendship, and how hard it is to find people you can count on.

Richard said those were all good values to have. I was surprised he could find them acceptable. There was nothing too lofty about any of them.

We talked about the call the night before. He said it was the only time in months that he had forgotten to turn off the telephone at night, the only time he hadn't let the answering machine take a call.

"Do you know what a coincidence that was, Jon?" he asked. "The odds against my picking up the phone at that hour . . . "

I figured it might have had something to do with the phantom feelings that urged me to call him in the first place. I had never experienced a feeling like that before, and I wanted to tell Richard about it because it was one of those weird things he was so interested in. It might explain the coincidence. But I didn't say anything about it.

We talked a bit about college and final exams. I wanted to ask him about the problems with Kris, Rob, and Erica, but I didn't want to get an answer like "That's between them and me." I didn't want to make him think I was prying into his business.

And that was the conversation. We hadn't mentioned a single thing about divorce or problems with family. It was just father and son shootin' the breeze.

After our talk, I hung up the phone and immediately started putting together a letter, a tangible restoration of a written communication he and I had started so many years ago. He showed me he could be down to earth, so I wanted to show him I could be philosophical.

May 9, 1989
Hello Richard,

The door is open and I'm trying to find the doorstop in that huge pile of emotions, preconceptions, bricks and rubble that comprise my picture of you. It's a little wood wedge now, but I think it'll be larger and steel over time. I've started to find the strength and courage to keep holding the door open.

The slate is not clean in terms of my perceptions of you. It's my job to be objective (as a reporter) and I'm hoping the skill is refined enough to maintain a relationship with you without letting preconceptions get in the way.

We have communicated the first few drops of a reservoir of feelings I have. It is a powerful amount of water as you may know, so hang on. . . .

I finished the letter and sat at my desk.

Maybe I'll send him some of my columns, I thought. *That'll give him an idea of how my style has progressed.*

It was strange to be sitting at a desk that symbolized my achievements in student journalism and have a compulsion that felt centuries old.

On the wall, the second hand on the clock moved as it always had.

I took the calculator from my desk and punched numbers:

Six hundred sixty-two million, two hundred fifty-six thousand seconds brought me to this point. Give or take a few million. All of it boils down to this second. What do I do now? What happens next? Does it mean anything?

Logic told me I had the freedom at any time to back out of this new relationship. Logic would support whatever I did.

Conscience told me it was very "adult" to resolve differences between him and me. It would never leave me alone if I backed out now. It'd haunt me, nag me until I went insane or did the "right" thing.

Emotion was cynical. Writing the letter was like practicing dull piano lessons on a beautiful Saturday. I didn't want to have an open mind. Emotion asked me: was my life all that bad before I called

Richard? Did I really have to call him? Emotion called me a traitor. It reminded me of Richard's kind response to my hate letter and my silent responses to him.

But while Logic, Conscience, and Emotion battled for the driver's seat of my mind, along came the innocent warrior Curiosity, who sat down behind the wheel.

Curiosity reminded me that my father had written a book I was named after—a book I had never read.

CHAPTER FORTY-EIGHT

Ten minutes later, I walked into the University of Maine's Fogler Library and checked out a softcover edition of *Jonathan Livingston Seagull*.

I opened to a page marked "Part One" and read the next page after it.

> It was morning and the new sun sparkled gold across the ripples of a gentle sea.

It wasn't just a short book about a seagull who learns to fly aerobatics. Jonathan Seagull was a bird who wanted more than boring days flying around fishing boats fighting for garbage to eat; a seagull who stayed true to his desire to push the envelope of speed and knowledge and mysterious workings of time and space.

> He flew through heavy sea-fogs and climbed above them to dazzling clear skies . . . in the very times when every other gull stood on the ground, knowing nothing but mist and rain.

Forty-five minutes later, I finished the last line: "*His race to learn had begun.*"

I was stunned, stupefied, and amazed at how easily I could understand the philosophy. It wasn't rocket science or abstract ramble. It made tons of sense.

It was a book about Possibility.

I was named for this symbol, I thought. *And to realize today that I never question why I drink, that I don't know what my values are until I'm asked! Yikes! Do I want to know nothing but mist and rain?*

Or am I now just realizing that I can fly above the clouds, above the mist and rain too?

My own words sounded like something Richard would say, so there was just a tinge of regret—a fear that I was becoming someone more buoyant than a "down-to-earth" guy, someone different, someone too much like Richard.

But I couldn't ignore what millions of people must have seen in Jonathan Seagull. It was uplifting, empowering. The book was beautiful in its simplicity, brilliant with its message: we can do anything we want, if we want it bad enough.

I stared at the cover.

Jonathan Livingston Seagull in yellow letters, *by Richard Bach* in white, just as it had always been.

CHAPTER FORTY-NINE

A letter from Richard was waiting for me a few days later.

No iron ball in my throat this time, just quickened-pulse eagerness to read whatever Richard had to say, knowing for sure that this time I could understand what he said.

May 12, 1989
Dear Jonathan,

When they tell you that you can have anything you want if you're willing to work for it, they ought to add that after you have it, you don't know how to stop working! It's like driving a Kenworth up a long hard hill in compound low gear, finally making the top and rolling down-grade at last, then discovering the brakes have failed. A million calls and letters .from people who expect that you are obligated to respond to whatever permission or offer or proposal they feel like making, seven days a week, and all you want is six hours off. Whine, whine, whine.

A thought on my feelings about peer pressures. One additional reason I cringe at the image of you becoming one of the good ol' beer drinkin' boys. For most of my life, I've observed that the good ol' boys are not too swift of wit, that they have macho buttons waiting to be pushed by anyone who chooses to manipulate their actions. They'll do anything not to be called a sissy, they'll buy anything you tell them a real man ought to have.

Remember when you were a kid and the guys said, "Last one in the water is a monkey's uncle"? (or an old maid, or a horse's ass?) When you ran like mad to hit the water first, or at least, not last?

What that line means, I now realize, is: "Last one in is different,"

185

and whoever says it is depending on the assumption that no one wants to be different from the rest. No stakes when it's a child's game. When you're grown up, though, you've got to learn your way beyond the game or you will be manipulated mercilessly by anyone who would control you: beer and cigarette and drug salesmen, businesses and nations who want you to act as they wish.

The simple way around any manipulation, of course, is to call its bluff. Stroll up to the dock after everyone else is in the water and say, "I guess this makes me the horse's ass" (or the sissy, or not-very-macho because I refuse to suck their cigarette, or unpatriotic because I refuse to cremate Leningrad). It's saying, "I guess that makes me different," and that is absolutely right. It is our difference that is our gift, and to deny that difference is to submerge ourselves in a sea of mediocrity.

If you choose any activity for your own well-considered reason, if you would choose to smoke or drink if peer pressure were against the choice instead of for it, then it's your own action you're making and not one picked for you by some Budweiser account executive on Madison Avenue, c'est vrai?

Now show me an alternate viewpoint on this. I assume that smokers, drinkers, machos of all kinds (including myself at various times in my life) are stupid conformist sheep, yet you are not stupid. Therefore, I must be wrong. Some light on this please?

Different subject: I want to reiterate that if you would like to learn about who your father is, you'd do well to study *The Bridge Across Forever* and *One*. They may not make the most comfortable reading you could pick, but if you could read them with a dispassionate journalist's mind, it could be remarkably instructive.

I'm glad you understand a little more about Leslie. Anyone I ever might have been close to would in Bette's mind have been her rival and therefore despised, even though she came into my life many years after the divorce.

By now I've been divorced from your mother for 19 years—six years longer than the entire time I was married to her. Why her bitterness (possessiveness? jealousy?) persists is a mystery to me, but it's an attitude over which I have zero control. If that bitterness has the same effect on her that it had on Leslie's mother, hating her ex-husband after 40 years divorced, Bette has a sour, bleak future indeed. It didn't have to be . . .

You might ask Jim, the next time you talk, of his personal experience with Leslie and his observations about who she is. See how they match what you've been told about her. Erica knows from her visit to California that Leslie talked long and caringly with her at home with me and alone with Erica on shopping trips to town. How does personal experience get smothered by what somebody else says? Must fact get its heart torn out on hearsay's altar?

Thank you for the copies of your stories! It's fascinating to see the contrast between the working newswriter and the essayist catching ideas way out in right field. Both are commercially successful for now, but my hope and my bet long-term is on the guy in the grass.

With love from your father,
Richard

It was as if no time had passed from his first letters to me in 1980. And just like those letters, I was inspired to write immediately after reading his words.

May 15, 1989
Dear Richard and Leslie,

You write an interesting letter. I'm going to take the liberty to analyze it bit by bit, if I may. First you say that people expect you to respond to whatever permission or offer or proposal they feel like making. Why not simply ignore it as you would junk mail? Technically, that's what it is anyway, unless it's a request that appeals to your very soul and moves you to the depths where it prompts some action. You are not legally bound to anything but your own personal legal system. To use an overused expression: "Don't worry, be happy."

About the coincidence of your not turning the phone off on the night I called . . . I believe that whatever force that determines destinies was in fine form that night. The same force determined that

Beth and I should stop our fighting and get along more harmoni-
ously than ever before in our lives in the days before the accident.
If your number had been busy or forced me to leave a message, I
probably would've continued the misconceptions I've had for so
long about you. In fact, it probably would have reinforced them. So
chalk one up to fate and forces and divine powers that have decided
that communication between Richard and Jonathan be reestablished. It is one event in a long list of not-readily-explainable ones
which I have experienced. I concur, although more emphatically
and deeply, with your comment: "Go figure."

Regarding peer pressure: Ah, this is a tough one. I can't say "If you
were in my shoes . . . " because you have been there on a much
broader scope: your experience with fellow military personnel, 30-
odd years of experience with life which I haven't had yet, etc. But
there is something to be said for the psychological need to be
accepted. Some people drink to be accepted into a group—rooting,
I think, from a deeper fear of being an outcast or rejected. Again, on
a psychological note, I feel more relaxed when I'm holding a beer
and drinking it in the company of beer drinkers than I do when I'm
holding a can of soda.

I suppose there is a psychological and philosophical explanation,
but, I haven't figured it out yet. Anyway, take heart. Your son is not
an alcoholic. In fact, since we talked, I have done nothing but drink
soda in the bar I go to. It has made the people around me feel
uncomfortable. Some tease me, I think, because it brings attention
to what they're drinking and they feel they really shouldn't be drinking and it makes them realize they don't have the willpower to go
against the norm and drink soda with me. A few bartenders even
give soda for free!

Curious. You've brought to my attention a whole realm of psychological experiments that can be done dealing with reactions to
non-drinkers in a bar, peer pressure, and people's realizations of
their own weaknesses. I admit I do succumb to the pressure occasionally, because sometimes when I drink soda, it draws too much
attention. I mean, when I'm the only one drinking soda at a table of
four, that's the topic of conversation, ridicule, etc. for countless

minutes which detract from what I want to be talking about. Much like what questions about the family do to you when you're lecturing on infinite, parallel lives. Frankly, I'd rather avoid the attention and just relax and talk about the gripes I carry around in my mind, and listen to others' too.

It's a topic that we can discuss at great length, and frankly, I think you have made some excellent arguments and have plenty left to spare. In that sense, you have me at a disadvantage in that I have no great and glorious counter-arguments. I agree with you more than I am able to successfully disagree with you. But then, you do have just a few years more experience than I do.

About Leslie: I view Leslie as an unopened can of fruit. I see the picture on the label, some, but not all of the ingredients, yet I know that it is probably sweet and beneficial and will most likely improve my vision and add vitamins to my diet, but I have not tried it. Well, if you'll excuse yet another analogy, I have a can opener at the ready.

Now about Mom. I love her in a lot of ways, for a lot of things she has done. But her grudge against you is something I have not fully understood and something which is very inconsistent in her personality. I'm not proud of that aspect about her. She is a tremendously complex and strong woman, though.

I enclose some more columns from much, much earlier in my newswriting career. If you have the time, read them, try to enjoy them, and give me some enlightenment on concepts that I may have overlooked.

Well, it is late, even for me. I'm down at my office and I hear my bed calling me to get some sleep so I can wake up successfully at 6 a.m. and drive to work. Hope to hear from you BOTH soon.

Your son,
Jonathan

I read the letter a few times to make sure it read like I wanted it to read and discovered that this philosophy stuff was really cool. The voice in which I read surprised me, too. I sounded like an intellectual!

Was that really me who wrote that? Was that really *"Your son, Jonathan"*?

I sent the letter the next day, felt like I was making a deposit in a bank.

Why does it feel this way?

I reasoned that although it's nicer to have money in my wallet than a newly deposited envelope in a dark night-deposit slot, having money in my wallet won't increase my bank balance.

I wrote the thought on the back of an empty deposit envelope as I walked out of the bank.

The interest, will be the letter or the phone call I get from Richard. Gradually I'm building an "account" with him, just as he is with me.

All that day, it was hard to concentrate on work at the *American*. I had finished a small story about the town of Calais and its annual chocolate festival and opened a new computer file to spill the events of the past few days.

May 20, 1989

Okay, no disruptions. I've got to document a lot of stuff.

Barriers, obstacles, stories to tell. After my conversation with Jim the other night, I felt the need to finally put my barriers and preconceptions aside and get the job done. I equate the open door with Richard to taking medicine you know is good for you but tastes awful. We've talked about fame and writing, writing what's in your heart and not worrying about diction or prose, responses from the public, perceptions and learning.

I called Jim and he was pretty psyched. He said he was proud of me, because he didn't think I was going to call. He said he knew it took guts.

I called Erica and told her what happened. She was surprised to hear how receptive he sounded and said she'd call him then. Now that door is opened.

I called Rob too and learned that he had just called Richard. Apparently he saw my relationship with him as a good sign, but Richard told him that he didn't want to hear from Rob until Rob understands why there are problems between them. Apparently it has something to do with loaning money. I just hope Rob understands the way Richard thinks. Good advice for myself, now that I think about it. Understanding seems to be the key to forgiveness. An open mind helps.

Mom seems to be slightly supportive of my new communication with him. Had an awkward talk with her—a lot of brief silences. She seemed like she'd lost a battle and was acquiescing. She gave kind of a calm support.

"I'd always wanted you to know your father," she said.

But I sense that she's got some regrets and some reservations. I don't know what exactly, just a feeling. She listened without saying much, except a few "hm"'s now and then. Her reaction was very calm. Maybe it was because I didn't give her much chance to say anything. I talked fast and was excited and optimistic. I was proud of what I had done and I guess I called her to get some validation of that. I wish she could be excited for me, but I understand what she's gone through when it comes to Richard. Maybe in time she will.

I don't know how I managed to get up such courage so quickly and still manage to keep it and not feel like I'm betraying myself.

Kris and I talked for a few hours about her and Richard. She says she doesn't like to call him and feel like she has to say something important or relevant. Apparently, she had called him at a bad time and Leslie was real abrupt about not wanting to talk. I guess I can understand her not wanting to communicate if he's going to be too busy for her, but at least that hasn't happened with me yet. I guess I'll know more about that problem as time passes. I have to be careful about communicating. That's where problems always seem to arise with Richard and the family.

Time is a big factor. Being honest, not changing my personality for the hope of a meaningful relationship, letting sleeping dogs lie are all challenges. I can feel a change, though. I seem to be writing a lot more, thinking about more.

Across the room, the other intern, Steve, heard me typing my thoughts. Usually, I typed slowly and methodically as I perused my notes for a story. He'd heard me typing eighty words a minute for the past few minutes.

"That must be one hell of a chocolate festival story," he said from his desk.

"Yep," I said without taking my eyes off the keyboard or losing my typing rhythm. "This is front-page stuff."

CHAPTER FIFTY

May 27, 1989
Dear Jonathan,

Your analysis is right about not being obligated to respond to mail. Given that, what does one do when some of the mail says, "Unless I hear from you to the contrary, I assume that you have granted me permission to offer my screenplay of *Illusions* (or *The Bridge Across Forever* or *One* or some other book or story or article) to every director in Hollywood"?

There are a raft of these little legal timebombs, any one of which can mean weeks or years of your life down the drain. So we choose to answer. One day we won't care; not yet.

What a pleasure to see your mind at work, and to watch your action because of what you're thinking! A fascination, that you would experiment with drinking soda in a bar . . . there's a self-designed test that requires the courage of a true experimenter. Leslie noticed it in Hollywood when her friends were slipping heavily into marijuana . . . they'd be nervous with her around because there was a straight mind in the room watching their consciousness change. Almost as if she represented the rational part of themselves that they were seeking to elude in the smoke. Didn't last long . . . she and they went their separate ways and never got together again.

I didn't have that problem in the Air Force. I'd tease the other pilots about demon rum and they'd ask me how I could stand up after my fourth ginger ale. Beneath the banter was a grand respect between us because we trusted our lives to each other, flying formation every day. And I think that they admired and even envied

193

me a little for having the same courage that you have, to stand there with my Canada Dry. No, you show more courage. You don't have the balance that I had then . . . the unspoken Other Level of my relationship with the squadron: I may drink ginger ale, but I'm nevertheless as good a pilot as two-thirds the guys in this room. Lacking the other level, you have to stand against peer pressure on sheer inner knowing of your own excellence. Brave, my son!

Hey, I don't mind you agreeing with me! Curious thing about age . . . I'm just as eager as ever to learn new things, to test what I believe against those who challenge not only my belief system, but my ability to be sharper than knives, making it clear. We can agree about an idea, yet still illuminate each other with different aspects of it, with different incidents and examples showing the idea in action. Though it's no competition, you're right that just living and thinking for a few years longer than you might give me a greater stock of examples that I've already studied and catalogued. But I wouldn't bet a penny that you haven't had experience and insight that never occurred to me.

About drugs. To experiment with drugs requires its own belief system about identity: I am a physical machine, not spiritual master of a magical lifeform, and my being will be affected by this substance as a machine would be affected by physical changes in its environment. That belief to me is boring . . . what do I have to learn from somebody convinced he or she's a helpless passenger in their body? Makes me itch to get out of there, find the company of those who are interested in exercising their power to change their lives and worlds into the highest they know. The active and the unique is so much more fascinating to me than the passive and the herd. Not to say that there are no interesting things to be found in herd-minds, but I miss the scintillation!

At this point Leslie walked into the office and said, "What are you doing?" and for the first time I read her your letter to me, and my reply to this point. She found your ideas charming and true. I typed fast as I could as she replied:

"Aside from being apart from the group, it's not only watching others lose consciousness that's distressing . . . it's that when you drink, you lose yours! Once I liked myself, I was never as high on alcohol as I was being sober. I loved life so much that I'd never do anything to diminish it. Drinking alcohol was like listening to music with earmuffs on."

She laughed at your description of being the topic of conversation for 20 minutes just because you weren't drinking. "The trick to deal with this is: ask for a 7-Up with a twist and a cherry or an onion or an olive that makes it look like a drink . . . as long as it looks like a drink, everyone will assume it's a drink and leave you alone." This works at cocktail parties, she says. She doesn't know about bars. "You may become a social pariah to drinkers, but a fascination to non-drinkers, who are really exciting people."

She has led an extraordinary life, Jonathan . . . grinding poverty in Manhattan slums, foster homes galore, outsider in small-town school vowing to get out of domination by those who considered themselves her keeper. Then grand success, klieg lights and flashbulbs and gossip columns, riches and glamour and personal friendships with the world-famous. Then sacrificing it all to be among the very first actors to protest that wicked war in Vietnam, demonstrations and police riots in the streets of L.A. and Chicago, and ultimately winning the battle.

Your newspaper columns have the tone of conversation and that's why we read columns. The more intimate and personal your columns become, the more irreplaceable, the more interesting and necessary they will be to the intellectual life of the community. Not the way to become part of the herd, I'm afraid, but you've got to make your own peace with that.

More to say, but it's late with much more to do before dawn of a busy day tomorrow.

Love,
Richard

I put the letter inside the envelope.

It seemed that Richard believed in ultimate personal freedom. He'd understand if I was skeptical or down to earth or practical or whatever the hell I called myself. He respected my freedom to be who I was, and that made philosophy fun. He said I even had the freedom to be wrong in my perceptions and my analysis of the obvious, that I could be as cynical and skeptical as I wanted.

As philosophy became my new friend, it seemed I was now flying formation with Jim, the superglider. I felt I could survive in that open field now, as Jim had. It looked safe to come out from behind my transparent steel walls.

CHAPTER FIFTY-ONE

It was mid-July, and my days at the *American* weren't all that exciting. But it was three college credits and a decent wage, so I didn't quit.

It was a tempting thought, though. Things were happening at the paper that tested my patience. A few members of the staff accused me and fellow intern Steve when files started disappearing from their computer disks. I guess they figured that since we were the new guys, we were bound to be the culprits.

The managing editor told us that we were ambassadors for the *American* and had to wear pants and button shirts instead of shorts and T-shirts—even though the July days were hot and humid and our job was to be "out and about."

The folks who worked in the composing room, where the paper was laid out every week, didn't like us much either, even though it was part of our job to be there. They were the pros and we were the goonies. We could never do anything that pleased the staff.

I was having second thoughts about a career in journalism.

Now that Richard and I were talking every few days, I felt comfortable complaining to him about the headaches at the newspaper. He was always insightful, always had thought-provoking questions.

"What does being a journalist mean to you? What are you working toward? If your ambition is to be a great journalist, these are great experiences you're having, as boring or frustrating as they may be."

He reminded me that I had the option to quit at any time, that there were many kinds of journalism and reporting that didn't have to involve working in offices or writing mundane assignments.

Everything he said seemed simple and obvious, but it was brilliant and true, just like his writing.

Communicating with him was too easy and it made me nervous. I tried to keep myself from telling him too much about my feelings or my life for fear of slipping into a relationship with him that might hurt me.

I had let Rachel and Tempest hurt me, and I had no intention of letting anybody else close enough to do more damage—not even my new friend Richard Bach.

I told myself it wasn't going to hurt to do some research on the guy.

I looked at the calendar and realized a month had passed and I still hadn't read *The Bridge Across Forever*. I rummaged through a box of books in my closet, looking for the copy Richard had given me at the reunion. The cover was a little crinkled, but inside were the same words that had bothered me five years ago when I couldn't get past page 50.

I was certain that the page wouldn't bother me now.

As I lifted the book, I felt a slight energy, an electricity surging from a feeling that the book had waited patiently for me. It seemed to be happy that I was ready to read it again.

Before the first page, there was black felt-tip ink.

"Jonathan!" the markings said triumphantly. *"So happy for who you are! Love, Richard and Leslie."*

CHAPTER FIFTY-TWO

August 1, 1989

In our last phone call, Richard asked if I wanted to fly out to see him for a few days. I don't think the *American* will let me off work.

I'm on page 116 in *Bridge Across Forever*. I feel older, more in touch, more aware of who I am and who Richard is. I feel strangely grown-up. A feeling I didn't have when I started reading the book.

I feel stupid for waiting this long to read it. Well, then again, I did try once. There were just too many emotions in the way. So why didn't I read it a month ago? Same thing. It's like there was a line between then and now. A thin line. One day. One phone call.

Do I like the change? Is it temporary? What does it mean? Why am I so eager to fly out and see him? What is it about him that affects me this way? Jim used to seem a little flaky to me. Now I see him as downright practical, like me. He seems so normal now, he knows both worlds of mysticism and practicality. I'm new to the business of having room for both. And then Mom, sometimes her hidden resentment shows. Am I betraying her? I feel like she's somewhere back deep in my past. Somewhere in the cobwebs of memory. It hurts to write that. I really have to explore the feeling sometime.

There are times when I'll be reading *Bridge* and I'll come across something that will make me say "Ah yes!" I fold the top corner of the page and mark it as something to talk about when I get out there. That part of me feels like a real journalist, doing homework on a subject before writing a story, doing research before interviewing a source.

I feel so hazy, trance-like, as my mind decides to take long vacations with these thoughts.

Why am I changing so fast, why tonight, why this time in my life, how long will it last, what effect will it eventually have? I want to see myself, my future self, but I realize that hindsight is no match for foresight. Lots of adventures and infinite choices.

199

I broke from writing to let my mind rest with some TV.

On the screen, a dark-haired, frantic guy held a gun to an older guy's head and demanded that he be given his memories back.

"I can't. I just sold them," the hostage said.

The younger man cocked the gun and demanded that he be given something to replace them. The hostage, a shopowner whose business was apparently buying and selling memories, said, "Okay, I'll see what I can do. There is a way, but it's not perfect."

The next scene showed the younger man sitting at a job interview talking about his experiences.

"Well, in 1905, I graduated from Princeton," he said, "then in 1950 I graduated from Harvard, but I only spent a year in college because in 1920 I traveled to Europe before the First World War. That was after I graduated from Yale last year . . ."

He continued to babble to the confused interviewer about his contradictory experiences. The camera shot pulled out and began a fade to black.

Then a voice:

"Milton Foster. A man with pieces of other people's lost dreams. A man who makes us realize we truly are the sum of our parts. A very special resident of the *Twilight Zone* . . . "

I looked quickly for a pen and paper and wrote.

> A coincidence on TV: Milton Foster and how we are the sum of our parts. Is it a coincidence that I turned the TV on at that moment and found something so relevant to what I'm learning about? There's relevance in anything if I choose it. I guess I choose that scene on TV to have meaning for this moment in my life. I am the sum of my parts: Jonny Ground Crew, Jonny Young Writer, Jonathan Journalist, Jonathan Whoever.
>
> Is it really just a coincidence that Richard and I like to write? A coincidence I'm his son?

In *Bridge*, Richard had written about the end of his barnstormer life, his intolerance of loud music, his ignorance about money, and the judge within himself who evaluated his performance on everything from parachute jumps to the airplane crashes he survived. He showed the reader, showed *me,* how his ignorance, stubbornness, his escapist instinct melted away as his life changed, enhanced by this fascinating woman named Leslie Parrish. The woman he called his soulmate. The woman who convinced him that marriage was not an evil thing, that he could love and trust someone again, be married again.

I read and learned because I was *ready* to learn. It was that simple.

Do I want to fly out there? Last month I would have recoiled in reluctance. Two months ago I would have recoiled in terror. Now I'm excited and only a little anxious. I told him that'd be cool, but I'm not sure if I really want to be that excited. So many changes, so fast.

I paused, looked up at the ceiling over my bed.

What's the worst that can happen?

CHAPTER FIFTY-THREE

I looked at my watch.

6:47 A.M.

Five minutes until the flight leaves and there have been no announcements. I wonder if I'm doing this right.

I looked around me. There were no other lines to wait in.

A man in a United Airlines uniform came down the stairs leading up to the airline gates. He passed under the Bangor International Airport sign and stopped short of the line of people I was standing in. He shouted: "It's going to be at least another hour or so for anyone departing on United flight 251 to Chicago!"

Groans from the line of would-be passengers faded away as some of them took their baggage upstairs. Some chose to sit at their place in line. Some decided to sleep. Some, like me, had books to read.

I followed the upstairs crowd. The gift shops, the restaurants, and the phones were all up there.

Phones.

Oh, yeah. I'd better call Richard.

A minute later, nervous energy helped me tap a pen against the metal phone booth.

The phone rang, then answered.

"Hi. We're away for a while, but if you'd care to leave your name and number, we'll call you back as soon as we can."

A few more seconds and a beep.

"Hi, Richard, this is Jonathan. I'm . . ."

"Hello! Hello, Jonathan!"

My father was barely awake. I had forgotten it was not yet four in the morning out there.

"Sorry to get you up. I thought you might like to know my flight's delayed. There's a rumor about a malfunctioning part on the plane we're supposed to be taking."

"Oh . . . okay, then."

He took a second to think.

"All it means, I guess, is that I'll be an hour or two later. That is, if I make my connecting flight in Chicago," I said.

"Yeah . . . well, okay. Whenever. Consider us informed. We'll be in Seattle an hour later then."

"I'd like to say I'm on my way, but, well . . . you know airplanes."

"No, I don't, actually. Could you tell me a little bit?" he said with a sleepy laugh.

"I'll fill you in on them when or if I get out there."

I let him go back to sleep.

My bags sat in the airport terminal seat next to me as I turned to page 200 in *The Bridge Across Forever*.

An hour passed without announcements.

The uniformed guy came up the stairs. He shouted: "Flight 251 has been postponed for another two hours. We're waiting for a part to be flown in from Portland. When it gets here, there'll be another brief delay and hopefully, then, the flight will depart."

I called Richard again.

No machine this time. He gave a more awake hello.

"Oh. Hi. Uh . . . hello. It's me again. I expected the machine to kick in."

"Oh," he said. "Sorry. I can put it back on if you like."

"No, that's okay. The guy on the machine isn't much of a conversationalist. Um . . . I hope I didn't wake you up again . . ."

"No, no. After you called the first time, I rolled around and tossed the sheets off the bed, woke Leslie up and then she couldn't get back to sleep either so she decided to go downstairs. That woke Jim and Kim up and now they can't sleep. So we're all up talking about you. That noise woke Seattle up and now a few hundred thousand people are restless."

Jim's out there? All right!

A few Christmases had passed since I'd seen him.

"Tell them I'm sorry, will ya'? I didn't know they were out there visiting you."

"I will. So what's new?"

"They've grounded us indefinitely. Something about the airplane being overdue for its annual. They're out there right now taking it apart bolt by bolt."

"Oh no!" He laughed again.

It was great to be able to speak Airplane with Richard. It was as if growing up around airplanes prepared me for this moment where I could feel comfortable with him.

"I'm taking the bus out there. Uh . . . bus number six. Should arrive there in about fifty days. I'll be in the one with the Greyhound emblem on the front. I figure it'll be faster than flying."

I heard Leslie's voice in the background static. Richard cupped the mouthpiece and I heard a muffled, "He's taking the bus out here."

Richard's voice again, this time loud and strong.

"Okay, we'll be at the bus station waiting. We should be eligible for all kinds of senior citizen discounts by then."

I smiled at his answer.

"Seriously, they're waiting for this part or something to be flown in from Portland. It's going to be a while."

Richard relayed the information to Leslie and they talked for a bit.

"Okay. Leslie wants to know if there's another flight to Seattle or to Chicago with an adjoining."

"I can check, I guess. It's going to take some finagling, but I'll see what I can do."

"Okay, we'll be waiting by the phone. Hey, let me give you a credit card number to book a reservation in case you find something."

Wow. Richard's credit card. Thing's probably got a million-dollar credit limit on it.

"Cool. That really helps. I'll find some way to get there, don't worry."

Passengers were beginning to line up at the United counter to make other plans.

"Okay, I gotta go. See you sometime in the next twenty-one years."

"Ayyyyyy! Try to do better than that!" he said.

Being eighth in the line downstairs meant hearing the best flights out of Bangor. There was one other flight to Chicago. Delta flight 105 in another two hours. I made a reservation and called Richard again.

"Hi. Me again. The latest word is Delta 105 to Chicago. Picks up with 213 to Seattle, arriving eight thirty-one your time."

Leslie joined my conversation with Richard. She was determined. She was charged with a mission. There would be a solution. There was no other alternative. This was definitely the Leslie in *Bridge*. The Leslie that didn't take any doubletalk, who was determined to keep the Bureau of Land Management from cutting down trees, determined to recover Richard from bankruptcy and his problems with the IRS. She found solutions, period. I was glad to have her on my side.

"Jon? What flight did you get? I might have something better."

It was the first time I'd heard her voice in five years.

I swallowed past my lumpy throat and told her my flight number.

"Well, let's go with that one then. I've done some checking on my end and it seems that's the best way."

Checking on her end? Already? I bet she did. I bet she could find a direct line to Seattle. A private Lear jet flown by Mr. Lear himself.

We were a team with a goal. If there was ever a motivated team to be on, it was with these two.

"Okay, we'll try again," I said and went back to my seat to pick up my reading.

Forty-eight pages passed. No announcements.

Another hour, fifty-four pages.

I guess we should be boarding any time now.

Just like in the movies, a voice on the p.a. answered my thought.

"Delta announces the delay of flight 105 to Boston and then continuing service to Chicago."

I called my father again.

This time, Leslie answered. She seemed too businesslike to be humorous.

"Delayed?" she sighed. "Well, I've been doing some more calling. We're going to get you out here even if we have to come and get you ourselves."

I pictured them doing just that.

She gave me a flight number and times. Apparently she had called every airline there was. I pictured some airline manager at Delta, cowering under his desk, having just dealt with Leslie Parrish-Bach. I imagined a lot of "Yes ma'ams" in response to "That's a lousy way to do business" and "I suggest you find a better way to handle this problem."

As I hung up and again returned to my seat, it appeared we were winning the battle, in theory, but it didn't look as if I was going to leave the ground anytime soon. And soon it was just past three in the afternoon—eight hours past the time of my original departure.

The next announcement over the p.a. sounded incredibly out-of-place.

"Jonathan Bach to the United ticket counter . . . paging Jonathan Bach."

At the United desk, a cute blond woman with royal blue eyes worked with a passenger. She was stunning, even in uniform, but I imagined her in a much different outfit. One less confining, less formal, just plain less. J-U-L-I-E was inscribed on the tag over her left breast.

I lost interest in the phone call.

"I'm Jonathan Bach," I said to her, sounding as businesslike as I could to impress her.

She handed me the phone without diverting attention from her reservation computer in front of her. She wasn't impressed.

"This is Jon," I said to the phone.

It was Leslie again.

"I've got you on something else," she said. "Delta 113 to Logan leaving in fifteen minutes. Can you get on it?"

"Fifteen minutes? Geez, I'll give it a shot."

"Well, do your best. If you can't, you can't. Don't worry, we'll get you here, I promise."

I didn't doubt her. Leslie's promise seemed to be the stuff on which skyscrapers were built. In that capable voice, there was care, support, a friend. I had a feeling this latest flight would take me right to their door.

We said good-bye again, hoping it would be the last time we had to call each other about flights.

Julie was done with her client. She had no one left to help.

"See you later, Julie."

She looked up from her computer.

"I hope you get there, Jonathan."

Her answer startled me so much that I almost tripped over my feet as I walked away. She had said it so sincerely, like she'd been a lifelong friend who knew it had taken me years to make this flight.

"Uh . . . thanks. I appreciate your help."

I thought of something more to say. There was a tremendous compulsion in me to ask her out. Maybe she was my soulmate—a word Richard used to describe his perfect female partner, Leslie, in *Bridge*.

She smiled and turned to help a new customer. I didn't have time to say much else to her. I had to go to the adjacent ticket counter to try to make the flight.

After a five-minute wait at the Delta ticket counter, I was booked on the Delta flight.

I took one last glance at Julie as I passed her and went up to the gate.

This was one of those forks in the road of life. I could see myself asking her out. She says yes and my world changes. She says no, I keep going on the path I'm on.

Tempest, Rachel, both of them changed me. For the first time I could be involved in a relationship with my new intellect, my new state of mind, my new sense of capability. None of the past codependent crap.

As I walked by her, I watched to see if Julie was going to give me another second or two worth of meaningful glance.

She concentrated on her keyboard.

Oh, well. She's too cute not to have a boyfriend anyway.

My priority, then, was Richard Bach.

I laughed slightly at my crazy thoughts about the goddess at the counter. Maybe I was going overboard trying to find meaning in any little thing. But I couldn't ignore that it was fun, interjecting possible Purpose everywhere. I couldn't remember the last time my mind had been so active or I'd felt so intellectually energetic.

How could I think of doing anything else right now than getting to know Richard? I answered myself in remembering that phrase: "*You are unilaterally free to . . .*"

Choices, choices. A million choices. To the Jonathan-Sitting-on-the-Edge-of-His-Bed-Deciding-to-Call-Richard and the Jonathan-About-to-Get-on-This-Plane-to-Seattle, one of the more difficult aspects of life seems to be deciding what to do with all the choices. The second most difficult is reminding myself that I have choices.

I paused in my thought.

Sounds like something Richard would say.

His latest book, *One*, was in my hand as I boarded the plane. I had no idea what it was about. The only description on the back of the dust jacket was a question:

"*I gave my life to become the person I am right now. Was it worth it?*"

CHAPTER FIFTY-FOUR

Twenty minutes later, I was in the sky.

I put my notebook away after recording some thoughts and silently read the inside of the book's dust jacket in my father's phone voice:

What if space shifted and time bent and we could meet ourselves as we'll be twenty years from now? What if we could talk face-to-face with the people we were in the past, with the people we are in parallel lifetimes, in alternate worlds? How would we change if we knew what waits beyond space and time?

Here is his journey with his wife, Leslie, to a realm where survival depends on discovering what other aspects of themselves have learned on roads they never took; where imagination and fear are tools for saving worlds and destroying them; where dying is one step to overcoming death.

As the world may not be what it seems, suggest the Bachs, so might we be more than we appear to be. Their book is a curious loving fantasy in harmony with science and spirit at once, a startling door ajar on a path to finding ourselves.

I was awestruck.

My dad *knew* me.

He spoke to *me,* not the millions of other folks who could walk into most bookstores in the world and read his best-selling words. His book was a message for me—to get me to think about the magnitude of my decision to travel across the country and meet my father. It was just a coincidence that my father happened to be *him.*

The most striking thing to me was how the message of the book had been consistent with what I was thinking minutes before I opened it. Or was it that on some deep, mystical level I *knew* what I was doing when I opened the book? Did some mysterious force put these words in front of me? Was it coincidence that they came from my father? Did it mean anything or nothing?

My choice. I could answer all of those questions many ways.

I had barely passed the third page and I liked his book. And somewhere in the gloom of an alternate August 5, 1989, another Jonathan Bach worked at his dull internship, the back of his mind thinking about his distant father and the call he wasn't brave enough to make.

Chapter Fifty-Five

I landed in Boston, searched frantically to find the connecting flight.

I had only a minute or two to find which gate it was leaving from. After I found it on one of the schedule monitors, I hustled and just made it, the last one on a crowded 737. This one would take me to Chicago to make the connecting flight to Seattle.

The stewardess closed the door behind me and I looked for my seat on this bigger plane. It was way down the aisle. The plane was packed, too, but the two seats next to mine were empty.

Good, I thought. *I like space.*

But as I got closer, I saw two kids in both of those seats.

Damn. They're going to drive me crazy. I've got reading to do.

"Hi," I said as nice as I could. It was hard to hide my disappointment. They were too young to be offended anyway, even if they noticed that I wasn't too thrilled about sitting next to them.

I put my baggage in the compartment above us. Everybody around me watched.

Holding *One,* I sat down and buckled my belt.

"Hi," the boy said. "My name's David and this is my sister, Jen. We're going out to see our dad."

"Heh. That's funny. I'm going to see mine," I said, amazed at another coincidence. I was more amazed by the boy's tone of voice. It was mature, direct, just as if I were talking to a forty-year-old.

"Is he away on business like our dad?" he asked.

"You might say that."

"Might? Why, what's he doing?"

What kind of answer should I give?

Play it straight. No harm in that.

"Well, he writes books."

"Wow! Science fiction books? Like Bradbury and Asimov?"

Geez, I would have pegged him for an eight-year-old. Maybe he's a few years older.

"No, not really. Mostly stuff involving flying and . . . "

I thought about what I had just been reading, thought of how to explain to him so he would understand.

" . . . well, some recent stuff about parallel universes."

I expected him to ask what they were.

"Cool!" he said, fastening a Lego astronaut to a Lego spaceship.

"Hey, Jen." He poked the little blond girl next to him. She was busy trying to rip a paper doll from a book of perforated cut-outs.

"What, David?" she asked calmly.

"His dad writes books about flying *and* parallel universes! Isn't that cool?"

"Yes," she said.

"Do you know what one is?" I asked the boy.

"Sure, um . . . let's see, it's like . . . it means that there is another world just like this one but different, y'know? Everybody, like, has their own variety of them, y'know, and um . . . there's like a lot of, uh . . . sections of alternate people, y'know?"

"Uh . . ." I said, stunned that he knew the basic idea. "That's about right."

He held up a Lego pirate. "Like this pirate guy here. He's a pirate here and now," he said, holding up the astronaut, "and this is his parallel self who decided to be an astronaut."

"Two different guys?" I tested him even though I was still new to the concept.

"Yes and no. Like I said, the same but different."

Hearing him explain was like hearing a dolphin speak perfect English without a dolphin accent.

I shook my head in pleasant amazement. I liked this little adult.

"How do you know about parallel universes?"

"There's a book about it."

Stupid question.

"I guess I've seriously underestimated the power of reading," I said, thinking of what Richard said in one of his letters so many years ago about me being able to bring "a fresh, unboring gift to the world" as a twelve-year-old author.

If only I'd stuck with it. The jump from then to now was one second. One second didn't seem like a long time to wait. Somewhere there was a parallel me that stuck with it, who has lived the life of an established author at fourteen.

"You know, you ought to write a book," I said. "With a sharp mind like yours, I bet you could write about anything and people would pay lots to read it."

"I'd rather be a pilot," David said, building a plane out of the other Legos in his lap.

I suddenly wondered if Richard hadn't transported his soul into this young boy—to test me, to test my budding philosophies.

He wants to be a pilot? Parallel universes?

"Have you ever heard of Richard Bach?"

"Oh, sure. He wrote *Jonathan Livingston Seagull* and a bunch of flying books."

I shook my head, half in surprise, half in envy of his intelligence.

"That's who I'm going to see," I said.

"You mean on this flight? Right now?"

"Well, after I make the connection to Seattle, yeah."

"Really? Wow, that's neat! Hear that, Jen?" he said, poking her book.

"Yes," she said, not losing an ounce of concentration on her doll book. "What's your name?"

I told her and thought, *here comes another great conversation. What would she say to me? That she liked my name and how it was neat that it was the same as the seagull, which embodied a whole spirit of being free, flying away from the flock, being true to your heart and believing in yourself? Maybe her expertise was time travel—knew a way to make it happen, built a time machine out of doll parts . . .*

"Jonathan, would you help me tear this doll figure out? It's not stamped very well. I'm afraid I'll rip it."

"Sure," I said, laughing.

"What?" David said.

"I thought your sister was going to ask me about time travel or something. You both seem so poised and mature. I figured she'd be brilliant too!"

"Mom says we are. Something about being pro-dijus or something."

"Prodigies?"

"Yeah, that's it. Prodigies. I always mix up that word. I'd still rather play with Legos, though. Since I'm too young to fly."

"How old are you?"

"Nine. My sister's only seven."

"Seven and a *half*," she said, unwavering in her attention to the cut-outs.

She reminded me of Beth. I missed having a little sister. Chills passed through me, and I smiled. Beth was sure to be a topic of conversation for Richard and me, but I had no idea how I was going to handle it. I felt she was going to be right there listening.

Amazing. I wonder how many kids there are like this in the world. So mature. Not fighting, not irritable. And we even had Legos in common. This ought to be a great trip after all.

"Yeah, Legos are great, aren't they?" I said. "My little sister and I had Legos not too long ago. They're a creative way to pass the time, right? Never the same toy twice if you don't want. I never much liked those robot transforming things."

"Exactly. I hate those," David said.

I was still tearing the cut-out carefully from the doll book. Jennifer had been doing a better job.

A minute later I gave the book to her, minus the one cut-out which I handed to her separately.

"Thanks," she said. "Now you can go back to playing Legos with David."

I felt ten years old again. Permission to play.

I did what I was told.

David and Jennifer, two harmonious peas in a pod.

The three-hour flight to Chicago was Legos and paper dolls. They were both capable of brilliant conversation, they just preferred dolls and Legos. In spite of all their gifts, all of society's "plans" for them, all of its expectations, they liked being kids. What a great way to live! I hoped they would never lose that spirit, hoped anything as potentially crushing as a parent's divorce or a car accident or a distant father wouldn't bury their optimism or their ambition.

They got off in Chicago, but their spirit lingered with me. They had quite a head start on life. They could be anything they wanted if someone didn't convince them they should be doing anything else than what made them happy.

And what if they had been "normal" kids—arguing, fidgety, complaining next to me while I read? I couldn't have tolerated it. I would have felt trapped, distracted, just like writer Dick Bach with a house full of kids.

It was as if that thought had been written on the back of the airline seat in front of me. I jotted it into my journal during the initial minutes of the flight to Seattle.

I may be more like Richard than I thought.

And with that thought my pen ran out of ink.

Chapter Fifty-six

"The day had barely begun," said the last line of *One.*

The end.

Thoughts came about the day I was just ending and the new one I would begin with Richard tomorrow.

The man next to me noticed Richard's book on my lap.

We talked about what an interesting writer he was.

He said his name was Spaulding. I said mine was Bach.

"Oh, really?" he said.

And for the next few minutes, I told the story: *Time* magazine, the letters between me and Richard, the day in Burlington, the reunion, the accident, the hate letter, working at L. L. Bean, the talk with Rita Farley and the phone call to Jim that led to the phone call to Richard, and the letters and phone calls in the three months since then.

" . . . so he offered to fly me out to see him and here I am doing just that."

And I didn't feel bad. I had a handle on my feelings, despite the amount of material Richard and I had yet to talk about.

Mr. Spaulding was overwhelmed. He had nodded a lot during my talk, didn't say much, but now he spoke.

"Seems to me this is a right courageous thing you're doing, Jon. I'm hard pressed to give you any advice about it, but it sounds like you're doin' the right thing."

"Yeah, I guess so. I'm really curious to see how it'll go, as you can imagine. I just hope it isn't too awkward, y'know? I mean, in some ways I feel more comfortable talking with you than I'll be when I talk to him!"

"That's natural, I would think. What I would do if I were you is just tell him what's on your mind. Right up front, straight honest, is the way I'd go. Sounds to me like it worked for you before in that phone call and that letter you wrote. Least, like I say, that's what *I'd* do."

"Yeah, that seems like good advice for me too. Appreciate the insight."

I started to write about our conversation, remembered my pen was dry.

Before I could form the first words of my request, Mr. Spaulding handed me a spiffy, heavy silver pen from his jacket.

"Noticed those circles you were drawing as you talked and figured you'd need some help."

"Hey . . . thanks!" I said, impressed at his perception.

"No problem at all. 'Sides, I wouldn't want to miss seeing this story in a bookstore someday, right?"

I laughed uneasily at the thought. The story, that hate book which had seemed so simple and felt so right before I had called Jim, was much more complicated now. But there I was, trying to sort it out for this stranger.

"Right," I said disparagingly. "I can't imagine that'll ever happen. I haven't sorted enough out yet. That, and I don't have the discipline to work on something that big."

I drew some circles to get the pen flowing and tried to imagine me working on a book.

No way, I wrote.

There's still no way I'll quit college three years into my degree, throw away the skills I've learned, all the money I've invested, just to do something I could have done without a day's worth of college. I'd have to say, "Gee, guys, this journalism stuff has been fun and all, but I want to be an author now." They'd laugh me out of the newsroom like some English-major volunteer writer who writes a hard-news story like a journal entry. Nice way to end college. Right when I'm going to be editor this fall!

No way. There's no way I'd quit now. No way I'm subjecting myself to living that typical struggling-writer cliché where my diet would be rice cakes and rejections from whatever free-lance stories I could throw together.

Journalism and a steady paycheck is the practical thing to do. And that's me—even with these new philosophical moods, I'm still practical down to the bones.

And what would Mom say if I quit? She'd freak out. She'd give me one of those short, polite, but perplexed "oh"s, holding back what she really thought: "I've lost a son to this strange man called Richard Bach."

Then a flash feeling left me anxiously stranded as if I were watching the last boat home drift away swiftly from the dock.

Something was bound to go wrong, just like it had for Erica, Rob, and Kris. Maybe something had even happened between Richard and Jim, something Jim hadn't told me.

And what about Leslie? There were times in *Bridge* when she got really angry at Richard because he'd been acting so selfish. They had argued, and he had dealt with it by escaping.

Maybe the *worst* thing I could do for myself was visit Richard and get close to him! What if I got hung up on evaluating whether or not he could qualify for "dad"? It might offend him or anger him and he'd banish me to some kind of philosophical purgatory. He could suddenly turn cold or run away, never caring what I felt, because, after all, he says we have the right to do *anything*, even if it's abandoning children and running away just as he had in 1970.

I thought of Mom again. I was her son before I was Richard's. Her words ("Daddy won't be called 'Daddy' anymore. His Daddy-part died") lingered strong. It was easy to imagine her saying: "Jonny Bach was the sweetest little son, but his son-part died. I don't recognize this *Jonathan Bach* character."

CHAPTER FIFTY-SEVEN

I was disguised.

I hadn't planned to be wearing a University of Maine baseball cap, glasses, and a mustache when I saw him, the look just invented itself. The mustache was a change; something different to spice up the reflection in the morning mirror. The glasses were just as new because two weeks before, I had noticed things getting blurry. I didn't wear hats much, but it was a piece of home.

The people from the plane moved quickly up the ramp.

A million needles touched me and disappeared.

Inhale.

Exhale.

I walked through the huge doorway and into all kinds of people hugging each other under fluorescent light.

There he is.

Just then, a man shouted my name and threw me to the ground.

"Hey, bro!" he said.

Jim had wrestled me to the floor. It must have started as a quick, clumsy hug.

People tried to walk around us. Some were probably calling airport security, telling how a suspicious-looking man in a disguise was being assaulted by a professional wrestler.

Jim was a playful, but huge, pup. I wasn't prepared to be physically challenged. Especially in the terminal. With people watching. With guards with guns watching. With Richard watching.

Jim didn't care.

So be it, then. Wrestle we will.

He may be older, but I've gotten stronger since I last saw him. I'll show the slimeball!

The wrestling match lasted only a few seconds and then we met each other in a clumsy hug. Jim's wife, Kim, was there, and then to her left, Richard and Leslie.

I approached my smiling father as Leslie stayed behind him. He looked shorter than when I had last seen him, but he was thin, like me. He still had his mustache. He dripped smooth intelligence as I thought of all the pages I'd just read about him. He carried immense knowledge in that vault behind his blue eyes and I felt like a prepared interviewer, ready to tap into that bank with a list of a million questions, proud of myself for taking the time to research this man who approached me with outstretched arms.

I approached my father and hugged him.

In that three-second hug, he was a real person, not a theory or an idea or some abstraction.

I put my arm around his waist and did the same to Leslie as she joined him at his side.

Jim and I talked about my flight, and our excited brotherhood energy dragged me slowly ahead of Richard, Leslie, and Kim. I could sense they were observing me. Every movement, word, joke I made, mannerism, height, weight, face, glasses, hat, mustache and all. Richard and Leslie were vacuums, collecting information.

I was glad Jim was there.

The five of us talked about the trials of airline travel and how we were going to make up for the hassles of delayed flights.

In the parking garage a few minutes later, Leslie punched in the code for the electronic door locks on an otherwise plain-looking, down-to-earth, sensible Ford Taurus. I had expected a Mercedes or something.

"You hungry at all?" Richard said.

I lied, didn't want to tell him I was too nervous to eat. "No, no. I had stuff on the plane."

Good job, Jon. What happened to "right, straight up, honest"?

"We could find an all-night place," Leslie said. "There's plenty around."

"No, really, I'm fine."

Leslie drove. That seemed to make sense. I suspected Richard didn't care much for ground travel.

He looked back at me from the front seat.

"Well, Jonathan! Welcome."

He smiled and I smiled back.

"Thanks."

"Yeah, you guys have a lot to talk about," Jim said strongly.

It was like hearing the tone my pager made when there was a fire call—danger somewhere that required me.

No matter how many fire calls I went on, there was always a brief second when I heard that tone and asked myself, "Do I know what to do?"

CHAPTER FIFTY-EIGHT

The car was a burning building.

It was hot as I sat in back diagonal to Richard, who was in the passenger seat up front. There was a danger that Richard would ask me a question I couldn't answer, a chance he could see through whatever feeble, uninspired response I gave. There was a danger of awkward silence, a fire that could scar and paralyze me.

I made myself look my father in the face, ready to answer his questions honestly, no backing down or "I don't know" answers. I was worried that I would get flustered or confused or exposed, worried that Richard could see right through to my faults, my inconsistencies or any part of my life I had left unexamined. The car burned hot with the danger of me feeling inadequate.

But as I talked with Richard, my firefighting training was coming in handy.

I had been taught, like most firefighters, that safety is the highest priority. I was taught over and over and over to look for dangerous situations, assess them and take measures to stay alive, even if that measure was to escape. There were hours of videotape that showed the consequences of ignoring danger: third-degree burns, electrocutions, radiation and skin poisoning, instant respiratory failure from inhaling insidious polymers. The buddy system was a cornerstone of firefighting and it was never questioned. We were warned against being freelancers—working alone, ignoring your buddy, taking the situation into your own hands, being a hero, going for glory in spite of obvious danger. But they never trained us how to ignore someone who is about to be burned alive, hanging out a thirty-story ledge, and the only way to get to them is to go through fire and caustic chemicals. I'd never heard of any firefighter who stopped during a two-hundred-stair climb, turned to his buddy, and said, "Y'know, Joe, it's really hot in here! Let's go back down." It was almost always that you had a job to do and you did it.

The car was ablaze, and I ignored the danger of silence, concentrating on the firefighting, talking. A few times Jim interjected some wisdom to clarify what he thought I meant. Having him there was like having an experienced fire chief with me.

Five miles had passed without silence. I'd told them my thoughts about Julie the counter girl, little David and Jennifer, Mr. Spaulding, thoughts about *Bridge* and *One* and how each of them prepared me for this Seattle meeting.

Everything I spoke about was fresh. Nothing bound my words, and I was discovering that very quickly I had reached a point where nothing could *stop* my words. There was no feeling inadequate, no awkward, new-kid-in-the-class feeling.

I was manic, talking a mile a minute about everything I felt on the trip. I burned with my own fire and I never felt more alive.

CHAPTER FIFTY-NINE

Richard opened the door to his huge condominium overlooking downtown Seattle. There were no fancy furnishings inside, no expensive antiques, no rare artwork on the walls—just four folding chairs and a folding table. Steel-gray marble floors paved the entryway and the kitchen to the left, plush cream carpet lay unweighted in the living room that overlooked the Seattle skyline.

"Excuse the place," Leslie said as she opened the heavy wooden door. "We haven't moved in yet. There just hasn't been time."

My father carried my suitcases into a room to the left. I followed.

The room was bare except for a lamp and an air mattress. Large windows on the far wall framed a section of the entrancing, twinkling, midnight lights of the city.

"Geez, Richard . . ."

"Pretty neat, huh? Best view in the building. That's a million-dollar view there."

I bet that's what this place cost.

Leslie came in with some sheets and blankets. I saw her reflection in the glass and turned to make sure she didn't start spreading them out on the mattress without my help.

"Oh, thanks," I said. "I can just lay these out later. I'll be up for a little while looking at this view. I assume you guys are tired and everything."

Richard unrolled a layer of egg-crate-shaped foam material he took from the closet and put it on the mattress.

"I bet you're tired," Leslie said.

"Not really . . ."

"Not after all the airline headaches and travel you just lived through?!? It's also three hours later for you out here."

Both of them started making the bed.

"Oh, that's right," I said. As I tried to think of a better comment to describe what I was feeling, I helped them make my bed. I didn't feel like making a fuss out of telling them not to make a fuss.

"Well, you ought to sleep good on this egg-crate stuff," Richard said. "It's amazingly comfortable."

Leslie echoed his comment.

"Oh, I'm used to a lot worse," I said. "College mattresses that are a hundred years old, sleeping on desks at the campus newspaper, I even slept on top of the firetruck at the station, right in the hose bed. So you don't have to go to all this fuss or anything."

"Well, this is a far cry from hose beds," Leslie said.

"Yeah, I'll bet. By the way, I'm up on my fire safety training, so if anything happens in this high-rise, just follow me."

"Well, I know we'll sleep soundly knowing there's a qualified fireman in here," Richard said, tucking the sheet between the mattress and the floor.

The three of us went out of the room as I told them an ounce of the few million pounds of information I knew about fire safety.

Got to keep it meaningful. Make sure I don't get bogged down in practical things without meaning.

I tried to think of the last time I felt as awkward. It was in L. L. Bean, trying to tell the short version of the Richard story to a customer. I didn't like the feeling then either, but there didn't seem to be any way around it.

Leslie separated from us and disappeared into the master bedroom. I followed Richard into the kitchen, adjacent to the expansive living room where Jim and Kim sat at the card table. My father offered me a soda from the fridge and I took it. Leslie called him into the next room for something, he excused himself and followed the call as I took the empty seat next to Jim and Kim.

"Well, bro, isn't this place cool?" he said.

"Yeah, man, I'm majorly blown away by the view!"

"Yeah, it's pretty wild, all right."

"There's the famous Space Needle," Kim said, pointing northwest to a two-inch-tall futuristic monolith on the north edge of the skyline.

It had 500-foot vertical arches supporting a spaceshiplike structure.

"Huh. The Space Needle is what they call it? Kind of looks like its name."

As I stared at it, I slipped away from Jonathan Bach and into someone familiar, but nameless. I had never seen a city skyline and the view of this new world made Maine seem like a place I had only dreamed about. The lifetime when I was the son of a female pilot was just the first of a million others. Nothing mattered except feelings, learning, the pursuit of answers in this lifetime which was just beginning, but felt ageless.

"What if space shifted and time bent . . . "

Never mind "what if." A more useful question for me would have been *"What do you do when . . . ?"*

A feeling answered me.

Anything you want.

"I heard you giving Richard your fire safety lecture," Jim said.

I snapped back into a Seattle condominium in 1989.

"Yep. Just one of the many fringes of a college education, I guess."

"Hm."

"So any special reason you're visiting Richard?" I asked.

"Well, Kim and I haven't seen him in a while, and since we knew you were coming out, we decided to come up earlier."

"That's good. I'm glad you did."

"Well, that's another reason. This is a big step you've made, and it helps having family around."

"Yeah, thanks. Still, it ought to be pretty interesting."

He and Kim agreed.

I told them the latest happenings at the newspaper. I wanted to get in a little ordinary event-telling before Richard came back into the living room and we'd have to start talking philosophically.

I was in the middle of telling Jim about the Jackson Lab fire when Richard and Leslie walked into the living room and sat at the card table. I ended the story even though I wanted to tell Jim about other feelings I had about the internship.

"So anyway, it's a learning experience," I said, knowing Richard would like that phrase.

I waited for Richard to ask me something. That was the easiest way to know what to talk about.

"What kind of experiences do you think you would've had if you weren't in college?"

Hm. Neat question.

"Tough to say. I suppose I would be just as practical as I am now, regardless."

"Jon thinks he's too practical to be a philosopher," Jim said to Richard.

"Yeah, well, I *am* practical," I said. "But not as much as I used to be, I guess."

"Well, yeah, but it's not like you're averse to philosophy either," he said.

"Well, not these days."

"That's not true," Jim said. "Remember how we were talking on the phone about Beth's ascension about a week after the accident?"

I remembered.

"We talked about the letter she wrote in the chain?" I asked, knowing the answer.

"Yeah, exactly. You seemed pretty fascinated by it."

"I guess I was kind of philosophical, but that's because it was weird and kinda interesting."

"Exactly my point. So tell Richard about the stuff you told me about that night. The stuff you call 'weird and kinda interesting.'"

"You've never heard this?" I asked Richard.

"No," he said, sounding interested.

For the next five minutes, I told the story I remembered telling him the night in the hospital. He acted like he'd never heard it. Maybe he'd forgotten. Maybe I only thought I'd told him the coincidences of that night.

" . . . and it was the weirdest thing," I said in summary. "She never took off her seat belt, but she chose to take it off that night. Not only that, she wasn't scratched after she hit the windshield! I mean, nothing.

No blood, nothing. And there I was with my belt on and I get a broken wrist, shattered nose, broken collarbone, and a cut lip. I can't understand it."

"Whoa," he said quietly. "Fascinating."

Everybody around the small table was transfixed as I spoke. I wondered if they were feeling the chills of Beth's presence like I was.

We talked about other coincidences—how there was no such thing as chance—and I believed it.

I couldn't believe what I was hearing myself say. Choosing to die, the concept I couldn't grasp not too long ago, made perfect sense. I started to suspect I'd understood the concept all my life—that it was the reason I didn't cry about Beth after the night of the accident, the reason I felt such an easy peace about her dying. I must have known that there was a good reason she chose me to be her witness, that she even had the courtesy to die without making me see her bloody and suffering and that I'd make my own choice to die someday and would talk with her then about why it all happened.

Richard said there were many books about the subject of life after death, choosing to die, and incredible coincidences. Lots of books. He said he had a whole bookshelf full at his island house.

I didn't doubt him.

Richard was quiet as I took the reins of the conversation, taking us through a talk about newspapers and what truth meant and firefighting and the importance of being a rescuer and L. L. Bean customer service and what it meant to help people and why I found each job interesting. I spent the next hour finding meaning in all kinds of practicality.

Energy, energy, energy! It came from nowhere, took my nervous, hollow feeling and spun it into confidence.

I needed a pen and paper, but I didn't want to interrupt the flow of conversation. My father saw me suddenly edgy, looking around for something to write on. I took my plane ticket from my shirt pocket.

"Need a pen?" he asked.

I looked at him quickly.

"How'd you know I was looking for a pen?"

"Oh, just a guess. You looked like a guy who's just been told to remember Christie Brinkley's phone number."

The laugh that followed broke us out of a conversational trance. Leslie remarked that it was four in the morning, which none of us could believe, so we tried to find a way to freeze the momentum of the talk to thaw out the next day.

None of us wanted to stop talking, especially me. I had been awake for twenty-four hours and I wasn't tired. I got my energy thinking about Richard, discovering he hadn't been "too philosophical" and I hadn't been "too down to earth." We were equally fascinated about things, had equal urges to explore.

That small, wooden doorstop I had written to Richard about was starting to show characteristics of steel. Three months ago, I'd been trying to find the courage to "keep the door open." The door hadn't closed an inch since then. Now it looked as though it could come off its hinges for good.

CHAPTER SIXTY

I woke up five hours later. Not an ounce of me was tired. I had never felt that kind of energy the morning after going to bed so late, but with that feeling came a bit of regret, like the morning after I called Richard in May—as if I'd been drunk last night.

I was still dazed by the night before. I felt a little nervous, a little bewildered at how exhilarating I had found philosophy to be the night before.

Like a good friend with some coffee at the ready, my journal was there. The foot-wide counter near the window looked like a good place to write. It was bathed in Seattle morning sun.

Seattle. Morning, bright sunshine, journal on my lap. Yesterday was a 24-hour day for me, but here I am, up and ready for I-don't-know-what. Maybe it's because Richard and Leslie are in the next room. Maybe it's because only five hours of sleep has made me more anxious than normal.

Talked about stuff till 4 a.m. last night, about practical things that may not be as practical as I think. My involvement in firefighting might come from my desire to get through life-threatening problems, rescue the threatened, extinguish harmful situations, and that can be representative of my desire to resolve my relationship with Richard . . . and I guess I might like newspapers because of the honesty and the clarity in writing, the truth, the nobility and importance of disseminating accurate information, which could represent my nature to be open and direct and practical . . .

Finished reading *One* and *Bridge* on the plane. Feel like I already know these people. Too bad they don't have a book about me.

A knock at the door snapped me out of my conversation with myself. The voice was friendly, light, polite.

"Jon?" it said.

"Door's open."

Leslie edged the door open. The ex-movie star glamour goddess was dressed in pink sweatpants and sweatshirt. She smiled at me.

"Good morning," she said, her face turning into immediate concern. "Oh, be careful on that ledge!"

I hadn't realized I had been so perilously perched on the open windowsill.

It was something Mom would have said to me.

"Yep. I'm okay."

"Good."

There was silence.

"Sun's great, isn't it?" she asked.

"Yeah. The view's not bad either."

"Want some breakfast?"

"Sure, I guess. I'm just finishing up anyway. Getting in a little thought."

She smiled the warmest smile I'd ever seen. It was as if she realized Richard and his son Jonathan were more alike than they knew. It was as if she knew this similarity with Richard's writing mood would be just one of thousands of similarities between father and son.

"Take your time. No one's really up yet."

"Okay, thanks."

The door closed.

Leslie. What a sweetie. Voice was very warm, she's letting me take my time. I'm sure if I didn't answer the door she would have assumed I was sleeping and let me rest. A million good impressions in those 15 seconds.

I figured they'd be busy that morning. Richard would probably lock his door and wouldn't want to be disturbed for hours while he wrote, and Leslie would be on the phone to various metropolitan areas talking about book royalties or contracts or some other important aspect of author life.

I remembered I had brought ten years' worth of Richard's letters to me. They stayed tucked in the manila envelope that had grown as much as I had.

I spilled the letters onto the mattress and looked at the collage of familiar print styles and colored paper.

I read the first letter I saw. It was a scribbled early draft of my first letter to him.

September 2, 1980
Dear Captain,

I wanted to write you and say that I am writing a few stories. Your books are on the shelf with the other flying ones, but I haven't read them yet. I want to be a writer too someday . . .

Good ol' Jonny. The kid had a lot of heart. It was just one of the many Jons staring me in the face.

The old Jonathan, the one that never called Richard that night in May, the Jonathan loyal to Mom, the Jonathan who would surely be the best journalist the *Portland Press Herald* ever had, the Jonathan ready and willing to be the best newspaper editor the *Daily Maine Campus* ever had, sat as audience to the Seattle Jonathan as he made sense out of whatever was going to happen next.

"*Traitor*," the old Jonathan said. I didn't know how to respond to him. He had a good point. I *was* a traitor.

CHAPTER SIXTY-ONE

Inhale.

Heeeeeeeere's Jonny!

"Mornin', guys," I said to Jim and Kim. He looked out the window while she folded the sheets on their air mattress.

"Hey, bro," Jim said as I headed for the large windows to see a more panoramic view of daylight Seattle. Things are always so different in daylight.

Kim gave a soft hello.

Through the reflection in the glass, I saw Richard come out from the bedroom. He was freshly shaven, and was completely dressed and awake as if he had a business lunch to go to. I turned to see him only for a second and returned to the view.

I wore my blue Oxford shirt and my gray pleated chinos, some popular brand-name sneakers. Would he ask me why I blindly followed the traditional dress of society? Maybe he knew that's what most upscale college students wore these days and he'd ask what my clothes meant to me.

I watched him, the factory that made my Y-chromosome: my height, facial structure, urge to write. I watched the container for all this as he talked to Jim about the day outside.

"Morning, my son," he said to me.

"Hi, Richard," I said, turning around.

"Have you given any thought to what you want to do first? See Seattle maybe, catch a movie, go flying, eat breakfast, go skydiving?"

Leslie came out as I answered him.

"I don't know. I'm open to whatever," I said meekly.

"We could just hang out," said Jim boldly. His volume was deep and strong to my sleepy ears. It's always deep and strong. "You guys have a lot you should be talking about."

Richard looked at me and raised his eyebrows.

"Jon . . . ?" he said, clasping his large hands together softly. "Sound okay to you?"

"Sure, whatever. That's cool."

"Want some breakfast first?"

"Yeah, I guess."

I say that too much. "I guess." Maybe he'd ask me why.

"Cereal's good," I said.

I feel like I should have prepared an itinerary or something. Maybe he'd remark about my consistent awkwardness of not knowing what to say, where to start, how to stand, what to eat, what to think, how to express myself. There's got to be a way to make this easier. I wonder if he has any ideas.

Jim talked to Richard about computers. Like in the car outside Jim's motel room, seven years ago, I was thankful the spotlight was off me. I let them talk as I ate breakfast.

We finished breakfast, talked a little bit about Seattle, and packed everyone's stuff into the car, ready to take Jim and Kim to the airport to go back to California.

He got in the back with me and Kim. That's when I remembered why they'd come to Seattle.

"Thanks for being here, guys," I said to them. To know he came out here for me, that was true brotherhood.

"No prob! It's just too bad you were delayed so much. We could have had more of yesterday to spend."

We dropped Jim and Kim off at the airport, hugged them good-bye at the gate. I hugged him a little harder than I had hugged him yesterday, thankful to be related to him. Richard, Leslie, and I watched them walk away until they disappeared behind the corner of the gate.

I sighed an excited sigh and flash-wondered again where to start.

"Jim's a cool brother," I said to Leslie.

And that's where we started.

We talked about Jim and the importance of "true family," friends that mean more to you than your own blood relatives. We talked about how especially wonderful it is when your "true family" happens to be your blood relatives. We talked about choosing our families and the experiences in our lives to make us stronger.

We talked about so many things, building that house on that new site of common ground. There was so much yet to build, though.

"Where are we headed now?" I asked Richard as he pulled out of the airport parking lot.

"The island," he said. "But to get there, we need to go over to the other airport—Renton. That's where Daisy is."

CHAPTER SIXTY-TWO

Daisy. She's some secretary, maybe. No, that's Stacy. A pet hamster?
A friend of theirs they wanted me to meet? A half-sister I was never
told about?

"Daisy?" I asked.

"Daisy's a Cessna Skymaster," he said.

I'd seen a few Skymasters during my days at Sugarbush airport
helping Mom behind the counter. They were two-tailed, high-
wing monoplanes with one propeller in front, one in the back. Very
powerful things. They were as loud as any L-19 towplane I'd ever
heard.

"Why do you call her Daisy?"

"Because that's her name," he said. "She's bright sunbeam yellow
and white, and very pretty."

And fifteen minutes later I met Daisy, watched my father preflight
the airplane just as I had seen a million pilots preflight theirs. He
walked around the plane slowly and methodically, checking the rudder, the ailerons, drained a half ounce of gasoline from the valve at the
bottom of the gas tank.

Everything he did before takeoff was the same as Big Jon had
done with our Cessna 170. He, too, had a checklist of items to remember, laminated and clipped to the control wheel. When he and
Leslie and I were strapped in and the propeller was spinning, Richard looked over his shoulder at me in the back seat, like Mom and
Big Jon used to, to see if I was ready to roll. I nodded to him like
I'd nodded to them.

I reminded myself I was about to fly with a world-famous pilot, a man who never seemed to write anything that didn't have something to do with flight, a man who had flown antique biplanes, supersonic fighters, high-performance gliders, and ultralight aircraft with fabric so thin you could see through it.

My life was in my father's hands, and I was strangely and completely comfortable.

CHAPTER SIXTY-THREE

We landed forty-five minutes later at a little island airport. I helped Richard put Daisy in the hangar for the night as Leslie got into a shiny Subaru sedan and pulled it closer to us to unload our baggage.

Five minutes of conversation later, we arrived at a huge house overlooking Puget Sound.

I knew I couldn't get too comfortable. This was Richard's private space, the fortress on his island of isolation. For a brief second, though, it felt like home.

Richard turned the key and held the door open for Leslie and me.

The place was very spacious and very beige.

There were a few pictures of surreal scenery on the wall, lots of pictures of planes. One picture framed a photograph of the old Parks P-2A biplane from the cover of *Biplane* and *Nothing by Chance*.

The ceiling was sixteen feet above us, two skylights cut in it.

In the open living room, there were two eight-foot L-shaped couches. A piano sat just behind the back of the L; in front of it was a marble coffee table that would easily hold a five-thousand-piece puzzle. The table was barren except for a chessboard.

Body-length windows encased the whole scene.

There was an outstanding view of serene Puget Sound below, of the line of distant mountains. My first impulse was to find where the sliding glass doors opened to the deck.

A seaplane flew about a half mile away, level to our altitude in these hills.

Fifteen feet below the deck was a garden that spanned the perimeter of the house. We were surrounded by nature.

To the left, a kitchen was separated from the dining room by a barlike partition that could seat four, a little tightly but comfortably, as if put there to allow guests to watch whatever cooking took place.

It looked big, but it wasn't a mansion. More like an ambassador suite in a formal hotel.

I tried to think of a better word than "wow," but that's all that came. Everybody who visited there must have said the same thing. You'd think a journalist could come up with some new phrase to describe being impressed.

"Wow."

On the wall, I saw a framed list of six signatures: Johann Ambrosius Bach, Johann Sebastian Bach, J. C. Bach, W. F. Bach, C.P.E. Bach, Von G.C.F. Bach, and then Richard's. Below that was the proclamation: *"Ingenuity often runs in a family."*

I thought of my L. L. Bean name tag. Was Richard just as proud to be a Bach as I had felt sometimes? I imagined him behind a counter answering questions about whether or not he was related to Johann Sebastian.

I didn't want him to ask me what I wanted to do first. I didn't have an answer yet.

"Wow," I said. "This is cool."

I tried to think of a better word than "cool."

"I mean, this is impressive."

Richard started down the little set of stairs to the right, carrying my luggage.

"Pretty neat, eh?" he said.

Leslie hadn't made it past the plant near the door. She was feeling its soil, examining some leaves.

"It's so nice to have you here, Jonathan, and I'm going to try to stay out of the way while you and your father talk," she said.

I took off my shoes.

"Really? I hope not. This isn't just between Richard and me, y'know. I mean it is, but you're part of that framework, right? That's what I figure, anyway."

She glanced up at me for a second and smiled.

"That's sweet," she said, returning to her plant-examining. "Unfortunately, there's going to be some work I have to do. But I'll try to get it done as quickly as possible."

She squinted her eyes at a limp yellow leaf toward the top. "Okay."

She plucked the leaf from its dry stem.

"Well, you're welcome to jump in anytime," I said. "I imagine I'm going to want to know about you sooner or later. That is, apart from Richard and everything."

She stopped her scan for more ailing leaves and looked up at me. "Really? Well, that's good to hear. I was wondering if you'd feel that way. It was heartening for me to see that in one of your recent letters to Richard, you were wondering why you never heard my voice."

I looked at my socked feet and remembered the exact words I had written: *"I wonder what voice I will hear when her pen has done the talking . . ."*

"I'm curious about you, too," she said. "I didn't get in on a lot of your phone conversations with him because I was respecting your time together. That, and I was also pretty busy."

She paused and seemed to wait for me to say something.

"That's too bad," I said to my feet. "That you were busy."

She plucked another leaf. "Truthfully, I didn't want to have anything to do with this," she said.

Richard came up the stairs and brought a few moments of silence with him when he reached our level.

I didn't know whether to be hurt or intrigued at what Leslie had just said, so I was both.

CHAPTER SIXTY-FOUR

Leslie explained what she meant.

After investing great energy to have loving relationships with Kris, Rob, and Erica, and experiencing the frustration of having miscommunication and bad feelings crack the foundations of those relationships, Leslie had been afraid that something similar was going to happen with me, that I wouldn't be able to get beyond my anger at Richard, that it would make for another fresh batch of heartache and frustration. She said she hadn't wanted to invest her energy in another doomed relationship with another of his embittered children.

I stood next to where my luggage used to be, leaning against the wall, daring myself to ask what had happened between them and Rob.

I dared.

" . . . If that's okay," I said. "I don't mean to pry open a can of worms or anything."

Richard sat on the couch. It looked as if he didn't want to talk about it. Leslie came over and sat next to him. I sat on the floor as she started to explain.

She said that two days before the family reunion in 1984, Rob and his pregnant wife, Cami, had wanted to meet with them to discuss a "business proposition." Rob asked them to invest ten thousand dollars in a new business he was thinking of establishing—all he needed was a new computer to get started. At the time, Leslie and Richard were trying to get out of bankruptcy, trying to scrape up the money to heat the house past fifty-five degrees in the winter. They had no money to invest, but Rob was desperate. He and Cami only had two dollars in the bank, and his job wasn't paying the bills.

"We told them we could lend them a thousand dollars," Leslie said. "They said it would do no good. We tried to come up with some jobs they might do to sustain them while Rob changed jobs. They said it wouldn't be enough. They needed $10,000—that would pay for the baby's delivery, buy the computer to start the business, and would sustain them for the next six months."

She said she and Richard had $1,500 which they gave them right away. They set to work to find more money as quickly as possible, and after nine days had the other $8,500 for them.

"The uncertainties in Rob and Cami's immediate future were such that it seemed almost impossible to write a meaningful loan agreement and set out a payment schedule for them," Leslie said. "No need, we thought, because we loved and trusted them. They knew we were in financial straits as well. But as time went by, Rob not only didn't quit his hated job so he could build the computer business, he increased his time at work. His computer business went nowhere. He talked to us about vacations he and Cami were taking and a new car and an apartment building they were planning to buy, but never mentioned paying back the loan. We asked them for paperwork about it but we never received it. We eventually had to get a loan from the bank to see us through, which was hard because of the bankruptcy."

Eventually, harsh discussions about money led to a stop in communication between them.

"We wanted two things: to have a warm relationship with Rob and Cami, and to conduct business with them. We felt including them in the second would enhance the first. It only caused strife," Leslie said.

They took turns telling me about other specifics of the problem. The bottom line was that they felt Rob had compromised their relationship for ten thousand dollars.

I didn't see how Rob could do such a thing, especially knowing how much he valued his relationship with Richard—always calling him "dad," traveling to Arizona to fly gliders with Richard after he had just learned to fly, naming his second son Fletcher after Jonathan Seagull's feathered friend.

I understood Leslie and Richard, though. I knew from reading his books that they both had been burned many times when it came to money and trust.

"You see, Jonathan," Richard said, "money is a lovely child which comes with a smile on its face, flowers in its hand, and a pack of snarling monsters behind it. Pick up the child and there you have the monsters: jealousy, betrayal, resentment, hatred—and a host of other horrors to bring agonies to the heart. We walk through a spiritual minefield each time we reach out to anyone on *any* level for any*thing*. We must be careful to be absolutely precise, to anticipate everything and spell it out clearly. No matter how much we give, how generous we are, people think we have more and they have less, and they don't like it. Agreements seem to shift and change to disagreements in the most bewildering way. Lawsuits are spring-loaded to jump on us, no matter how carefully we do business."

Leslie nodded. "Once we were taken to court for nonpayment of a bill by a person who had refused the certified letter we sent with timely payment enclosed! The judge opened the letter, found the check and gave it to her, and then found in her favor!"

"Geez," I said, understanding that there were often *more* than two sides to every story.

Richard continued.

"Even things as simple as friendships are frightening to us. Like the poor plumber we had befriended and helped financially all through last winter when he didn't have food on his table. He lied in court on behalf of the woman who refused to accept our payment and smiled happily as he left the courtroom! It doesn't seem to anyone that 'rich' people can hurt. Fame makes it even worse."

I looked out the bay window.

"That explains why I see you as so private and isolated. Because you have to be."

"We don't *have* to be, no. But it makes our lives less complicated. If we lived on Main Street in Seattle, we'd be slaves to whoever decided they had a right to knock on our door or get our autograph or pop in for coffee."

"But isn't that escaping?"

"It sure is. But there's nothing wrong with that. There's no problem so big that you can't run away from it."

"Isn't that kind of cowardly?"

"Not cowardly, just exercising our right to privacy from people who think I'm obligated to serve them in any way they see fit. I don't want my private life to belong to someone else."

Leslie reminded me that I had done my fair share of escaping.

"There were times we'd write you and get no reply for months, if at all. I remember a very powerful letter you wrote in 1987. As I recall, Richard was happy to hear from you and wrote immediately to tell you so, but we didn't get a reply to that either."

I felt ashamed about that hate letter. She had a good point. I had refused his cheerful offer of communication. I defied his logic. I didn't want his good suggestions. I didn't want him to be sensible. I didn't want him to be a nice guy. I wanted him to make a move just so I could reject him.

"Yeah . . . I guess you're right," I said, looking at the floor again. There had to be some way to rationalize my actions, or, to use my hate-letter terminology, my non-actions.

I remembered silently telling Richard, "I'm not interested in therapy."

Is it bad to deny help or logic or sensibility? I had denied it and eventually acted on my frustration, caught by my self-imposed Catch-22: wanting help but not wanting help.

Richard read my mind again.

"But there's nothing wrong with escaping, Jon," he said. "Sometimes it's very necessary. If I had stayed with the family despite Bette's mistrust, I would have self-destructed."

"Yeah, I remember you telling me that at the reunion."

"Okay, good. Then you also remember me telling you there was a consequence for leaving. I didn't get to be a part of your lives for a long time and I had to risk you being bitter toward me for a long time."

Leslie spoke.

"In the years after the divorce, Richard tried repeatedly to make contact with the family. His journals from the early years after leaving home are full of you kids and talks with Bette, and, as he got money, gifts like the Tiger Moth, a house for you guys, and other things. But your Mom's bitterness made it impossible for him to have a relationship with you. That's why when Jim left the house, it was easy for us to communicate with him. There were no barriers.

"Finally, we felt that if any of you expressed good feelings toward Richard, you would jeopardize your relationship with your mom. Richard saw that you were in an unreachable position and decided to let Bette tell you whatever made her comfortable—that he was dead, that he was a monster, whatever—to let the children think whatever she thought appropriate until they grew big enough to understand. At that time, it was most important that you have a good relationship with her. His relationships would have to wait.

"I was sure this wasn't necessary and I persuaded Richard to reach out to Bette again. She was as negative as he had said she would be. But he hung in there. This went on for years. In 1981, I finally wrote her a long, long letter begging her to put the bitterness in the past for her own good, to please let us be friends for the sake of the children."

"Did she write back?"

"She sure did. She said that the sight of our postmark on an envelope made her sick and told me to leave her alone."

"Hm," I said. I could believe Mom would say that.

"But you see, we were damned if we wrote and damned if we didn't write. Letters came from you and Beth for a while, to your father's delight and mine, and he answered every one on the very day he received it."

Richard nodded.

"We gave them top priority," he said. "No matter what the legal problems, the agony of deadlines in those days. Your letters came first."

I realized it was true. None of my letters to him had gone unanswered.

"Yeah, I appreciated the letters," I said. "It was the only mail I got. I mean, I felt special to get them because Kris, Rob, Erica, and Jim knew you guys so well, but it was the only way I knew you."

"That's why we wanted to fly you out here in 1978. We asked for you to visit right after Erica and Jim came to see us. But Bette told us you were afraid to fly and couldn't make the trip."

At first I was surprised to hear that. Me, a little boy raised around airplanes, afraid to fly? But again, I could imagine Mom saying that. All those times I didn't want to fly with her on those windy, bumpy, turbulent days must have given her the impression I was afraid of flying. Or maybe there was something in the language Beth and I shared which showed through to Mom—something like the reluctance we'd both had in the driveway before pedaling to see Richard at Jim's motel room.

"If we'd known you wanted to come, we would have brought you here in a second! We wanted you, believe me. As much as we thought, 'Bachs afraid to fly?', we had no choice but to take your Mom's word for it."

"At the reunion, we mentioned it to Bethy," Leslie said. "She looked disgusted and said, 'Aw, c'mon, gimme a break!' and we had our first indication that it might not have been true."

In my mind I heard Beth say it. Hearing that voice made me feel like she was with me, getting to know Richard too.

"Another time we had to go by your Mom's word was when Bethy died," said Leslie. "Erica called us in the middle of the night to tell us what had happened. She was a marvel of self-control and explained carefully what she knew. At a time like that, all thoughts of Bette's bitterness vanished. We felt Bethy was her favorite, that she had found a vicarious glamour and fulfillment through Bethy's skating perform- ances that she was unable to attain on her own. Richard was filled with compassion and concern and would have done anything to support her through that awful time."

She turned to him.

"Forgive me for speaking for you, Richie," she said.

"No, no . . . you're right on," he said, taking her hand.

He spoke to me, continuing where Leslie had left off.

"I called Bette to offer to come home, to help in any way I could, but she told me that she didn't want *anyone* coming home, that it would be like having company, and she sure didn't want that. Which, when I think about it now, is contrary to her statement to us that the house would always be open to you children.

"Each of you was entitled to a share of the house I'd bought for you. Bette sold that house after she remarried and moved to Alburg. When you didn't get your share, when Bette decided that your money should be tied up in her home, we decided that you'd be better off if we deposited the extra money we sent into your own accounts. When you turned eighteen, you could do whatever you wished with the money; it would be your decision and not hers. That's why you started getting financial statements."

I thought of the day when Beth tried to explain the statements to a friend of hers who'd seen them on the kitchen counter and asked about them. I didn't remember Mom ever saying anything about them.

"Well," I said, "I knew Mom was upset when you decreased the support to the minimum amount you could get away with."

"We *never* cut your support," Leslie said. "We were paying triple the amount required plus extras like private high school for Kris and Rob, summer camp, Jim's computer, Erica's college, doctors. . . ."

"Triple?"

"To Bette, it might have seemed that we cut the support," Leslie continued, "but we simply diverted the extra two thirds we sent each month to your account and Beth's. We didn't want more of your money going to the Fineman estate."

I could understand that money channeled into our special accounts might not give Mom much comfort. From her point of view, she had less cash available for daily necessities.

"It would have seemed even less to her after Jim had moved out, since we were sending his support directly to him," Leslie added.

"Ohhh." I nodded.

"Anyway," he said, "Bette told us there wasn't going to be a gathering for Beth. They'd sprinkle Beth's ashes on the mountain and that would be that. So I decided that I shouldn't go. My presence would only make things worse."

"He was very quiet in the days following Bethy's death," Leslie said. "He was really concerned about the family and reached out to be as supportive as possible. I never saw him cry, but he lost four pounds the night he got the news. For a long time he looked very, very old. We talked together about the breathtaking pain in our chests each time we thought of Bethy, and there were times I went off alone to cry so I wouldn't make him hurt more than he already did."

"Wow, Richard, I had no idea," I said to him. It was like seeing him that first time at the motel and discovering he wasn't in a wheelchair.

Leslie said it was understandable that I had no idea how Richard had felt. "But what did you think Richard was feeling?" she asked.

I told them I knew he used philosophy to explain Beth's death, but I couldn't relate to it at the time. I told him I was mad that he had said the combining of my and Beth's accounts was "what Beth would have wanted." They answered that by saying they wished they could have known her better, but they couldn't because Beth was under Mom's authority.

We talked for another few hours about the bankruptcy, though I'd learned why he'd had to declare it from reading *Bridge*. It went back to the conversation we had just had about Richard's feelings about money, trust, friendship, and his own ignorance about financial matters.

I asked him, if he had truly been bankrupt, how had he been able to pay child support, help Erica with college, and buy Jim the computer?

"Richard *was* bankrupt," Leslie said. "None of you understood that *I* was paying his bills. The child support, Erica's college money, the hundred dollars you and Beth got at Christmas—that was from me. None of you understood that Richard was wiped out—and I mean wiped right out. Left with five hundred and sixty-three dollars in the world."

I was surprised and I respected their hard work turning their financial problems around, but I wasn't too surprised or too full of respect to thank Leslie for coming through like that.

"Oh, Jonathan . . . what you've said, that just means so much to me. I tried so hard to keep things open and loving for all of you. I've been through that kind of pain in my life, thinking I had a father who didn't care about me, and I knew it didn't have to happen to you."

She explained about her childhood, bouncing from one foster home to another after her parents divorced when she was eight. Her mother had had nothing but awful things to say about her father, and it took Leslie forty years to renew her relationship with her dad. She discovered he was the sweetest man she had ever met.

"Dammit!" she said, pounding her fist lightly but firmly on the couch armrest. "None of the problems between Richard and you kids had to happen. None of them! After the reunion I thought we'd finally worked through to understanding. I thought the chain letter would keep communication current and prevent new problems!"

Another surprise.

"The chain letter was your idea?"

She nodded emphatically.

"So why'd you stop it?"

She shook her head and frowned. "See, that's another thing . . . we didn't stop it. One of *you* did!"

One of us?

I didn't know what to think about reality anymore. The reality I had lived by for so many years was coming apart. I was afraid to say anything for fear of getting an extreme dose of "That's not true!"

But already my perception of Richard and Leslie had changed dramatically. Bad feelings for Richard dissolved into a mix of shame for not knowing the truth and pride in myself that I had taken brave steps to be here, learning it now. Feelings of not knowing what to think of Leslie melted into a respect for her pain and an appreciation of her misperceived compassion.

There was so much to explore. Everything I considered to be truth was subject to re-examination. My experiences had been truth to me. The stuff I had heard about Richard had been truth, the stuff Mom had said, the stuff Rob and Erica had said. How ironic to be a journalist, disseminating truth to thousands and not examine what truth was in my own life!

Are experiences truth? Or can experiences be reexamined and reinterpreted, like a picture of a beautiful young woman who turns into a hag when stared at intensely enough or from a different angle? Is an experience at age ten the same experience at age twenty, forty, one hundred? Maybe experience isn't always truth.

I can see Big Jon as a bad guy for being strict or I can see him as a good guy for teaching me the value of practical responsibility. I can understand that he was trying to do his best as a first-time father with six kids who weren't his own and I can understand that his values came from the way he was brought up.

My mind was wildfire. Any old truth was up for re-evaluation.

I asked about the misconception with Kris, and Leslie told me it had started with a phone call. Kris had called during a time when Leslie was very busy so she'd been very abrupt on the phone. She had also called them collect and they told her they couldn't afford it.

"Ever since then, we've heard nothing from her except for her part of the chain letters, which didn't mention us. Now she treats us to outright silence. It's as if she was looking for an excuse to get us out of her life so she wouldn't have to deal with feelings too difficult for her to handle. We've worked the problems through with her many times, but it never lasts."

What about Erica—their letter to her that harshly criticized her for turning Catholic and joining the military?

They told me there were no harsh words in any letter to her.

"That letter only asked her about those issues. It didn't *condemn* her for them," Richard said. "She had been following the study of Christian Science, as far as we knew. When she told us she had decided to convert to Catholicism, I told her that I didn't understand her decision and asked what made her switch. I was just curious. But the main problem between us had to do with withdrawing our financial support for college. We pleaded with her to understand that I was going bankrupt and Leslie had run out of money and we had no more to give her. Apparently that upset her, and we haven't heard from her since."

Misunderstanding. That's all it was. Hurt feelings that stood in the way of communication. I had been guilty of it too.

Richard reminded us that we had to eat sometime if we wanted to have energy for these long talks.

Leslie said she had to close up some things downstairs in the office and I sat at one of the stools at the kitchen counter while Richard fried some fish.

I hadn't shown much reaction to their side of the family problems. I was still trying to sort it all out.

Richard looked up from the frying pan.

A few seconds passed without a word from either of us. Then he looked up and frowned at me.

"Why are you here?"

CHAPTER SIXTY-FIVE

An uneasy chill passed through me like a strong riptide as Leslie came up from the downstairs office.

"Hey, darlin' . . . there's fish a'fryin' here for ya'," Richard said.

I couldn't believe the question he'd asked me. Flying me out here, getting to know him and the truth behind all the family problems had been his idea.

"Uh . . . why am I here?" I asked with a nervous chuckle.

"I just asked Jon what he's doing here," he said to Leslie.

I was glad she was there. Maybe she'd see what game Richard was playing and stop it. There were times in *Bridge* when she wouldn't play Richard's games. She used her determination, put her foot down, and said, "I won't be treated like this!" when Richard suddenly acted cold. Now she was on my side.

"What a great question!" she said with a smile, looking straight at me.

"Uh . . ." I swallowed.

"Maybe a better question would be: what kinds of expectations do you have for the next few days?" Richard said.

The confusion dissolved. I realized Richard wasn't asking, "What the hell do you think you're doing here?" He just wanted to know what I wanted to learn!

I saw firsthand what could have happened between him and Erica to make her feel condemned. Richard's curious inquiries could have sounded threatening. He seemed to have a deliberately strange way of phrasing questions.

I was energized. Out of the momentary trauma of misinterpretation, I felt the exciting challenge of answering Richard's question in the most creative way possible.

"Why am I here . . ."

I thought reflex-fast, scanned for the most creative way to describe the feeling—did being out here feel like anything I've ever felt before?

"Okay. I've got it. . . . There are these two sunbathers enjoying a sunny summer day. Suddenly some clouds appear and drift in front of the sun. This happens all day—clouds, then clear, clouds, clear. Finally one sunbather says, 'Enough! These clouds are driving me crazy! I want an *unobstructed* sun with *unobstructed* warmth!' The other sunbather says, 'What's the big deal? Just enjoy what sun there is.' "

Leslie leaned against Richard's left shoulder and held his waist. Both were smiling.

"See, I'm one of those agitated types who needs an unobstructed sun. And since I haven't found another way around it, I guess I'm here to learn to fly—to get above the clouds once and for all, so I don't have to be a slave to them on the ground. I'm here to learn stuff about you so I don't get riled when someone mentions your name."

Leslie gave an emphatic "All right!" as Richard laughed, surprised and seemingly enlightened by the analogy.

I liked it too.

I scanned the counter, then looked at the dining table a few feet away.

Richard knew what I was looking for.

"You need a pen again," he said, flipping the fish and pulling out a drawer near his waist. He threw a little note pad and pen to me.

"Thanks, pal," I said, writing the analogy.

"If you're going to keep coming up with stuff like this, we should all have pens and pads," he said.

And for the rest of that evening and into the early hours of the next morning, we had pens and pads by our plates, in our pockets, on the coffee table.

In the same way I had taken notes and quotes as a student journalist, I took notes and quotes about life, the universe, anything.

We found metaphors for everything, explored obvious issues like what does it mean to be human, why is family important, is "selfish" such a bad word?

He asked if I believed in soulmates. I told him yes, especially after reading *Bridge*. I told him about Rachel, Tempest, and even the few seconds of thoughts I'd had about Julie. I told him that emotional walls weren't terrible structures to have and how I agreed with him when I was reading *Bridge* that my walls might be the very things that prepare me to meet Her.

He asked how I felt about being a journalist. I told him I was still deciding if I wanted to be one if it meant dealing with an office life like the *American*'s.

He asked what I'd do if I were rich. I told him that after hearing all the problems he'd had with money, I didn't know what I'd do or who I'd trust.

It was my turn to ask him some things. I had a perfect first question. "Why do you fly?"

He looked pensive for a second, then looked at the ceiling in another second thought. Leslie had her head on his lap, about to fall asleep.

"If you ask me tomorrow, I can give you a better answer," he said. "You're giving us a real workout."

"Yeah, I know. I'm sorry," I said.

"Oh, Jon, don't apologize. As tiring as all this talking is, it's a pleasant workout," he said.

Leslie gave me a hug good night, and as she went into the master bedroom, Richard took me downstairs. Their office had two bays for desks like a two-car garage, separated by a knee-high counter, another little conversation area with a couch and an easy chair next to a fireplace, and a bathroom and bedroom where Richard had put my luggage. Bookshelves along the back wall, another little office where Stacy answered the phone and assisted Richard and Leslie with corporation work, a small laundry room and an exercise area separated from the office by sliding glass doors. The place was modest compared to other celebrities' homes on TV; no gold fixtures, porcelain statues, or cascading walls of water. It was easy to be comfortable.

My room had a king-size bed, a wall's worth of bookshelves and an access to the deck overlooking Puget Sound.

I hugged Richard good night and thanked him for dinner. I tried to think of him beyond the label "Richard," just as I had progressed to thinking of him as beyond "Captain."

I was content with addressing him by his first name.

"You're welcome, my son. I'm delighted you're here . . . though I don't know if we're going to keep up with your schedule. You never sleep, do you?"

"College life did it to me," I said. "And as far as I'm concerned, this is Richard and Leslie 101."

"Well, there will be a final exam when you leave, so be prepared," he said with a chuckle as he went upstairs.

I took off my shirt, forgetting I had twenty note-pad pages of ideas and insights in the breast pocket. I let them spill onto the bed.

—every activity can have a metaphor, a lesson, a comparison if I choose

—physics experiments can go wrong, mistakes are inevitable, but they are proof of possibility just as they are proof of impossibility—we are what we experience

—someday I'll wish I was 22 again, that's what I have now so I'm not wasting time, so I'll have few regrets when I'm 40—I'm exploring while I have this body and this energy because it won't last

—disasters can be blessings and vice versa

—things to strive for in writing: UNPREDICTABILITY, EN-TERTAINMENT, EMOTION, DESCRIPTION, EXAMPLE, TRUTH

—no rules but my own—I can paint a room pink if it helps me write, hang stuff on walls, music or no, sleeping in, dining out, walking, ANYTHING that helps to create a mood for writing

—we all have our versions of reality—what one would call crazy, another would call normal—it's what we choose to do with our standard that determines our character and our happiness

—important aspects of life are desire for learning, happiness, willingness to admit you're wrong, right, sad, happy, honesty, courage to stand your ground overall, look adversity and scorn and ridicule in the face and say, that's okay, do what YOU want, I'm doing what I want. Be yourself—keep your ideals in the face of social pressure, skepticism

—if you forgive someone for what they did to you, THEY have to live with how they feel about it, not you.

—who says I can be a writer? What do I know? ANSWER: I know what I've experienced and how it felt, all I have to do is dare to write it down and revise it if necessary, stick with it

—loving what you do is important—*Ellsworth American* is not the fun it used to be. Don't think it'll be that way with editorship, want to go in right now and get things done because I like it, because I know I can make a difference and affect people's perceptions of the paper and maybe make them learn something—trying to make it a good place to work for everybody. My door'll be open to hear problems, communicate with staff and their ideas

—Richard said he feels a little guilty about getting the good results of Mom's hard work to raise me—he wants the animosity gone between them, but only if Mom chooses—she chooses her pain—if she would let it heal, her awkwardness when Richard called or came up in conversation, it would be no big deal

—how do you know life isn't an illusion? We have memories, but how do we know for sure that they happened?

—memories are tools to build yourself

The notes didn't have a purpose other than to indulge my journalistic compulsion to jot them down as if they were notes for the most important news story of my career. When I took notes in class, I told myself that ignoring anything a professor had to say was academic suicide. It was the same with Richard. I realized being on the island was not to be enrolled just in Richard and Leslie 101, but also in Jonathan's Future 101.

I turned the light off and thought of the Jonathan of a little over twenty-four hours ago who was just about to land in Seattle. I thought of everything I'd tell him if I had the chance.

And what would I tell the Jonathan of three months ago? What would I tell the Jonathan who has just called Jim and is debating whether or not to call Richard as he holds the silent receiver?

I tried to figure out a way to talk to him telepathically. Richard had hinted it was possible.

I imagined Jonathan sitting there, sent him the first words that came to me:

Just call him.

CHAPTER SIXTY-SIX

Richard talked through the next five chess games. And while we talked, my nervousness disappeared for good. Unlike previous times I'd talked with Richard, when I was trying to put meaning in whatever I said so Richard wouldn't turn off, the talking became effortless. I could be excited to tell him any thought that came to me.

I was discovering that Richard wasn't a philosopher. The label was too boring to describe him. He talked about things that mattered to him and he wanted to know what mattered to me. That's the way I liked it too. I didn't want to talk about things I didn't care about. It was impossible anyway.

I was starting to understand his way of talking. When he labeled himself a "free-breather" instead of a nonsmoker, it was because he didn't believe in labeling himself after someone else's destructive behavior. "If you were a loyal, dedicated employee at your newspaper," he said to me, "would they label you a non-embezzler?"

I liked his style. He was never boring and always creative.

I let Richard know that I wasn't nervous anymore. He said it was great to hear that I had stopped giving my consent to feeling anxious around him. Perfect perspective! I was nervous not because I had to be, but because I let myself be.

I suspected I could allow myself not to be nervous in other areas in my life. Was there something else I could experiment with? Some situation where I was usually uncomfortable?

There was.

CHAPTER SIXTY-SEVEN

We took a break in our games to drive into town. When he asked if I wanted to go, I figured it was for a grocery run. But when we got to town, he turned off the main street and onto the airport driveway.

I remembered I had asked him, "Why do you fly?" and I had a feeling he was about to show me an answer. I just hoped it would be calm up there and I wouldn't get sick.

I tried to remember what Richard had said about choosing not to give consent to nervousness. It wasn't working.

When he opened the rusty metal doors of the hangar, I saw his sleek seaplane, a Lake Amphibian. It was my favorite airplane. Streamlined, an engine in the back, low wing and high rudder, floats on the wings—essentially a flying boat. Whenever they landed at Sugarbush, I got as close as pilots would allow me to come.

As I took a closer look at the red and yellow plane, a familiar smell hit me—high-octane gasoline and old airplane oil. It was perfume to me. That smell brought me back to the days when I'd help Mom drag out the Tiger Moth.

For a second, I was home.

I stepped out of the hangar and looked up at the sky. No clouds, a few hours of daylight left. Nervousness was disappearing.

He didn't need my help during preflight, he said nicely, but I knew he'd definitely need me to help him roll the thing out. After so many millions of times rolling out the Tiger and other airplanes that had come and gone in the family, I was a practiced hand at the aircraft-pulling-out process.

Richard was done with the preflight and seemed to be ready to ask me to help.

Before he had to ask, I walked toward the trailing edge of the left wing.

"Nope, nothing like that. I've got it covered."

"You've got it covered? Don't tell me you're going to prove your manhood by dragging this thing out by yourself!"

"Yes, that's exactly it."

Not many muscles, I thought, staring at his arms. *Maybe he's stronger than he looks.*

Richard went to the back of the hangar and brought out a block and tackle that trailed what must have been thirty feet of quarter-inch cable.

He passed me at the wing and strolled out to a spot ten feet from the nose. There was a little hole where asphalt met grass. He put a stemlike thing connected to the block and tackle into the hole. Then he connected something to the nose gear.

"Oh, I see now," I told him and walked to the edge of the hangar to watch him pull.

"You see now?"

He tightened up the cable slack, passed me again, headed toward the back of the hangar and picked up something that looked like a remote-control device.

Clang, whirl, ting, ting, ting, ting.

The plane started to move forward.

A few seconds later, the plane stopped at the edge of the asphalt a foot from that little hole.

The noise stopped.

"I've never seen an electric winch used for that," I said.

I figured it was one of those devices rich people used to make life more convenient. I would have preferred to see him pull, reminiscent of the barnstorming days he wrote about in *Nothing by Chance,* when the only pulling power was the strength of muscles.

"Well, Leslie isn't always with me, y'know. It comes in handy."

Of course! This wasn't a convenient extravagance. Can't pull out a ton of airplane when he's alone. This made perfect practical sense. I felt stupid for thinking otherwise.

In another few minutes we were sitting in the alive Amphibian, waiting to be pointed in any direction. Just like with Daisy, the engine spoke to us from behind.

Seat belts on, run-up checklist out, canopy still open. I didn't think it'd be noisy. It looked too sleek and clean.

"Headphones?" he said as he handed them to me.

Headphones were things that only Mom or Big Jon wore. It was a thrill to have this greatness bestowed on me. I could hear and try to understand what was going on with navigation, have input on where we were going instead of being an idle, ignorant passenger.

Richard's voice was electric gravel as he announced every step of the run-up. Maybe he spoke aloud to remind himself. I hoped he wasn't talking to me, expecting me to remember every item on the list.

Taxiing. Grass and flowers passed under the wing at fifteen miles an hour.

Then the end of the runway until we stopped over a big painted-white 34.

And nerves.

All those hours of flying with Mom and Big Jon and I never got rid of it. It was a fear not just of getting sick, but of feeling powerless if I suddenly wanted to get down. It was claustrophobic energy. Having my father next to me, a man I had gotten to know for the past day or so, made the energy a little stronger than usual.

"Ready to go?" he asked.

"Sure," I sighed.

"Put your hand on the yoke."

"What? My hand?"

He's kidding. It's so hard to tell when he's serious.

"I'll follow you though it," he said.

This was definitely a switch. I wasn't going to be a passenger, but a pilot? When we pulled into the airport driveway and I knew we were probably going to go flying, I hadn't thought it meant *me* taking *him* flying, *me* with *my* hand on the control wheel.

I had told Richard that one of the first steps of any relationship is trust. We agreed it is usually the toughest step, too.

I put my hand on the wheel and it was forbidden territory, as if I were reading someone's diary.

"I don't know . . . you'd better do this."

"It's okay, I'm with you. Now put your left hand on the throttle and let's go."

The throttle now? Geez . . . I don't know. Besides, I don't know where . . .

He saw me looking.

"Right up here."

He guided my hand to a T-shaped lever on the ceiling between us.

"Just inch it forward."

All those hours flying with Mom and I'd never touched a throttle. I touched this one, just a little bit of metal, but it felt different from any metal I'd touched. This piece was connected to a huge engine with a deadly propeller that hurled a ton of airplane into the air.

"But I'll crash us."

I was ready to take my hand off when he rested his hand over mine.

"No you won't. Just ease it up. I'm with you all the way."

I eased it forward. His hand rested pressureless on mine.

More power, more noise.

Rolling faster.

I didn't think I was pressing hard enough to really do anything, but as we started to roll even faster, there was a slight feeling that I was sewn into the engine, that this plane was as much a part of me as my left arm. I didn't seem to be pressing on the throttle with any noticeable pressure, but our ground speed was already seventy miles an hour.

Maybe he had a secret throttle he was pressing.

I didn't have time to look for one. I assumed it was me.

"Good, Jon. Right down the line. Now we'll see if she flies."

The nose came up and she flew.

The left wing dipped as the weight of plane-on-ground disappeared. And as quick as a decision, I turned the wheel right and the wings came just a bit more level.

The stick, the throttle, every movement was liquid. Everything moved smoothly, easily, sensitively, more responsively than any car.

The ground was three hundred feet below us now.

"Good, Jon! You're a natural, you really are! Now pull out the gear lever and move it up."

I'd spotted the lever when I strapped my seat belt on. It was a lever in a slot with two notches. It looked just like the one I'd never touched in all my rides in Big Jon's Navion.

I moved it up like he said.

From beneath us, a whirring. The nose dropped a bit. Bump directly under us as the gear came up. Another two seconds, then a bump on the right.

"Sounds good," he said over the headset, sounding like someone very official at an air traffic control tower.

I could dial any frequency and talk with any controller in a hundred-mile radius if I wanted to. Though there was probably some legal consequence for saying, "Hey, Seattle Approach! What's sha-kin'?"

"Now do the same with the flaps. All the way up."

"Got it."

The flaps came up.

"Good. Watch your nose. Not too steep."

I inched the stick forward.

"Verrry nice. Verrrry good. I'm impressed."

It felt natural. Maybe it was just all those hours of riding and watching. This time I had all the power. Richard wasn't touching the stick, the throttle, or anything I could see.

He wasn't even facing forward. I saw him reaching in the backseat for something.

I watched the instruments until I realized that I should be looking for other planes to avoid.

I looked to my left, out Richard's side window.

He was filming me with a video camera he'd brought.

Wow, I really am flying! I could smash us into the ground, pull us straight up, roll it over if I wanted!

He pointed the camera out the window and narrated.

"These are the beautiful San Juan Islands in beautiful Washington State . . ."

He panned the camera to me. I watched him out of the corner of my left eye.

" . . . and this is your pilot, Jonathan Bach. A natural master."

Flying. It was so easy! It was like learning a language. At first the words are intimidating, but when you learn what the words mean, you can communicate. It was that obvious. I was communicating with this airplane, taking me and this pilot, this famous pilot, a thousand feet above the ground, cruising 140 miles an hour.

A few times Mom had let me do turns and line the Champ up on base leg to turn final for the runway. But this was different. Richard was a passenger, *my* passenger. Richard, the pilot with a zillion hours in old biplanes, twin-engines, supersonic jets, author of four books about flying, writer for *Flying* magazine, former Air Force pilot, was too busy being commentator about the scenery below us to fly.

Flying with him was like going to church with the pope.

I looked at the instruments. I really didn't need any of them. I preferred to fly by feel. I throttled back a little so it sounded like all those times when I was passenger. Richard didn't stop me.

The altitude and the compass varied on my whim. I was careful to watch out for other traffic in the sky, careful to keep us from diving too fast or climbing too steep. Other than that, there was nothing else to be concerned with.

Just watching myself—the way I checked for planes, the way I checked airspeed and altitude, the way I countered a yaw to the left by pressing on the right rudder, the headset, electric gravel voice—there seemed to be no difference between me and all the pilots I had ever seen in action.

I had power, choices, freedom.

I had wings.

I was immortal.

Richard had stopped his narration but continued to film. I wondered how he felt being a passenger in his own airplane, how he felt having the son who had stayed out of his life for so long in the seat next to him doing what he had written so passionately about.

Richard's life was in my hands and he was completely comfortable.

I gradually brought us down to a hundred feet over the water to get a feel for speed. Richard didn't say anything.

Flying at three thousand feet felt like airline flight—not a terrific sense of speed. The ground moved too slowly. At a hundred feet, things moved considerably faster.

Fifty feet would be even better!

I dropped the nose over Puget Sound to where seagulls flew higher than we did.

The engine was my third arm. Add ailerons and rudder and it felt as if I had twenty more. I was part of this airplane. Imagine the metal gone and I was just as light as any bird, insect, dust particle in a sunbeam. My body, a most unaerodynamic thing, had turned super-glider.

The sun was getting low on the horizon, so I pulled the nose up, climbed to a thousand feet to see more of it.

"Okay, I guess I've had my fun. Did you want to go anywhere in particular?" I asked him.

He had put down the camera and was just looking around—the truest compliment he could give me. Maybe he knew that. He's too creative a guy to just say, "I feel comfortable with your flying, Jon."

"Do I want to go anyplace in particular? . . . hm . . . Well, not really. There's a nice spot over to the left, though. Bearing three-six-zero."

I turned a shallow left, lined up the directional gyro until the needle pointed to 36.

Another fifteen seconds in that bank and I dipped the left wing to see a little inlet, a freshwater lake with foothills surrounding it.

Richard took the stick.

"Here, I'll just yank it around to base. Bring the power back a bit to fifteen hundred rpm."

The takeoff was easy; landings were much different. It's one thing to go from zero to one hundred twenty miles an hour, but do it backward?

"Uh, I don't know . . ."

"Just one step at a time. Power back."

Power back.

"Flaps down."

Down.

"Wiggle toes."

"Wiggle toes?"

"Yep. Try it. Wiggle your toes."

"Okay."

I did it. For those few seconds I was a passenger.

"Helps you relax. Am I right?"

"Hey! That's cool! It works."

"Makes you aware that you're still human, that the airplane doesn't have control of you."

Sure enough, I had been caught up in exactly that, letting myself be an airplane.

It was quieter now with the throttle back.

"Stronger on your left rudder."

I pressed hard and we came around faster.

"See the waves? That's where the wind's going. Right into it now. You want it about eighty miles an hour. Just ease it back."

I throttled back.

"Not too much."

I gave it a little more.

"That's it."

The water got closer.

"Not too steep of a glide, now."

Five hundred feet, four hundred . . . three hundred . . . two hundred. A few bumps at a hundred feet . . . fifty . . . twenty . . . ten . . . eight . . . five . . .

"Give it a little flare."

I was sweating.

I'm not part of the airplane. It controls me. I am a powerless human. Mortal.

I lost track of how far we were above the water. Up there, things moved slow; the speed I'd craved so hungrily a few minutes ago was now the *last* thing I wanted.

His hands were on the stick. He pulled it back, flaring the plane, nose up at the last second. It was a smooth touch. Gradual, just the right amount of nose. It was so perfect, it was like the plane had been programmed to guide itself down.

Then BANG!

Water smashed around us. Water hit us so hard I thought we were going to break apart. There were violent bursts against the nose as we became a speedboat.

Slowly, but violently, we decelerated.

"Ugh," I sighed when it got quieter.

"Almost had it there. I could tell you were a little nervous."

"A little? Heh. Yeah."

We settled into the water. He unlatched the canopy release and we breathed fresh air. Water splashed up over the nose . . . or was it the bow?

Richard turned off the engine.

The world was a very silent place. As we slowed to a drift, I took the headphones off. The sound of water lapping up against the metal fuselage penetrated the invisible cotton in my ears.

"Now I know what I've been missing all those years as passenger on trips here and there. I've never touched the throttle or the trim or anything substantial. I mean, just a few times Mom let me take the stick, but I guess I was too nervous to really feel anything else."

"Yes . . ." Richard said slowly, waiting for more.

I remembered yesterday.

"Oh, yeah . . . I *know* why you fly. This is awesome!"

He looked pleased.

"Now you know," Richard said, leaning back in his seat and unclipping his seat belt.

He stood up and sat on the top of the cockpit as I climbed out on the black strip on the nose.

"If I had a plane, this is what it'd be," I said. "There's no place you couldn't go. Nothing like having total freedom anytime."

He shaded his eyes as he stared into the setting sun.

"That's the idea."

A plane flew nearby. It wasn't loud like planes usually are when they fly over your head. This one sounded idled back for landing.

"Looks like we're not the only ones to find this spot," Richard said, squinting his eyes over his left shoulder.

I could see the little plane now. It was a Super Cub on floats. It made its final approach and landed more smoothly than we had, then taxied over to us and cut its engine thirty feet away.

Its door opened as it slowly drifted parallel to us.

"Hey, you folks wouldn't be needin' any help, would ya?" yelled the burly pilot.

"Nope," Richard yelled back. "I'm just sitting here enjoying some time with my son. But thanks anyway!"

The man nodded, looked at the gauges on his control panel. He probably thought Richard and I had done this every weekend since I was born. For a second, I thought the same thing.

"Hey, would you be Richard Bach?" the man asked.

"I would."

"Heard you lived around here. Recognized your plane from the back of one of your books. Nice to meet you! I live just up the inlet here. Seen you round a few times and wondered if it was you. Now I know."

Richard nodded.

"Yes sir. I wouldn't be anyone else."

Large ripples from the Super Cub's landing gently rocked our plane as nobody said anything.

"Well, just thought I'd check in on ya'. Have a good 'un."

"You too," Richard replied.

The Cub's engine came alive again, gave us a little spray of wet wind as it turned around. Throttle thrust forward and the plane roared into the setting sun. The roar echoed off the mountains around us, making it sound as loud as the L-19's roar bouncing around Sugarbush Valley.

We watched his ascent and his eventual disappearance into the pink sky.

I thought about the times people had asked about my name. It was weird to hear someone ask *him*. It was like I was golfing with Jack Nicklaus or sailing with Dennis Conner.

I thought, *Hey, I'm with a celebrity!* It was as if the wheels of my journalism career were still turning and I had an exclusive interview with Richard Bach!

"You can't get away from it even out here, huh," I asked him in reporterlike style.

"Nope. The plane's a trademark. Remember it from the back of *One?*"

I said I did and there was silence for a few seconds.

"It was nice of him to stop, though," he said.

"Yeah, that was considerate. Is everybody like that up here?"

I dipped my right hand in the water while I hung on to the canopy with my left. Richard was standing in the cockpit now, leaning against the opening.

"Pretty much."

Hm.

"Anyway, like I was saying, I think I know why you fly."

He looked down at me on the bow.

"Really? Why do I fly?"

"You fly because when you're up there, you're reminded that in another dimension, you're just as light and free. That you've chosen this life on this ball of dirt to appreciate that and express it in a fun way."

There was a pause. I sensed I had overdone my explanation. "Or . . . not," I said, looking up at him.

He was smiling.

"No, you're right on. For those reasons *exactly.*"

I was glad to be "right on."

"I fly because of that," he said, paused a second, "and because it's more fun than flying in airliners."

"Ah, I see," I smiled in reply, sounding as wise as I could. Flying the Amphibian *was* more fun than riding in airliners.

In those minutes of understanding my father, I was suddenly glad for Mom. I was happy that she'd been a pilot for so many years, able to feel just as free, not bound by the reality of divorce or raising children. I imagined her flying by herself sometime long ago when I was three or four and standing with my brothers and sisters as we watched from the gas pumps. I imagined her vacationing, just her up there in her biplane.

"I guess I was destined to be the son of pilots," I said to my father. "All my experiences, especially those of these past few days, converge on this moment, this feeling," I said.

He smiled curiously as I dipped my hand in the water.

"And what feeling is that?" he asked.

I lifted my hand out of the water and tapped the friendly airplane.

"Learning to fly."

CHAPTER SIXTY-EIGHT

The next day, after a sleep-in morning and big brunch to fuel our intense talking, Richard and I went target shooting—a skill Big Jon had taught me out in the fields near the runway in back of the house.

With Richard's .38 Special and a .22 caliber pistol, we took turns reducing milk cartons to confetti. I was surprised such an advanced thinker could find target shooting the least bit interesting, but I reminded myself that Richard had surprised me a lot in the past few days.

Most of my misconceptions had dissolved, and not just my misconceptions about him. I was a true philosopher now, not as grounded to the earth as I had been. I was also an airsick-passenger-turned-expert-pilot, a dispassionate-journalist-turned-passionate-writer, a distant-son-turned-understanding-friend.

At the house later that day, I thought hard about the discoveries I was making about Richard and myself. I experimented with an electric treadmill in the small fitness room as he cleaned the guns in the room next door. We were separated by a sliding glass door.

Words I had written on a somber night in Gannett Hall played like a recording. *Dad. Father. Some father I have. Purely biological.*

I had been another person when I wrote those feelings. They didn't fit anymore. Like Dick Bach dying in 1970, Jonathan Bach 1986 writing those sad thoughts in his journal was no more.

But that Jonathan 1986 is part of me, I thought. *And Dick Bach is part of Richard. Is it really accurate to say that those parts of us are DEAD?*

It was another "truth" to reexamine.

A flash-feeling came again. It brought an answer: *No, those parts of*

268

us are not dead, just assimilated into our character as Jonathan 1970, 1977, 1980, 1984, 1987, Jonathan 1989-Sitting-on-the-Edge-of-His-Bed and Jonathan 1989-Just-About-to-Land-in-Seattle.

From where come these flash-feelings? From where comes realization? From where comes insight and understanding and inspiration and idea?

Do they come from the same place as *"Just call him, Jon"*? Do they come from *ourselves*?

My interest in the treadmill ended and I slid open the door to Richard's office. Potent fumes of gun-cleaning fluid made my eyes water. It smelled like turpentine gone bad.

"Whew!" I said.

Richard looked up.

"Yeah, better watch it, m'son. These fumes will knock you right over."

"You said it . . . I couldn't smell a thing in the exercise room. Then I opened the door and bang! Wow."

"That's all it takes."

"Hm."

I took a few seconds to think. There was a possible analogy in everything.

"I just thought of something. The door is a concentration gradient. Strong fumes on one side and nothing on the other. I open the door, and it equals out, right?"

"Yes . . ."

"Just like the decision to call you. I open this door and all this stuff equals out. I get a dose of the fumes and the air gets lighter for you in here. Bridging the gap changes things for both of us . . . I guess . . ."

I lost my train of thought. I didn't want to sound too philosophical. That old Jonathan was still watching me.

"I don't know. Something like that."

Richard laughed a bit and nodded.

"Sure, I can see that. That's good. Very good. Can you develop that thought on the chessboard?"

He cleared the table he was working on.

"Chess? Anytime, pal!" I said threateningly.

He finished up his gun-cleaning as I studied the books on the bookshelf next to him.

I could beat him this time. I also knew that another chess game meant more talking: more fun than any checkmate.

That old Jonathan is watching me because he's a part of me.

I continued thinking, following Richard as he started up the stairs. My train of thought started its own chain reaction of conclusions until a mental shock hit me—a shock as if I had been unexpectedly introduced to make a speech in front of the world.

Dick Bach is part of my father.

Dad may not be dead.

A million needles touched me and vanished.

"Richard, uh . . . can I ask you a question?"

He was on the landing to the next bit of stairs.

"Of course," he said.

He was about to take the next step up.

"Would you mind if I call you Dad?"

Chapter Sixty-nine

He suddenly stopped.

I looked at each carpeted stair as I climbed it. I took another step up.

He turned to me and didn't move for a second. I almost ran into him, looking up just in time to see him standing there.

"I wouldn't mind it one bit."

I took another step and joined him on the landing above the bottom five steps. There were five more steps to the second-floor living room.

We were at eye level, equal height.

He put his left arm around me and spoke again.

"Do you mind if I call you 'son'?"

I laughed and looked at the carpet on the stairs as we stood there. I wish I had a nickel for all the times he'd called me son.

"Ooooh, I'll have to think about it . . ."

He chuckled a bit. "Well, I just thought I'd return the question. Let you have the option to say no."

"Yeah, DAD, as if I would!"

He laughed. "Just making sure."

We climbed the rest of the stairs, his arm around my shoulder, mine around his back.

In his touch were wrestling matches and father-son picnics and treehouses and snowmobiles and maple-tree tapping and baseball playing and thousands and thousands of meaningful Father's Days.

CHAPTER SEVENTY

"Checkmate, m'son."

"Not again. There's got to be a way out," I said, studying the chessboard helplessly.

"I don't think so."

It was an appropriate death.

"Ready for another analogy?" I asked.

"Go ahead."

"Okay, I'll die this time. But I'll keep trying until I win. To do that, to get better and to finally beat you, I need to die a few times. Dying is very necessary sometimes."

I told him about the thoughts I'd had on the treadmill, told him about how I didn't think the old parts of me were truly dead and how I didn't think his daddy-part was truly dead and that was how I'd arrived at asking him if I could call him Dad.

My dad looked at me as if I'd discovered something he knew I'd discover sooner or later, but not this quickly.

He nodded. "You've got it!"

I sighed. I had reached the top of a mountain I'd started climbing when I was two. I had learned to fly above clouds of confusion and bitterness and miscommunication, learned to fly over the same sea-fogs that Jonathan Seagull flew over.

"The more you write your thoughts down, Jonathan, the more they'll become longer sentences and paragraphs and pages and chapters and books."

It sounded so familiar. It was something he'd probably written me when I was twelve.

I could go downstairs to my suitcase and read those letters in that manila envelope and they'd be the same words I was hearing now.

I shared the thought.

He nodded and smiled, that was all. I was dazzled at what I was discovering.

To me, it was amazing to realize the simplicity of his early letters to me in 1980. To him, it was no surprise, as if he had waited all these years for me to finally understand them.

I jotted the thought down on the pad of paper next to a few captured pawns.

At the end of another evening of solid conversation, I looked at twenty-five more pages of thoughts spilled onto my bed.

One stood among them: *Show what you live and you'll never have to struggle for something to say.*

I had a crazy idea of collecting notes about life—full-time—as a career.

But did I want to live like Dick Bach? Could I live without a steady paycheck? I could always get another job to support myself until the checks came for my writing. *If* they came.

I thought of the pledge I had signed as a member of the journalism society Sigma Delta Chi: *I intend to undertake journalism as my profession. . . . I believe in the ideas of the Society and agree to abide by the By-laws of the Society as they affect me either as a student member or as a professional member after I am graduated or leave school.*

No way! That pledge of honor that was so honorable was now incredibly, tyrannically restrictive. My code, my *new* code, was to live by *my* rules.

Am I deciding, then, that I want to be different and have rules of my own? I'm sick of being a print journalist at the bottom of the hierarchy on some newspaper. I want to make my own destiny, not be bound by time clocks or office politics.

"I want to write on my own."

I couldn't believe what I was saying. I knew that starving writers *starved.*

But everything felt right: my thoughts, my idea, my decision. In my heart, I knew I wanted more for myself than a college degree in journalism.

And just by thinking these innocent-sounding thoughts, I suddenly felt I was drifting away from my circle of acquaintances and college buddies. The same had been true for Jonathan Seagull. He'd been true to his desire to learn to push the aerobatic envelope and found he'd alienated his friends, was banished from the flock.

I made a decision there, that day. Just as I'd made a decision, listened to the Future Me who told me to call Richard. I remembered that decision hadn't killed me.

What then? Write what? Little stories like the ones I used to write about single-guy heroes and mowing graveyards? I need something to say.

I couldn't think of anything.

Better to just finish out the last year of college and get the degree— just in case. At least until I figure out what I'm going to write.

I imagined a possible nameplate on my desk—Jonathan Bach, Writer.

I liked the label, thought back to the days when Mom had solid confidence that I was going to be a successful writer. In his letters so long ago, Richard had indicated his confidence in my ability.

I used to be a writer then, those years when I couldn't wait to get to the keyboard. I was a true, honest-to-goodness writer.

I looked into the mirror over the dresser. Ten years were ten seconds.

CHAPTER SEVENTY-ONE

Dad, Leslie, and I landed at Sea-Tac International Airport after another flight in Daisy Skymaster. It was time for me to head back to the life I'd left on the other side of the country.

I hugged them good-bye at the gate as strongly as Jim had the day he'd left at the same gate.

They made a parting comment about how "it'll be interesting to follow the choices you'll make from now on." I told them I was going to be just as interested as they were to see what choices I was going to make from now on, and I said I'd definitely keep them posted through straight, honest, open communication.

I waved good-bye, turned and walked down the ramp to the air-liner.

In my hand I held *Illusions,* the only book of Richard's I hadn't read. In an hour and a half I finished it.

It was about a reluctant messiah who was tired of the throngs appealing to him to heal them. He just wanted to be a mechanic, a job that brought him true happiness. The book was a summary of all I had learned in the past three days. It contained insight that read exactly like the sixty or so note pages I had taken:

"The simplest questions are the most profound. . . . Learning is finding out what you already know. . . . Rarely do members of the same family grow up under one roof. . . . Argue for your limitations and sure enough, they're yours. . . . Your only obligation in any lifetime is to be true to yourself."

For this book to be the last one of Richard's I had yet to read was an astounding coincidence. It was incredibly relevant. I wrote some thoughts on the plane.

My thinking process is strong, clear feeling of love for my two new friends. I've found my dad at last and a good, wonderful friend in Leslie. It's all about honesty, love, happiness, and CHOICES—choices to fail, to learn, freedom to choose any life we want and learn from anything, problems especially. It's about being yourself and not being afraid to be alone or different and to attract people just by being yourself.

So little time and so much to do, it seems. I'm so glad I'm young! So many seem to say, "I wish I had known at twenty-one what I know now" or "I wish I'd listened to that urge to be a musician instead of taking that job as an accountant." Now I can continue my life, I hope as regret-free as possible.

I have this urge to write a guide to dealing with Richard for the family: be honest, communicate things that matter to you, talk about choices and adventures that made you grow, where you're going, what your goals are, what makes you tick, why you made the choices you did. Patience and communication above all. I don't know if things will work out between Kris, Rob, Erica, and Dad, but I know if they ask me, I can offer good advice on how to deal with him.

I wanted to talk to Rob about his side of why he and Dad weren't communicating. I wanted to talk to Kris and Erica about their perceptions of Dad, understand their feelings like I had come to understand mine. I wanted to talk to Mom more than anyone, to see how she really felt about the whole thing.

I feel like I just got a tune-up. New plugs, new life to my old battery, renewed zest and spirit for life, and a satisfaction of my need for a dad. And what a neat thing for that dad to be my father! No substitutes.

The little things I found about him are cool too. He puts peaches on his cereal, he was born in 1936, his favorite teacher in high school was a writing teacher named John Gartner and he gave Dad an A because he was the only student to have published a story. He hates coffee, doesn't eat red meat, cooks all of the meals, plays the flute. . . .

Wow, how different I am from a week ago! I have an acceptance and pride of who I am. Excited about future. It's all been my choice to hold the door open and get to know my dad. Somewhere there's another me in another universe that decided not to call Richard that night. He gave in to his embarrassment and went on with his meager existence, buried by confusion.

Whether I use all this new learning or not, at least I have a father I can call "Dad." But I don't want to think about "at least." I feel I've just been through something so profound, it deserves more than just a place in this journal.

Now I wonder what Mom's going to think of all this. Lots more truths to reexamine. It's like I don't want to carry around anything in my life that I haven't explored—no phantom baggage to carry.

My hand hurt from writing. I gave it a break, looked out the window.

A cobalt blue sky melted into the sun's last rays of the day. Pink light covered an ocean of cloud tops like icing on angel food cake. There wasn't a tremor of turbulence to ruin the violently serene mood it created.

I couldn't ignore it.

Above the clouds now, I wrote. *In more ways than one, I guess.*

Then a thought. Simple, obvious, familiar.

Nearly every story is this simple: somebody wants something, something stands in their way, this is what they do about it.

As the plane whined indifferently, I remembered what had melted my bitterness.

Write your book. Write every word.

That's it!

I wrote thoughts until my hand cramped, excited about an idea born from hate, now reborn from love and understanding—a book about me and the "real" Richard Bach.

I stopped writing, rested my hand.

But what should I call it?

The man next to me noticed I had stopped.

"That's a pretty good book you got there," he said, pointing to *Illusions* in my left hand.

I smiled, agreeing casually that it was a "pretty good" book.

The man said Richard Bach was "really something."

I agreed that Richard Bach was "really something," and chuckled at the understatement.

"Why do you say it like that?" he asked.

I took a few seconds to think of a short answer he could understand. There was only one way to say it.

"Because he's my dad," I said with an unflinching voice, a strong heart, and a clear mind.

"Oh, really?" the man said with raised eyebrows and a surprised smile.

I extended my hand toward his, looked him square through his glasses and into his green eyes.

"Name's Bach," I said. "Jonathan Bach."

EPILOGUE

I did not write what you have just read.

This story was assembled by three pretty decent guys:

Jonny, the eight-year-old writer, gets credit for always wanting to write a book. He was also the inspiration who kept the project alive.

Jon, the twenty-two-year-old somewhat inarticulate former journalist-editor, clumsily set the story to words. He's the clarity expert, he likes short sentences, but he's got problems remembering details.

And Jonathan, the guy who writes this epilogue, an enthusiastic twenty-five-year-old first-time author, will probably get credit for all the work.

I am four years older since that handshake on the previous page, and I continue to experiment with my new beliefs—that we create our own reality, that college classes are almost irrelevant compared to what college truly teaches you, that experience is the ultimate teacher, that failing is never a setback, that taking notes on life is more productive than taking notes in a mandatory economics class, and on and on—but nothing gets by me now. Nothing on the TV passes without my giving it a thought or two, from light-hearted thoughts about the purpose of war and whether all that killing is really necessary, to serious contemplation of whether there's some cosmic reason that most fathers on sitcoms have to be portrayed as idiots.

I love honesty, I love problem-solving, I love writing what affects me. I hate traffic, watery coffee, and people on talk shows who yell at each other. But as a result of my experience with Dad, I also know *why* I love and hate these things. I love peeling the onion of Why to get the core whiteness (and whyness) that influences what I do from day to day. I've driven my friends crazy with my questioning of everything and I've even discovered that sometimes you can't peel the onion any further—sometimes why doesn't have an answer.

I have lots to tell Jon and Jonny—information they would kill to know because they, like me, are in pursuit of answers.

If I had the chance to sit face to face with them, I'd sound like a Tibetan sage as I told them only generalities about their future: stay true to what makes you happy, do the best you can, ask lots of questions, listen to your impulses, and by all means, give yourself the option to quit.

Sounds like a certain father I know.

But it is very important to know I am not Richard Bach. It's clear from the book that his influence on me was strong, but not because he is my father or because he's a world-famous author, but because I, like millions of other people, like what he has to say and how he says it.

He does not provide answers, he provides fascinating, on-target perspective. He affirms what I am on the edge of believing on my own and he reminds me of what I may already know—I say we create our own reality, he says, "No, we create our own illusions." And I'll be darned . . . I agree.

It's important to note that I don't *always* agree with him. He and I disagree about birthdays, for one thing. He says we are never born, so a birth-day is irrelevant. I think birthdays are great ways to celebrate our choice to be sewn into space and time. While he doesn't eat meat because he doesn't want to cheat an animal out of a chance for a contemplative lifetime, I can eat a chicken sandwich and be confident that animals have souls too, and since a soul is never born and can't die, chickens are really just illusions anyway. I just wish animal illusions didn't have so much cholesterol.

Leslie Parrish is as much a part of me as Richard. I, like her, love music, frugality, and voicing my opinion on social issues. I, too, am good at managing finances, I'm a futurist, and I'd like to make a difference in the world. Leslie's advice is as valuable as Dad's, sometimes more valuable, because she's got different experiences from his which may be more help to whatever situation I'm in.

Above everything, differences or similarities, Richard Bach and Leslie Parrish-Bach are my friends. They are there to help me become more self-aware and I try in my clumsy way to return the favor when they need my advice.

But back to the story and to important updates since the last page:

From the airliner, I stepped back into Maine, back into one last boring month of a boring summer internship at the *Ellsworth American,* back into the last year of a four-year journalism degree. Since then, there has been no resurgence of any awkward feelings about being one of Richard Bach's sons. The clouds are below me. I know myself and I like him a lot.

So why write the book?

My answer is the same to: why be a writer? a journalist? a campus newspaper editor? an author? a volunteer firefighter? My answer is the same to: why stay alive?

Fun.

I wanted to go for it, take the opportunity I have in this lifetime as Jonathan Bach to write about one of the neatest experiences I've had.

As never before, it's a delight for me to tell the "family story" to strangers because it has this hopeful ending of reconciliation. There is enjoyment now, too, just as there was in being Mom's ground crew when I was little—to be a hero, to help people with my experience. I wanted to reach as many people as possible without having to invent new ways of telling the same old story each time someone asked about my name.

In the time it took me to organize and document what you have read, my sister Erica has reconciled with my father. She was one of the ones who supported what I had done with Richard. She liked my new self-awareness and confidence. But it wasn't until she read this manuscript that she called me and asked if I thought Richard would mind if she tried to contact him. And just as I would tell the past Jonathan-Sitting-on-the-Edge-of-His-Bed, I told her, "Go for it!"

Little Brother giving Bigger Sister advice felt a little awkward, but I knew she was similar enough to me to feel the empowerment I had felt when I called him.

She called, they talked. They are still talking today. She calls him Dad, too.

My brother Rob has also reestablished communication with Richard. He didn't call me the way Erica did, but he did read my story. And with a strong mind and honest heart, he called Richard too. And slowly, trust was built between them again.

Erica and Rob have their own stories to tell, should they choose to tell them, but suffice it to say there are four of us now who feel comfortable calling Richard Dad.

Kris says she is content without Richard Bach in her life. Richard is content with her contentment. He's not the type to go somewhere he isn't wanted. Only he and Kris know what's right for their futures, but Kris has a happy life, and so does Dad. They're a perfect example of why I believe that some estranged family, friends, lovers don't need to reconcile. Their happiness and contentment are the surest measure of that.

As for Mom, she's wary that I've chosen to be an author. She knows from her marriage to free-lance writer Dick Bach that it isn't always a steady paycheck, and I'm sure she fears my car will be repossessed someday when no one wants to read what I have to say. Even though she wishes I'd chosen some other subject for my first book, she's confident in my ability to write cogently and she understands this book is something I had to write, like a cat coughing up a fur ball. She has her own perspective on these events and I'm sure her story would be a lot different from mine.

But if it should happen one day that no one wants to read what I have to say despite whatever talent she thinks I have, I have myself to thank for hanging on to complete my work for a journalism degree at the University of Maine. I hung on, too, to feel I had accomplished something tremendous, because there was no guarantee I would ever get this book organized in my lifetime.

Mom remains happily married to Big Jon, who understands why I've needed to tell this story and bears me no ill will. He knows I still use his lessons about money and responsibility, and I'm pretty sure he's glad to have made a lasting impression. True to his philosophy, I live within my income and I don't leave cupboards open anymore, so I think he's pleased.

But all of this means nothing.

You have stories, too, far more interesting than mine, I'll bet, and you are just as capable of telling at least one of them, or even making new ones. I would love to return the favor of picking your book from the millions on the bookstore shelves.

Jonathan Bach

Afterword

When I met the teenage Jonathan Bach in 1984, at the reunion of which he writes in this book, there was no telling what was going on behind his eyes. Long practiced in building walls of my own, I judged his ramparts mortared solid courtesy to a stranger—thick enough to last a lifetime, I figured, gate locked from within. Impervious.

Who lives in there? I wondered. A decent person, I could tell, age 30 in a 16-year body, hard-working, respectful. So are a hundred million other young people whom their parents never get to know, every one alone, each striving to learn what can't be taught by strangers. Products of a broken home, and now the barricades are up, such a pity.

My wife, Leslie, Jonathan's stepmother, grew up that way, her mother hating her father after a divorce twenty, thirty, forty years gone. Everything dim but the bitterness. I leafed the scrapbooks she grew up with, old family photographs everyone smiling except her father, him the business suit beneath a blank square where his head had been cut away from the page, him a blank rectangle scissored out of the picture.

Leslie met her father when she was 40 years old and he 68, a dear warm gallant gentleman who kept decades of clippings from all over the world, every magazine cover, every interview of his actress daughter, read and treasured.

"What happened to me doesn't have to happen to your children," she said. She wrote her pain to my ex-wife, urging our bitterness be dropped: *For the love of your children, can't you and Richard at least be on speaking terms?*

No luck.

Even as we talked that gone summer day with Jonathan and his sister Beth it was clear we'd never know them as teens; with patience

285

and skill it could happen when they were grown, if ever they chose to crack their doors. I didn't imagine that Beth might not live to make the choice.

When Jonathan seared the telephone post-midnight long-distance torment and rage and courage, daring me to smother the truth he'd write about Richard Failure Son-of-a-Bitch Bach, I broke in silent agonized joy. My son had decided to live! He had chosen for the first time to recognize that Richard Human-Being Bach exists; his father, not some stalking hooded puppetmaster in old daggers and blood-stains. Chased by myths, he had turned furious at last to face whatever demon I was, to fight me if he had to and destroy me if he must. How I loved him for it!

He's kept his promise never again to shut the door between us, so yesterday I could laugh with my friend Jonathan muttering in frustra-tion whatever the hell happened to all those women said they'd give their heart to find a sensitive loving one-woman guy like me, not some macho jock with a cigarette tattoo on his bicep?

"You'll find her," I said without the smallest idea how; then knew in a blink I was watching a Jonathan Bach all at once grown through his early tests, ready for more. Even though his parents divorced and he didn't find his father till he was 21, this open outgoing funny guy beside me had turned down the chance to screw himself into a ball of greensnake neuroses, trained himself to write what he had lived and to become the human being he wanted to be.

If Jonathan's the product of a broken home, I thought, maybe we ought to break more homes in this country to fill the nation with striving youngfolk: the jails would go empty.

Yet he's no more the product of a broken home than I'm the product of a broken first marriage or a lovely second one . . . nobody's the product of circumstance. Each of us is the product of *our response* to circumstance, lovely as well as broken, we're products of our choices to become who we want to be because of in spite of every event that changes our life, our mind, our heart.

"Dad," he said, thumping his finished manuscript down on our kitchen table, "I'm so glad you left when I was two! It was my destiny! I could never have written this book if you'd stayed!"

With one stroke the young man vaporized my responsibility for an old divorce. Amazing I hadn't realized . . . I was but the pawn in a headstrong infant's design to become the child of a broken home and thus begin his career as a writer.

I savor Jonathan's revelation and naturally I'm glad that I've been of service to him. Still, I wish he hadn't written some of the things he has, wish he hadn't seen fit to include on these pages the details of antique personal history I'd rather not see in print. I also wish that he would use words exactly the same way that I do and that he'd put his commas where I would.

But there you have it: our next generation. What can we do but hope they learn that nothing happens by chance, and wish them luck?

Richard Bach